'Castle' Class 4—6—0 No. 5035 *Coity Castle* negotiating the tunnels on the picturesque section between Dawlish and Teignmouth with a Down express in the latter 'thirties. This may have been the Wolverhampton to Penzance service as *Coity Castle* was a Wolverhampton (Stafford Road) engine during this period.

L & GRP, cty. David & Charles

THE
GREAT WESTERN
IN SOUTH DEVON

BY

KEITH M BECK & JOHN COPSEY

WILD SWAN PUBLICATIONS LTD.

ISBN 0 906867 90 8

Published by
WILD SWAN PUBLICATIONS LTD.
1-3 Hagbourne Road, Didcot, Oxon, OX11 8DP

INTRODUCTION

'Castle' class 4—6—0 No. 5003 *Lulworth Castle*, with an Up local passenger train, viewed through the open window of Laira Junction Signal Box. Laira Junction was situated about two miles to the east of Plymouth (North Road) station. To the left is Laira shed itself, and the carriage sidings are just discernible to the right, behind the bracket signal. The numerous autocars serving the Plymouth district normally occupied those sidings seen through the front window of the box (just beneath the block instruments) when not in use.
R. C. Riley

The Great Western Railway meant many things to many people, from the quiet and leisurely progress of the country branch line train, with its small tank engine and rather elderly non-corridor carriages, or the friendly autotrain whose seats were as reversible as the train itself, to the 'Cornish Riviera Express' or the 'Torbay Express', and that indestructible survivor of the broad gauge, the Up 'Flying Dutchman', still leaving Plymouth for Paddington at 8.30 a.m.

For railway enthusiasts there was a wealth of meaning in the magical letters GWR. They meant Brunel's magnificent broad gauge and his equally impressive Paddington station and Royal Albert Bridge; both of the latter, mercifully, still with us, though the broad gauge is now but a legend. They meant that incomparable succession of engines with tapered boilers, unique safety-valve covers and copper-capped chimneys; immaculate green engines liberally bestowed with copper and brass, and, above all, carrying those huge, curved brass nameplates; 'Saints' and 'Stars', followed by 'Castles', 'Kings' and 'Counties' – and the 'Halls' and 'Granges' – a locomotive family that sprang from the genius of a Devonshire man, George Jackson Churchward.

For holiday-makers and enthusiasts alike, GWR meant that wonderful line along the coast, with its tunnels, between Dawlish and Teignmouth, followed by the sinuous course of the railway as it climbed up and down over the southern spurs of Dartmoor. Somehow, it was the epitome of the whole Great Western; though it was, and is, far removed from the original Great Western Railway running between Paddington and Temple Meads. There was, and is, no other line in the country quite like that of the GWR in South Devon; certainly no other main line had such an astonishing, and almost disastrous, beginning.

I was privileged to be born within the sound of the GWR in South Devon, even if it was not the main line itself. However, the Branch (as it was known) serving the Torbay resorts of Torquay and Paignton, as well as Dartmouth by means of its steam ferry, was little short of being a minor main line. Where else did 'Kings' regularly work over a single-track line? Some of my earliest memories are of those gleaming green engines with their copper-capped chimneys and huge curved nameplates, of the sound of the succession of trains on summer Saturdays fighting their way up the bank from Torquay to Torre, and of the trains at Goodrington – much to be preferred to the supposed delights of the sands! It was at Torre station that I worked on the GWR during the final months of its long life.

This present work is an attempt to convey something of the history and the atmosphere – and even the 'Atmospheric' – of the Great Western Railway in that part of the country I have known and loved so long, South Devon.

Keith M. Beck
Coventry

Designed by Paul Karau
Printed and bound by Butler & Tanner Ltd., Frome

Blackpool Sands in the 1930s, epitomising the ideal of 'Glorious Devon' and the 'Devonian Riviera' promoted with such vigour by the GWR publicity department. Blackpool Sands are some 3½ miles south of Dartmouth and could be reached by train to Kingswear, GWR ferry across the River Dart and the GWR road motor service from Dartmouth to Kingsbridge. *National Railway Museum, York*

CONTENTS

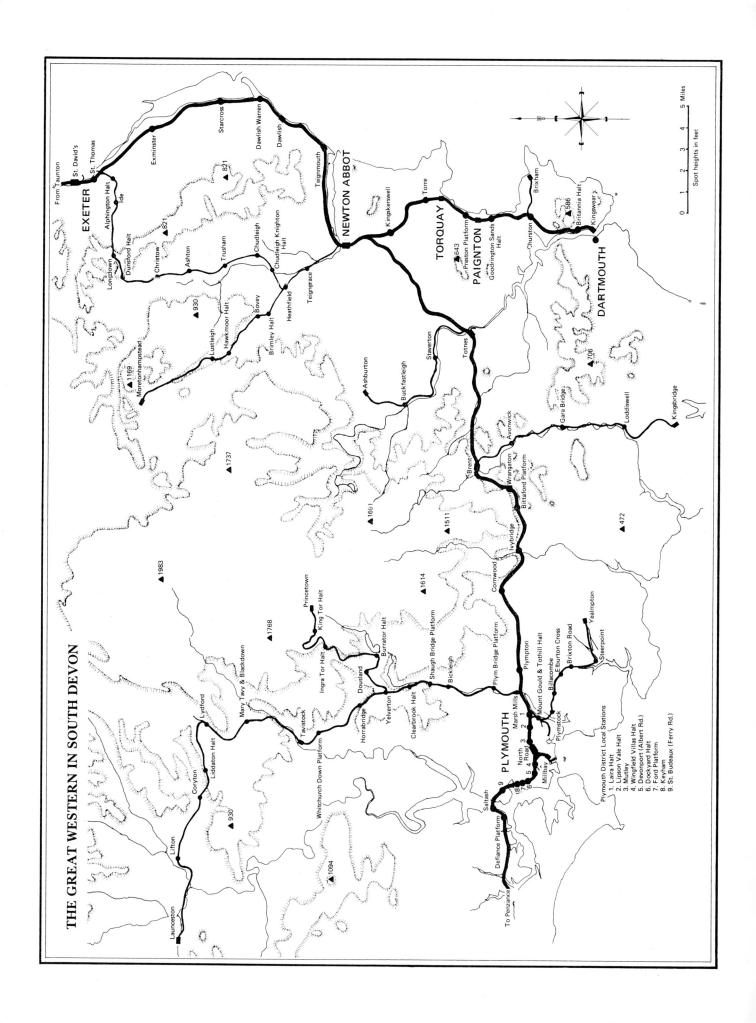

THE GREAT WESTERN IN SOUTH DEVON

CHAPTER ONE

THE SOUTH DEVON RAILWAY

The most spectacular section of the Great Western Railway's main line from Paddington to Penzance, the coastal journey from the Exe to the Teign, followed by the tremendous gradients and curves between Newton Abbot and Plymouth, had little in common with the magnificently graded line linking London with Bristol or its continuation south-westwards to Exeter. Such was the contrast that it is difficult to realise that the same engineer was responsible for such dissimilar lines. The reasons for such differences were not to be found in the very different terrain of the Vale of White Horse, the Somerset Levels and the southern slopes of Dartmoor, but in the origins of the Exeter to Plymouth section – not least in the means of propulsion originally envisaged. The South Devon Railway was a local line whose trains were to be propelled by an 'Atmospheric System'.

Hardly had the Act of Parliament authorising the Bristol & Exeter Railway been passed in May 1836, than proposals were made for a railway from Plymouth to join the new line at Exeter. Throughout that summer, Brunel was engaged in surveying the country; however, enthusiasm for such a venture did not extend to its financial support, so that nothing further was done until 1843. When the proposal was revived, it was due to the GWR, the Bristol & Exeter and Bristol & Gloucester Railways being induced to subscribe to the project.

The proposed 'atmospheric system' influenced the route taken west of Newton Abbot, including the gradients over Dainton and Rattery as well as the formidable climb from Plympton to Hemerdon which faced eastbound trains. Brunel's original plan had been for a coastal line from Exeter to the Teign, followed by the crossing of that river and a route via Torquay, across the River Dart and through the South Hams. An alternative, inland route by way of Crediton, Okehampton and Tavistock, advocated by Francis Giles, received little support in Plymouth, though some Exeter people favoured it.

In October 1843 the prospectus of the Plymouth, Devonport & Exeter Railway was issued, among its claims being some of considerable significance:

> The course of the line has been selected with the idea of accommodating the largest amount of population in the district to be traversed. From the Station of the Bristol and Exeter Railway at Exeter the Line crosses the river and passes down the flat ground on the bank of the Exe, through Starcross, round the point opposite to Exmouth and thence along the coast by Dawlish and Teignmouth, and up the Valley of the Teign to Newton, a short distance beyond which place it passes within about 5 miles of Torquay, embracing consequently, in these 21 miles of line direct communication with all the most favoured Watering Places of the South Coast of Devon.

The latter claim may be seen as a portent of those days when the line would convey tens of thousands of summer visitors to the South Devon coast, while the GWR always refused to admit that it was possible to reach Exmouth except by means of the ferry from Starcross!

Nor was future extension westwards overlooked; it was claimed that the site of the Plymouth terminus allowed for 'the extension of the Line at any future period into Cornwall'. The line was to be double track and on the same gauge as the GWR, B & ER and B & GR lines, 'affording facility for working the same stock as is used on all or either of these lines'. It was also claimed that the route involved less engineering difficulties than on the other projected lines.

Before the Bill for its construction was deposited, the title had been changed to the South Devon Railway. The Royal Assent was received on 4th July 1844. The assent of the Admiralty had also to be obtained, as the line would encroach upon the shore. One result of this was the construction of the public walk on the retaining wall between the railway and the sea, to compensate the residents for hindrance of access to the shore: generations of holiday-makers – and railway photographers – have had cause to bless the memory of Joseph Walker, the Admiralty's engineer!

The company had a capital of £1,100,000, towards which the B & ER subscribed £200,000, the GWR £150,000 and the B & GR £50,000. In addition to the line from Exeter to Plymouth, the Company were authorised to construct a branch 'if they think fit' to the waterside at Millbay (over which locomotives were not to be used), and to alter the existing Plymouth & Dartmoor Railway (but not its gauge) with the consent of the owners, and of John and William Johnson, the mortgagees in possession. Powers were also given to purchase the ferry between Exmouth and the Warren from the Corporation of Exeter, and to sell or lease the whole undertaking to any of the three subscribing companies.

The first meeting of the new company was held on 28th August 1844 at Plymouth, with Thomas Gill, MP, in the chair. An announcement was made at that meeting which was to have a profound effect upon the life of the South Devon Railway: 'Your Directors, in the belief that it will be greatly to the interests of the Company, have resolved that the Atmospheric System, including the construction of an Electrical Telegraph, should be adopted upon the whole line.'

The atmospheric system dispensed with locomotives as such, and used stationary steam engines working large pumps to create a partial vacuum within cast-iron pipes laid between the rails, a 'driving' carriage being connected by a vertical plate to a piston which was forced along the pipe by the creation of the partial vacuum. The plate travelled within a slit in the top of the pipe which was normally sealed airtight by a leather flap, secured at one side of the pipe (this flap being known as the 'longitudinal valve'), and sealed at the other side by a grease composition to make it airtight. A series of small wheels, fixed to a frame of iron plates on the special piston carriage, opened and closed the valve.

Patented in 1839 by the Samuda Brothers in partnership with a man named Clegg, the system had been tried out on the West London Railway. It became the subject of controversy among engineers; George Stephenson dismissed it as 'a great humbug', but Brunel was attracted to the idea and considered applying it to the Box Tunnel Incline between Bath and Chippenham. It was to be employed on the Dublin & Kingstown's branch to Dalkey, in Ireland, while William Cubitt decided to employ it on the Croydon & Epsom line. Robert Stephenson followed his father in rejecting the system (proposed for the Chester & Holyhead line) and was a witness before the Commons Committee on the Croydon & Epsom Bill. He was opposed by Brunel, who was asked whether he intended to use the Atmospheric System on the South Devon Railway. Brunel replied that he was not yet determined on it and could not say. This reply was given on 20th May 1844; his report to the South Devon Directors was dated 19th August!

Brunel stated that the atmospheric system was capable of producing much higher speeds than locomotive power, also that the line could be single throughout because 'the system admits of the working of the single line without any danger of collision'. By this means, *and by modifying the gradients and the curves*, he proposed to save £207,000 in the making of the line. The cost of the apparatus being estimated as £190,000 compared with the provision of locomotives at £50,000, the actual saving would be £67,000. He also estimated that £8,000 might be saved each year in locomotive expenses, while there were also the advantages of greater speed, less noise and the absence of coke dust 'which is certainly still a great nuisance'.

Further considerations were that the gradients between Newton and Plymouth would restrict locomotives to a speed of about thirty miles an hour, which could hardly be maintained in unfavourable weather: however, 'with the Atmospheric, and with the dimensions of the pipes I have assumed, a speed of forty to fifty miles may certainly be depended upon'. He concluded 'For all the reasons above quoted, I have no hesitation in taking upon myself the full and entire responsibility of recommending the adoption of the Atmospheric System on the South Devon Railway, and recommending as a consequence that the line and works should be constructed for a single line only'.

Having received such advice, the Directors lost no time in making an agreement with the Samuda Brothers for the use of their patent rights, and letting contracts for the supply of rails, iron pipe, valves, six pairs of stationary engines and air pumps. Brunel sent out a general specification and drawing for the last two items, leaving the manufacturers to adopt their own method of construction. The tenders accepted were those of Boulton & Watt, Rennies, and Maudsley & Field.

Good progress was made with the works, though little had been done beyond Newton, when the General Meeting was held in February 1845. The lengthy viaduct through St Thomas', at Exeter, had almost been completed, as had the line as far as Powderham, though work on the sea wall had been delayed by easterly winds. Doubts were expressed about the sea wall being adequate to stand up to the onslaught of the sea during gales, but Brunel stated 'I think it is highly probable that very little of the line will eventually be reached by the highest tides'. Time was to prove that Brunel's sanguine attitude was not justified. Work at Teignmouth had only just begun, while between Newton and Plymouth the line was being set out and the land bought, though the Marley Tunnel had been started. Brunel stated, 'I see no reason to doubt the ability of the Contractors to finish the whole by the period fixed in the Contract, namely the 1st of June', and he expected the line to be open as far as Newton in July.

Despite Brunel's optimism, the line was far from ready for opening in July. Beyond Starcross the Cockwood Marsh was

to have been crossed by an embankment, but as the mud proved to be too soft and deep, a timber viaduct was substituted. The tunnels near Dawlish and the tunnel and covered ways on either side of Teignmouth were all incomplete, while the approach to Newton was held up because of the failure to obtain possession of some much-needed land.

Public disappointment at the delay was combined with attacks in the press on the safety of the line along the seashore and on the atmospheric system. As there was no prospect of the stationary engines being ready in the near future, the directors announced that they intended opening as far as Teignmouth for the early summer, for passenger traffic only, and using locomotives. The 15 miles of single line from the B & ER station at Exeter (for the use of which the SDR paid a rent) to Teignmouth were at last opened on Saturday, 30th May 1846, with engines hired from the GWR (who were working the B & ER). The intermediate stations were St Thomas, Starcross and Dawlish, and the service consisted of seven trains each way on weekdays and three on Sundays.

The principal works were the low timber bridge over the Exe, the St Thomas Viaduct of 62 stone arches, the river wall with the timber viaduct (200 yards long) over Cockwood Marsh, and the sea wall from Langstone Cliff past Dawlish to Teignmouth. The latter section also included five tunnels through the headlands beyond Dawlish (Parson's Tunnel being 374 yards long) and the East Cliff Tunnel at Teignmouth – an impressive total for 15 miles of line!

The Directors changed their minds several times on the subject of the siting of the terminus at Plymouth, which involved another Act of Parliament. Further powers were obtained to raise additional capital of £500,000; to make a branch from 'Aller to a certain field in the Parish of Tormohun' – the closest they were allowed by the House of Lords to get to Torquay; to make a branch to Sutton Pool from Laira Green and another to Devonport; to alter the course of the Millbay Branch (locomotives still being prohibited from crossing Union Street and Millbay Road); and for deviations near Newton, to allow work to commence on the erection of the station. The extension to Newton was opened for passengers on 30th December, the first train being hauled by *Antelope*, one of Gooch's 6 ft single engines.

Progress with installing the atmospheric equipment was gradual; though by August 1846 the pipes had been laid to Teignmouth, the engines were still far from ready, despite the engine houses having been erected beside the line at intervals of three miles. Situated at Exeter, Countess Weir, Turf, Starcross, Dawlish, Teignmouth, Bishopsteignton, Newton, Dainton and Totnes on the main line, and at Longpark on the Torquay Branch, it is doubtful if the last three ever contained engines – if so, they were never used.

Joseph Samuda and a staff of trained assistants arrived in the autumn. Every effort was made to get the stationary engines completed, and in February 1847 the directors were able to report that a piston carriage had been worked from Exeter to Turf and back. Experimental trains ran during the next six months and eventually reached Teignmouth, but no passengers were carried. Brunel's reports were now much less confident, while the Directors managed to avoid any reference to the subject in the Report to the General Meeting!

Goods traffic began on 1st May 1847, with one train each way between Exeter and Newton, while on 20th July the line from Newton to Totnes was opened to passenger traffic. The first train over Dainton was hauled by *Pisces*, one of Gooch's 5 ft wheeled 2-4-0s, and *Pegasus*, a 7 ft Single, and goods traffic to Totnes began on 6th December. Newton station, like that of the B & ER at Exeter, consisted of separate Up and Down train sheds on the north side of the line. There were no major engineering works between Newton and Totnes, apart from the tunnel at Dainton Summit, 272 yards long, and the timber bridge over the Dart, at Totnes.

At long last, on Monday, 13th December 1847, four atmospheric trains began to carry passengers between Exeter and Teignmouth. It was reported that the new mode of traction was almost universally approved of, and that the motion of the train was smooth and agreeable, also that passengers were free from the annoyance of coke dust and the smell from the engine. However, there were considerable delays at each station due to the need to re-engage the piston. The highest speed recorded was 68 mph, with a train only 28 tons, but with a train of 100 tons the maximum appears to have been only 35 mph. Atmospheric working was extended to Newton on 10th January 1848. Brunel was still confident that mechanical defects and other problems would be overcome, despite the service between Exeter and Newton proving to be anything but reliable.

Passenger services to a temporary terminus at Laira Green, at Plymouth, began on Friday, 5th May 1848, though goods traffic did not commence until September 1849. The first train was worked by two 2-4-0s, *Pisces* and *Cancer*, the first of these being driven by the great Daniel Gooch himself. The line was double from Totnes to Rattery, then single to Hemerdon, and double again from the summit down into Plymouth. At first the only intermediate station was Wrangaton, later known as Kingsbridge Road in response to a memorial from that town.

Kingsbridge was linked with the station by a stage coach service. Brent, Ivybridge and Plympton were opened a little later, the premises not being ready in time, while Cornwood was opened in 1852.

As well as the considerable gradients between Totnes and Plymouth – the climb up to Rattery from Totnes being 4½ miles and that from Plympton to Hemerdon 2¾ miles – there were also major bridges at Rattery and Brent, Marley Tunnel (689 yards long) and five viaducts. The latter were at Glaze, Bittaford, Ivybridge, Blachford and Slade; the tallest was that at Ivybridge – 114 feet, with a length of 252 yards, while Blachford was 293 yards and Slade 273 yards long. There was also the famous 'Cocked Hat' bridge over the main road at Wrangaton, a timber span 27 feet on the square and no less than 102 feet on the skew. The bridges at Rattery and Brent were built of stone, but the viaducts were of timber, resting on stone piers, and all except Glaze were on curves. The permanent way was of bridge rails on longitudinal timbers.

Meanwhile, James Pearson, the engineer in charge of the atmospheric equipment, and his staff were struggling daily to overcome the almost impossible difficulties in maintaining the service between Exeter and Newton. Chemistry and natural history were now involved; it was discovered that combined action of water on the leather and iron in the pipes resulted in the extraction of tannin from the leather and the creation of a sodden mess, while the local rats had taken to eating the grease used to keep the flap airtight!

Samuda being still responsible for maintenance, Brunel was directed to ensure that the valve was repaired and that no expense should fall on the company. His report on 19th August contained the ominous words, 'I cannot anticipate the possibility of any inducement to continue the system beyond Newton'. It was five years to the day since he had written, 'I have no hesitation in taking upon myself the full and entire responsibility of recommending the adoption of the Atmo-

SOUTH DEVON RAILWAY TIMETABLE
Saturday, 30th May 1846

Miles			Class 1, 2 & 3	Class 1, 2 & 3			Class 1, 2 & 3				EXAMPLES		
0	Teignmouth	dep.	7.10	9.10	11.10	1/15	4/25	6/45	8/45		Fares: Teignmouth—Exeter	1st Class	2/6d
3	Dawlish	dep.	7.19	9.19	11.19	1/24	4/34	6/54	8/54			2nd Class	2/0d
6½	Starcross	dep.	7.30	9.30	11.30	1/35	4/45	7/5	9/5			3rd Class	1/3d
15	Exeter	arr.	7.55	9.55	11.55	2/0	5/10	7/30	9/30		Children under 3 years old		Free
	'GWR' Exeter	dep.	8.0	10.0	12/0	3/5	5/15	–	9/35		Children from 3 to 11 years old		Half price
	connection to		Paddt'n	Paddt'n	Express Paddt'n	Day Mail Paddt'n	Swindon		Mail Paddt'n		One horse		6/0d
											Two horses		10/0d
	Connection			9.45	7.30	10.15	12/0	5/30			Two-wheel carriage		5/6d
				Paddt'n Express	Paddt'n	Paddt'n	Paddt'n	Paddt'n			Four-wheel carriage		8/0d
											each dog		1/0d
	'GWR' Exeter	arr.	–	–	2/15	3/20	5/32	7/35	10/5		Fish is carried by the 7.10 and 8/45 trains.		
			Class 1, 2 & 3				Class 1, 2 & 3	Class 1, 2 & 3			Parcels up to 14 lbs – 8d; to 28 lbs – 10d.		
	Exeter	dep.	8.10	12/10	2/20	3/25	5/40	7/40	10/10				
	Starcross	arr.	8.35	12/35	2/45	3/50	6/5	8/5	10/35				
	Dawlish	arr.	8.46	12/46	2/56	4/1	6/16	8/16	10/46				
	Teignmouth	arr.	8.55	12/55	3/5	4/10	6/25	8/25	10/55				

spheric System ...' As from 9th September the section from Exeter to Newton was ordered to be worked exclusively by locomotives, the staff in charge of the system being notified that their services would no longer be required.

No attempt was ever made to revive what is still known locally as the 'Atmospheric Caper'. No less than £426,368 had been spent on it, of which only £50,000 was recovered by the sale of the useless equipment. The piston carriages were converted to brake vans, while the engine houses were adapted to other uses – that at Exeter became the well-known pump house, Starcross saw service as a Methodist chapel, and Longpark had a long life as a pottery. Sections of the pipe still survived in the 1970s – as drain pipes!

The legacy was not only a gigantic financial loss, but also the great inconvenience of operating some 40 miles of single line (from Exeter to Totnes and Rattery to Hemerdon) and the difficulties involved in surmounting the severe gradients to the west of Newton, one being as steep as 1 in 36. Despite all this, Brunel continued as engineer of the SDR; but the chairman, Thomas Gill, resigned from the Board, as he was the only director who wished further experiments to be carried out. Thomas Woollcombe succeeded him in the chair. For some time the Board was fully engaged in pacifying the debenture holders and endeavouring to sort out the company's finances.

The Torquay branch was opened for passengers, to a station at Torre, on 18th December 1848. A separate shed was erected at Newton for the branch trains, making three distinct 'stations' there, and for the first mile as far as Aller the branch ran alongside the main line, but there was no connection except at Newton station.

Finally, on 2nd April 1849, the main line was completed to the terminus between Union Street and Millbay Road in Plymouth. The original plan of crossing Union Street on the level had been abandoned in deference to the views of the Board of Trade, and a bridge substituted – the latter had been suggested in 1844 by James Walker, though how the Admiralty's engineer became involved in affairs in the centre of Plymouth is not clear! This allowed the use of locomotives, which had been banned under the original plan. The only engineering works of note were the Mutley Tunnel, 183 yards long, and the cast-iron bridge over Union Street. The Millbay terminus was an unpretentious wooden structure, with the usual overall roof. Mutley station was not opened until 1871, while North Road did not come into use until 1877.

Anxious to increase their income and reduce their expenditure, the directors attempted 'to kill two birds with one stone' by simultaneously reducing the train service and increasing the fares! The only result was an immediate drop in the number of passengers carried, and thus in the revenue! From April 1850 fares were reduced to their former level, though the benefits were slow to emerge. Goods traffic was almost negligible, accounting for only £12,333 out of a total revenue of £98,745 in 1850.

The provision of locomotives was the chief item of expenditure, as the GWR was charging 1s. 4d. per train mile between Exeter and Newton, and 1s. 9d. between Newton and Plymouth. As the GWR had no suitable engines for the gradients and curves of the SDR, Gooch was forced to design the 'Corsair' class of 4–4–0 STs specially for the line. Brunel suggested an agreement with Charles Geach, an ironmaster of

---

SOUTH DEVON RAILWAY – OPERATING DIARY
11.30 a.m. 10th October 1854

Present State of Engines

Aurora	Broke clacks & pulled out fire at Kingsbridge Road this morning.
Ostrich	Tyres loose – not safe to run.
Comet	One pump won't work
Lance	Fire box leaks badly. On Sunday the fire of this engine was pulled out and a train stopped on the line. Again on Monday [yesterday] the fire had to be pulled out and a train stopped on the line.
Osiris	In shed – under repairs – may be out on Thursday.
Meteor	In shed for thorough repair – may be out in less than a week.
Orion	Ditto.	Ditto
Ixion	Ditto.	Now all to pieces.
Rocket	At work. Fire box leaks VERY badly.
Falcon	In good order.
Priam	Ditto.
Damon	In pretty good order.
Cancer	[Great Western little engine] In pretty good order – working on Branch – has worked long and well.

TRAIN RUNNING

7.25 a.m. Down – 50 mins late to Plymouth consequent upon there being no engine to bring it out from Exeter.

4.10 a.m. Down Mail – 60 mins late. Goods Engine broke down.

SOUTH DEVON RAILWAY
Abstract of coke consumption – week ending 4th April 1855

Engine	Enginemen	Miles run	Coke – cwts	lbs per mile
Passenger				
Aurora	North & Newcombe	161½	55	38.14
Comet	Smith	621¾	132	23.77
Damon	Little & Neville	642	132	23.02
Falcon	Neville	907	153	18.89
Lance	Hutchins & North	463	155	37.45
Meteor	Hutchins & North	689¾	171	27.76
Orion	Hutchins & Henderson	695½	137	22.06
Osiris	Swinney	856	132	17.27
Rocket	Tunstall	593½	106	20.00
		5630½	1173	23.33
Goods				
Meteor	Hutchins	41	19	51.90
Tornado	Simm	696	292	46.98
Volcano	Chatworthy	649½	277	47.76
		1386½	588	47.49
	TOTAL	7017	1761	28.10

Birmingham, who was ready to supply engines similar in design, and to work the line for 10 years.

Terms were agreed, at a slightly lower rate than the GWR had been charging, with the contractor having the use of the company's engine sheds. At the end of the contract, the company was to buy all engines and plant at cost price, less depreciation. According to the contract, Geach was to commence working the line from 1st July 1851; however, the first of his engines did not arrive until the end of October – while the last of the dozen 4–4–0 STs arrived in South Devon in April 1853(!) – and the GWR continued to provide motive power for some time. No goods engines were provided until the end of 1854, when two 0–6–0 STs arrived, two more following several months later. All these engines were designed by Daniel Gooch, who appears to have had considerable interest in the contract.

Looking south-west from Dawlish along the coast towards Teignmouth, shortly before the end of the broad gauge. Slotted post signals, like the one on the right, were a common sight on the nineteenth-century GWR.   *National Railway Museum, York*

New contracts were made, shortly before the opening of the Cornwall Railway, for 7 years from 1st July 1859, but by this time Geach was dead. Among the contractors was 'Daniel Gooch, of Paddington, Gentleman' (!). The charges were again reduced, but severe limitations of maximum speeds were imposed – 35 mph above Newton Abbot and 30 mph below, while no goods train might run at more than 20 mph anywhere. When this contract ended in 1866, the directors bought the engines and commenced working the line themselves; they found that the actual working cost was averaging $9\frac{1}{2}$d. per train mile and that the contractors had been making almost 50 per cent profit!

A branch down to the Millbay Docks was opened in 1850, and two years later the branch to Sutton Harbour on the eastern side of Plymouth was completed.

The original intention was to construct the entire route between Exeter and Plymouth with double lines, but most of the railway was built to single track by Brunel to show the economy afforded by the Atmospheric system. During 1854-55 the main line was doubled from Newton to Totnes, a very necessary piece of work considering the delays which could be caused by the inclines on either side of Dainton Summit. The Torquay branch line was used to provide a new Down line as far as Aller, a signal box being opened at what became Torquay Junction.

The sea wall had given little trouble during the first few years, thus confuting the critics and justifying Brunel's assertions of its safety. However, 29th December 1852 brought what was the first in a succession of serious troubles when heavy rain caused a landslip at Breeches Rock between Dawlish and Teignmouth, and part of the sea wall was destroyed. Passengers were carried by road for two days, and then had to transfer from one train to another at the scene of the breach for another four days. The 'Crimean' winter of 1854-55 brought severe weather, resulting in the foundations of the wall being completely washed away near Teignmouth. A temporary wooden viaduct had to be constructed and it was not until the summer that the wall was rebuilt.

Further trouble occurred in October 1859 and again in January 1869, when a breach of 80 yards was made in the wall at the eastern end of Dawlish station. Apart from some damage near the same spot in the winter of 1872-73, this seems to have been the last occasion on which the sea was successful in its attacks, though the remaining years of the SDR's existence saw constant work in progress in building groynes to collect the shingle and prevent the scouring by the sea along the base of the wall.

The first important extension to the SDR during its 'post Atmospheric' period was to Tavistock. The single line, just under 13 miles long, of the South Devon & Tavistock Railway was opened for passengers on 22nd June 1859, goods traffic commencing in the following February. Shortly before this, on 4th May, the Cornwall Railway had been opened from Cornwall Junction, just outside Millbay station, to Truro. The work involved the construction of Brunel's masterpiece, the Royal Albert Bridge across the Tamar at Saltash. Millbay was enlarged at the joint expense of the SDR and the Cornwall Railway; while the line was widened south of King Street and a new goods shed with a bridge over Millbay Road was provided, these works not being completed until 1863.

On 2nd August 1859 the first section of the Dartmouth & Torbay Railway was opened, for passengers only, from the end of the Torquay branch to Paignton, being worked by the SDR. Another 3 miles to Brixham Road station, near Churston Ferrers, was opened for passengers on 14th March 1861. The final section, to a terminus at Kingswear, opposite Dartmouth, was not opened until 16th August 1864.

The next addition was an extension from Tavistock to Launceston, the Launceston & South Devon Railway, which opened for passengers on 1st July 1865, and for goods in the following October. The SDR worked this line, as they did the section to Tavistock. The branch to Moretonhampstead, authorised at the same time as that to Launceston, took longer to construct, the 12½ miles of single line not being opened until 4th July 1866. This was also worked by the SDR, who absorbed the South Devon & Tavistock in July 1865, the Moretonhampstead & South Devon in 1872, and the Launceston Company in 1873. The Dartmouth & Torbay was leased in perpetuity from 1st January 1866 and absorbed in 1872.

Having tackled the urgent work of doubling the main line between Newton and Totnes, the section between Exeter and Newton was next improved. Exminster (where the station was opened in 1852) to Starcross was doubled in 1860, and the following year the section between Exminster and Exeter was completed. An iron girder bridge for the new Up line was built alongside the existing timber one over the Exe, the latter being used for the Down line. The doubling of the line from Teignmouth to Newton was finished in 1865, Newton station having been completely reconstructed in 1861. The final section completed by the SDR was from Starcross to Dawlish, in February 1874, so that the GWR took over 12½ miles of single track, from Dawlish to Teignmouth and between Rattery and Hemerdon. Later in 1874 a third line was laid from Newton to Aller, whereupon the Torquay branch again became an independent line and Torquay Junction was abolished.

The final extension undertaken was the small branch to the City Basin at Exeter, which involved laying a third rail on the Down line between St David's station and the junction for the branch. This was to allow access to the Basin by 'narrow gauge' traffic – namely, that of the LSWR which had succeeded by devious means in reaching Exeter. Although the branch was opened on 17th June 1867, the third rail – a condition for the granting of the Act – was not laid until March 1871.

In 1874 the SDR was faced with a demand by the Devon & Cornwall Railway that a third rail be laid between Lydford and Plymouth to provide standard gauge access to that town. The SDR had been required to do this by an Act of 1865, on receiving notice from the other company – the prime mover being the LSWR, despite that company being bound by an Agreement of 1862 not to promote or assist any new line in the SDR's territory. Having reached Lydford, the D & CR not only served notice on the SDR to lay a third rail – and to be ready to receive their trains at Millbay – but also deposited a Bill for the 1872 Session for new lines from Marsh Mills to independent stations in both Plymouth and Devonport! After heated arguments, an agreement was reached and this was embodied in the D & CR's Act of 1873. That company was to make the Friary and Devonport branches, but to abandon its running powers into Millbay in exchange for the use of a new station at North Road and a loop to allow direct running to Devonport. The SDR had to provide standard gauge sidings at Laira, double the Sutton Harbour line as far as Friary Junction and build the new North Road station.

In 1875 the Associated Companies – a consortium of the GWR, B & ER and SDR – acquired the Plymouth, Great Western Docks at Millbay, but were forced to lay a third rail from North Road into the docks; however, no running powers were granted to the D & CR, and it was not until June 1878 that any standard gauge trucks entered Millbay Docks.

The independent Buckfastleigh, Totnes & South Devon Railway, authorised in 1864 and opened from Totnes to Ashburton on 1st May 1872, was the last broad gauge branch to be built in Devon, though the Totnes Quay Tramway, also owned by that company, was not opened until 1873. The BT & SDR was worked by the South Devon Railway whose directors, like those of the B & ER, were convinced that the broad gauge was more trouble than it was worth and should be converted to the standard gauge as soon as agreement could be reached. Permission was obtained in 1875 to alter their line and that of the Buckfastleigh Railway to 'Mixed or Narrow Gauge', but nothing was done.

Competition from the LSWR at Plymouth, combined with increasing costs for maintaining and renewing the permanent way, induced the Directors to follow the B & ER in agreeing to an amalgamation with the GWR. On 1st February 1876 the GWR took possession of the SDR under a working agreement, but Parliamentary confirmation of this was not obtained until 1878, when, on 1st August, the SDR was dissolved after a life of 34 years. Although the company had managed to pay a small dividend since 1851, it was not until 1872 that a figure of 4 percent was reached, this then gradually declining to 1½ percent for its last year of trading. Thomas Woolcombe remained Chairman until 1874, having done much to extricate the company from its early troubles, and was followed by Alexander Hubbard who became a Director of the GWR (after whom 'Badminton' class No.3299 was named).

The SDR had introduced the telegraph in 1848, and it was installed throughout the system. No train was allowed to start from a station until the question 'Is the line clear?' had been answered in the affirmative by the next station. However, one train might follow another in the same direction after the usual time interval. The crossing of trains on a single line was fixed by the Working Time Table, any variations or the crossing of special trains being arranged by means of telegraphed crossing orders. The train-staff system was never introduced.

Fixed signals were of the disc-and-crossbar type, similar to those used on the GWR, though painted differently, having the front of the disc black with a broad white ring and the backs of both disc and crossbar white, while on the GWR they were red all over. Caution or fantail signals were also erected at Plymouth and Newton, with a special double fantail (unknown on the GWR) used for signalling the Cornwall Company's trains at the junction with the SDR. At some places, station signals were interlocked with the points quite early in the SDR's existence; the first locking frame was installed at Totnes in 1873, followed by others at Starcross, Kingsbridge Road, Dawlish and Dainton during the next couple of years. Most of the work in connection with interlocking was left to be done by the GWR who inherited the single-line sections on the main line, and the gradients and curves west of Newton Abbot, as a permanent memorial to the SDR's disastrous 'Atmospheric Caper'.

CHAPTER TWO
TRAIN SERVICES AND SADDLE TANKS

The South Devon Railway was conceived as a local line to connect Plymouth with Exeter, but soon became part of a main line from Paddington to Plymouth, and later to Penzance. Within a short time of the opening, an 'express' train was leaving Exeter at 2.30 p.m., reaching Laira at 4.40 p.m. after five stops. This was an extension of the famous GWR express, at that time the fastest train in the world, which left Paddington at 9.50 a.m. and took $4\frac{1}{4}$ hours to cover the 194 miles to Exeter. The corresponding Up train left Laira at 10.15 a.m. and Exeter at 12.20 p.m., arriving at Paddington at 5.00 p.m. As neither the B & ER nor the SDR owned any locomotives, the GWR worked the entire service between London and Plymouth.

When the B & ER took over the working of their line on 1st May 1849, the times were immediately increased by ten minutes between Bristol and Exeter, while another 5 minutes were added for the Laira to Millbay section which had just been opened. The journey time of 7 hours 5 minutes between Paddington and Plymouth continued until 1852, when it was further increased to 7 hours 20 minutes, at which it remained

for several years. However, neither of these increases were caused by the SDR.

When the service from Exeter to Teignmouth was introduced, local traffic was quite heavy. The first weekend of the opening, 30th May 1846, happened to be Whit Weekend, and the *Exeter Flying Post* reported that 1,500 persons went from Exeter to the sea at Teignmouth, requiring a train of 21 carriages, while about the same number forsook the seaside in order to visit Exeter!

At first, the SDR was generous both with its train services and its provision for poor passengers, but as early as August 1847 it was reported: 'Your Directors have been desirous to hold out every encouragement and facility to Third Class Passengers that might not interfere prejudicially with the amount of First or Second Class traffic, but the extent to which advantage of the accommodation thus afforded was taken by classes of persons for which it was not intended, has obliged your Directors, in opening a further portion of the line to Totnes, to reduce the number of Third Class Trains, and so

Lance at Newton Abbot on 23rd July 1883. Completed in February 1875 by the Avonside Engine Co., *Lance* was the penultimate locomotive built for the SDR and replaced a similar engine of the same name which had been withdrawn in 1873. The second *Lance* survived until May 1892 when she, too, made the one-way journey to Swindon 'dump'.
Rev. A. H. Malan

regulate the times at which they run to adapt them, as far as circumstances would admit, more exclusively to the wants of the labouring classes.'

Excursion trains were introduced early in the life of the SDR. They carried 1,000 or more passengers and were of such length that they were too long for any of the station platforms; thus early did a perennial problem come to light. There were all manner of delays to these trains, both in departure and arrival, 'Dispatched with tolerable accuracy' being the highest praise! In July 1852 the first excursion was run from London; this conveyed 1,500 people in 33 carriages and allowed a week's stay in a choice of resorts, the fare to Plymouth being £1 – while the journey took no less than 13½ hours!

After 1852, many of the alterations to the train services were for the worse, especially on the Torquay branch. However, ten years later that town received preferential treatment when the 11.45 a.m. from Paddington was introduced, this being the famous 'Flying Dutchman' which initially ran between Paddington and Torquay. Passengers for Plymouth transferred to a stopping train at Newton Abbot, finally reaching their destination 7¼ hours after leaving London. The Up service was even worse, as to catch the Up 'Dutchman' at Exeter at 10.30 a.m. meant leaving Plymouth at 6.45 a.m.!

In September 1864, the 'Flying Dutchman' was re-routed to serve Plymouth. Stopping only at Teignmouth and Newton, Millbay was reached in 1¾ hours from Exeter, giving a time of 6 hours 25 minutes from Paddington. The Up train left Millbay at 8.30 a.m. and had an additional stop at Dawlish; over a century later there was still an 8.30 a.m. from Plymouth to Paddington!

A glimpse of everyday SDR operations may be afforded by a brief look at local passenger trains on the line. The 9.45 a.m. Exeter to Plymouth on Tuesday, 3rd July 1866, consisted of two first class vehicles, four second class, one third class, a carriage truck and a goods van, hauled by the 4—4—0ST *Hawk* (engineman Little). Arriving at Newton just a few minutes behind time, the train was then delayed for 55 minutes by the connecting service from the Torquay line, the 9.53 a.m. Kingswear, the engine of which had broken down at the terminus. Having detached one first and one third class vehicle at Newton during the wait, *Hawk* finally got away to Plymouth at 11.40 a.m. In charge of the train was Guard Warren, SDR, assisted by a Bristol & Exeter porter, the train having originated at Bristol.

The Torquay branch trains also varied in composition. The 7.23 a.m. from Kingswear on the same day, for example, left with one first class, one second, two third class vehicles and a goods van, with a carriage truck and a horse-box being attached during the Torquay stop. The following 8.54 a.m. Kingswear conveyed just one first class and one second class coach, whilst the 1.18 p.m. Kingswear consisted of one first, two second, one third, and a goods van. A mixed train, the 1.40 p.m. Torre, carried one third class vehicle plus nine 4-wheel wagons.

To illustrate the full traffic picture on the main line of the SDR, here is the working timetable for the winter of 1866/7:

SOUTH DEVON RAILWAY WORKING TIMETABLE (ABRIDGED)
with connecting services, 1st November 1866

MAIN LINE

		Goods	Pass'r	Local Goods	Pass'r	Pass'r	Pass'r	Pass'r	Pass'r	Pass'r	Goods	Pass'r
Paddington	dep.	12.20	8/10						9.15	6.0	10.15	4/50
Bristol	dep.	8.30	12.40	9/0		6.45	9.50	12/33	11.5	3/5	4.30	8/0
Exeter	arr.	2/10	3.10	2.25		9.35	12/45	2/27	2/55	5/35	8.30	10/5
		(MX)		(MX)								
Exeter	dep.	12.15	3.20	4.0	7.10	9.45	1/10	2/35	4/40	6/25	7/30	10/10
Dawlish	dep.	(12.58)	3.44	5.0	7.43	10.15	1/43	3/1	5/17	7/5	(8/10)	10/31
Newton	arr.	1.45	4.5	5.47	8.5	10.37	2/5	3/23	5/40	7/28	8/43	10/50
	dep.	3.0	4.8	7.0	8.10	10.43	2/10	3/28	5/45	7/33	10/0	10/52
Kingsbridge Rd.	dep.	6.10	(4.51)	11.15	9.7	11.45	3/7	(4/6)	6/32	8/28	(12.10)	(11/28)
Plymouth	arr.	7.40	5.25	12/10	9.52	12/25	3/55	4/35	7/15	9/15	1.15	11/55
Plymouth	dep.		5.40		10.25	1/40	4/40	4/40	7/35			
Falmouth	arr.		8.40		1/37	5/5	7/25	7/25	10/45			
Penzance	arr.		9.35		2/50	6/10	8/20	8/20				

		Goods	Local Goods	Pass'r	Pass'r	Pass'r	Pass'r	Pass'r	Pass'r	Pass'r	Pass'r	Goods
Penzance	dep.					6.15		8.48		11.30	2/40	
Falmouth	dep.					7.20		10.0		1/17	4/0	
Plymouth	arr.					10.28		1/10		4/30	7/0	
		(MX)	(MX)									
Plymouth	dep.	5.0	6.20	6.45	9.20	10.45	12/15	1/30	3/20	5/0	7/20	8/5
Kingsbridge Rd.	dep.	6.10	9.7	7.27	10.0	(11.15)	12/55	2/12	(3/50)	5/45	8/0	(9/35)
Newton	arr.	7.35	11.25	8.20	10.48	11.51	1/45	2/53	4/31	6/38	8/43	11/5
	dep.	8.45	12/5	8.25	10.53	11.56	1/50	2/58	4/37	6/43	8/50	12.0
Dawlish	dep.	(9.23)	12/50	8.49	11.15	12/16	2/12	3/20	5/0	7/5	9/12	(12.31)
Exeter	arr.	10.10	1/50	9.30	11.55	12/45	2/50	3/50	5/28	7/45	9/45	1.17
Exeter	dep.	1/0	3/0	9.45	12/30	1/0	3/10	4/0	5/35	8/30	9/55	4.0
Bristol	arr.	5/50	9/10	1/0	4/5	2/50	6/54	6/25	7/35	11/25	12.25	11.15
Paddington	arr.	3.5	7.55	4/45	9/30	6/15	11/10	11/10	11/10	4.35	4.35	1/15

NOTES: 0.00 indicates a.m., 0/00 indicates p.m.
            (0.00) indicates time of passing station.
            MX — Mondays excepted.

During 1867 and 1868 there was a general economy drive on the GWR, at a time when, hard though it is to credit, the company was on the verge of bankruptcy! One of the victims was the 'Flying Dutchman' which was withdrawn from the timetables, though it was reinstated 18 months later. With stops at Dawlish, Teignmouth and Newton, Plymouth was reached in $6\frac{3}{4}$ hours: however, there was no corresponding Up train, the fastest service being the 10.25 a.m. from Millbay, which took 7 hours 35 minutes to reach Paddington. In 1871 the Down 'Dutchman' reached Exeter in $4\frac{1}{4}$ hours, and the SDR restored the Up service with a departure time of 8.35 a.m. Both Up and Down trains took 1 hour 50 minutes between Exeter and Plymouth, and this was to remain the timing until the passing of the broad gauge!

Any train which by the remotest stretch of imagination could be regarded as 'fast' was for 1st and 2nd class passengers only; those who travelled 3rd class endured a very different service. In 1853 the Plymouth 'Cheap', conveying 3rd class passengers, left Paddington at 6.00 a.m. and took 14 hours to reach Plymouth, while the corresponding Up service was no better. The timings were later reduced to between 10 and 11 hours. In 1860, another train for 3rd class passengers was introduced in each direction, departing at about midday. On the SDR, 3rd class passengers were allowed on the 'night train' from London (Paddington dep. 8.10 p.m.) which conveyed the Bristol Mails to the West and arrived in Plymouth at 5.25 a.m., a privilege which neither the GWR or B & ER allowed.

By the end of the 1860s, competition from the LSWR forced the GWR to make some concessions, and 3rd class passengers were admitted to the 9.15 a.m. from Paddington and the 2.15 p.m. from Plymouth, thus giving three services in each direction between Paddington and Plymouth. In 1876, the year of the amalgamation, 3rd class passengers were allowed to travel on the following trains:

Paddington
dep.   5.30 a.m.   9.00 a.m.   10.30 a.m.   8.10 p.m.
Plymouth arr.   2.50 p.m.   4.20 p.m.   9.40 p.m.   4.40 a.m.

However, the Up service was confined to two trains, leaving Plymouth at 6.35 a.m. and 2.15 p.m., and arriving at Paddington at 5.15 p.m. and 10.20 p.m. respectively. Of the ten Down trains and nine Up trains on weekdays between Exeter and Plymouth, three in each direction carried local 3rd class passengers.

During SDR days, all trains stopped at St Thomas, passengers to and from Exeter being encouraged to use that station rather than St David's, as the rental paid by the SDR to the B & ER for the use of the latter station was based on the number of their passengers using it. The SDR regarded St Thomas as *the* station for Exeter so far as local traffic was concerned, and, truth to tell, it was probably more convenient for the majority of passengers. The company was always Plymouth-based, having been promoted in that town, the principal offices being situated at Millbay.

Had Brunel's 'Atmospheric Railway' been a success, the SDR would have required only a few engines for shunting and goods trains. However, the manifest failure of the system resulted in the company turning for help to the GWR who were already working the B & ER. It was one thing to run the services over the B & ER's fairly level line between Bristol and Exeter, but a rather different matter when it came to the

section between Newton and Plymouth. The GWR had no locomotives that were suitable or adequate for hauling trains over the 1 in 40 gradients.

Daniel Gooch therefore arrived at a 4—4—0 saddletank design for use on the line, setting a precedent for passenger engines that was closely followed for the remainder of the SDR's existence, and indeed until the abolition of the broad gauge. The drawings reveal that they were originally intended to have been *tender* engines, which would have determined a very different future. As it was, the company possessed no tender engines throughout its existence and consequently bequeathed to the GWR very small turntables, which were an operating handicap. The first two engines, *Corsair* and *Brigand*, were not delivered until August and September 1849, by which time the line to Plymouth had been in use for over a year.

GWR engines known to have worked on the SDR during the period of the working agreement were:

> 2–2–2 'Fire Fly' class – *Pegasus*.
> 2–2–2 'Sun' class – *Antelope* and *Lance*.
> 2–4–0 'Leo' class – *Pisces, Cancer, Taurus, Capricornus, Dromedary, Scorpio, Aries, Stromboli* and *Libra*.
> 0–6–0 'Hercules' class – *Goliah*.

Of these, only the 2–4–0s and *Goliah* would have been of any use between Newton and Plymouth.

The agreement found little favour with either the GWR or the SDR, and a contract was signed with Messrs Evans and Geach for working the line for ten years from 1st July 1851. These contractors eventually provided twelve 4–4–0 STs (with inside sandwich frames) for passenger work, and four 0–6–0 STs for goods, all designed by Daniel Gooch and built under his supervision. As in the case of the GWR engines at that time, all were named but not numbered, a practice which was maintained until the amalgamation in 1876. In contrast, the B & ER – which appeared to have a puritanical streak in its make-up – used only numbers.

The passenger engines were built by no less than four different firms, while the goods engines were built by a fifth! The protracted delivery period did not suggest that the wide spreading of orders was due to any urgency being involved; the speed with which two firms, Longridge & Co., of Bedlington, and Haigh Foundry, Wigan, delivered their first engines (the contract not being signed until 3rd June and the engines delivered in October and November) suggests that someone had anticipated the likely outcome of Brunel's talks with Geach and Evans during 1850!

Comet, Lance, Meteor and *Aurora* were the Longridge engines, delivered between October 1851 and the following January, while *Priam, Damon, Falcon* and *Orion* came from Haigh Foundry at intervals between November 1851 and the following February. One engine, *Ostrich*, was built by William Fairbairn & Sons, Manchester, being delivered in August 1852, and the two remaining passenger engines, *Ixion* and *Osiris*, by Stothert & Slaughter of Bristol, were both delivered in April 1853. All were of Gooch's 'Corsair' design, and the first delivered, by Longridge & Co., were sent in trucks over the standard gauge from Northumberland to Gloucester, where they were tried out on the GWR's Cheltenham line. Two did not survive to be taken into GWR stock in 1876, the only SDR engines not to carry GWR numbers. *Osiris* went to Portreath, in August 1873, to be used as a stationary engine for the incline, while

One of the small ex-SDR 2–4–0 saddle tanks, No. 2137 *Prince*, at Brixham station. Built in 1871 by the Ince Forge Company, she found employment mostly on branch lines, spending periods at both Brixham and Ashburton. Converted to the standard gauge in 1893, she was renumbered 1316, and her nameplates removed; a further six years were spent in traffic, before withdrawal in 1899. Strangely, she then had an even longer life ahead, being used as a stationary boiler until finally scrapped in 1935.

Lance was destroyed in a collision, between Menheniot and St Germans, early on the morning of 2nd December 1873.

The four goods engines were built by Vulcan Foundry to the same specifications as a series built for the Vale of Neath Railway, for which Gooch also designed locomotives. *Volcano* and *Tornado* were built in November and December 1854, while *Goliah* and *Sampson* (the spelling of the former name being faithfully copied from that of the GWR engine which had worked on the SDR) followed in September 1855. They had the usual inside sandwich frames, the second pair having larger saddle tanks. *Tornado* lived up to its name by suffering a boiler explosion at Totnes on 13th March 1860, killing the driver, and also achieved notoriety by being involved in the running-away of a clay train between Burngullow and Par on 29th October 1872.

As the SDR's engines were delivered, those belonging to the GWR returned to their native haunts; most had gone by the summer of 1852, though there were then only eight SDR engines in service. However, *Cancer* was still in South Devon in 1854. Until the end of that year, the entire service, both passenger and goods, had to be undertaken by the twelve passenger engines. Some considerable difficulties were experienced, with only nine of these locomotives at work on the entire main line from Exeter to Plymouth and the branch to Torre, and, of these, only four in what could be regarded as a satisfactory condition!

Shortly before the opening of the Cornwall Railway, new contracts were made, for seven years from 1st July 1859, with Messrs Evans, Walker and *Gooch* (Geach having died). During this period, sixteen 4–4–0 STs and another eight 0–6–0 STs were added to stock. As the SDR was also working the Cornwall Railway from Plymouth to Truro, the total of 40 engines (not reached until December 1864) left very little in reserve. On 1st January 1866, the standard gauge West Cornwall Railway from Truro to Penzance was taken over by the 'Associate

Companies'. The line already had its own standard gauge engines, which were either converted or sold after the broad gauge rail was added between Truro and Penzance in March 1867. The 40 engines, plus one or two ex-WCR engines, had then to maintain the entire service between Exeter and Penzance, the Kingswear branch, the branches to Moretonhampstead and Launceston, the Sutton Harbour and Millbay Docks branches at Plymouth, and the Cornwall Railway's branch from Truro to Falmouth!

Another 24 engines were supplied under the second contract, all coming from Slaughter, Gruning & Co., of Bristol. The passenger engines were *Eagle*, *Elk*, *Hawk*, *Lynx*, *Gazelle*, *Mazeppa*, *Giraffe*, *Lion*, *Antelope* and *Wolf*, delivered between April and August 1859; *Tiger* and *Hector*, which arrived in May and August 1860; *Cato* of September 1863; *Dart* received in December 1864; and *Pollux* and *Castor* which appeared on May and June 1865. They were very similar to the earlier 4–4–0 STs, though their appearance was changed by the fitting of long tanks of 1,100 gallons capacity, extending from the back of the smokebox to the back of the firebox (the earlier engines had short 800 gallon capacity saddle tanks over the boiler barrel only). The driving wheels, of 5'6" diameter, were 3" smaller than on the first series.

The eight goods engines also had inside frames, 4'6" wheels (again 3" smaller than those built by Vulcan Foundry) and similar tanks to those on the passenger engines. There were considerable intervals between construction – *Dido*, *Hero*, *Hebe* and *Ajax* were built in March, April and September 1860, followed by *Brutus* in October 1862 and, exactly a year later, *Argo* and *Atlas* in October 1863, with *Juno* completing the class in December 1864.

The company purchased the entire stock of 40 engines from the contractors in 1866, and immediately added to their number six passenger and two goods engines, all built by the Avonside Engine Co. (the successors to Slaughter, Gruning &

Co.). The new 4–4–0 STs were the first SDR engines to have inside plate frames. The tanks were of the same capacity as those fitted to the previous batch, but the wheels were larger at 5′8″. *Gorgon, Pluto, Sedley, Sol, Titan* and *Zebra* were built between September and November 1866, and must have been a godsend to the company in its efforts to work the entire service between Exeter and Truro with the existing limited motive power. The goods engines, *Remus* and *Romulus*, were of the same design as those built between 1860 and 1864.

Between 1868 and 1872, the SDR acquired an odd selection of tank engines, most of them second-hand. There were, however, four new engines, all of different designs! *Tiny*, built by Sara & Co. of Plymouth, was a vertical boiler 0–4–0 engine, with a well tank holding only 80 gallons of water, and 3 ft diameter wheels. It was purchased for the Sutton Harbour branch, previously worked by horses. After withdrawal in June 1883, it became a stationary engine at Newton Abbot shops and remained there until 1927, when it was overhauled and placed on exhibition on the Down platform of the new station, the only original broad gauge engine in existence.

Taurus was another Avonside product, being an 0–6–0 ST built in May 1869, but differing in appearance and size from the 'Dido' class engines, having wheels of only 3′ diameter and a 12′ wheelbase (compared with 15′5″ of the larger engines). It was employed on several branches, including the Ashburton, Brixham and Sutton Harbour lines, and was converted to standard gauge in April 1894. *King* was also built by Avonside, being a small 2–4–0 *side* tank – the first side tank engine on the SDR (who had not commissioned its construction, hence the side tanks!). It had been ordered by the little Torbay & Brixham Railway who had been unable to pay for it. As its tanks held only 80 gallons, the same as *Tiny*, its range of duties was very limited. Soon after being taken into GWR stock, it was converted to standard gauge (in 1878) and given the number 2.

Prince was another 2–4–0 T, but was a saddle tank very similar in appearance to *Taurus*, though built by the Ince Forge Co. at Wigan. With 4′ diameter wheels and a wheelbase of only 12′, it was employed on similar duties to *Taurus*. Converted to standard gauge in 1893, it was withdrawn from service in 1899. Its useful life, however, was not yet over—it was then used as a stationary engine until 1935, when it was cut up at Swindon.

No less than 13 second-hand engines were added to stock in five years. Three, built by Slaughter, Gruning & Co., came from the Llynvi Valley Railway in South Wales, when that line combined with the standard gauge Ogmore Valley Railway to form the Llynvi & Ogmore Railway in 1868, being exchanged for four standard gauge engines of the West Cornwall Railway. *Ada* and *Una* were 0–6–0 STs, very similar to the SDR's own engines, whilst *Rosa* was a 4–4–0 ST with 5′6″ wheels, subsequently being converted at Newton Abbot into an 0–6–0 ST with 4′6″ wheels.

Etna and *Hecla* came from the Carmarthen & Cardigan Railway, which spent most of its life in the hands of a Receiver. They were built in 1864 by Rothwell & Co. (the builders of the fabulous B & ER 4–2–4 Ts with 9′ driving wheels) and were reputed to be the last engines constructed by the firm. They were 4–4–0 STs with 5′3″ wheels, arriving on the SDR in 1868

and 1872 respectively. *Heron* and *Magpie* also had associations with the C & CR, having been hired for service on that line. They were 4–4–0 side tanks, built in 1861 by Sharp, Stewart & Co., the only broad gauge engines built by that company. They were sold to the SDR when the C & CR was converted to the standard gauge in 1872. Needless to say, the SDR immediately converted them to saddle tanks! However, they were always the 'odd' engines among all the 4–4–0 STs and, despite the efforts of both the SDR and the GWR, they continued to look 'different' to the end of their days.

Redruth and *Penwith* were of Cornish origin, as might be expected from their names. They were ex-West Cornwall tender engines, which were converted to broad gauge saddle tanks at Newton Abbot. *Redruth* was an 0–6–0, built in 1856 by the WCR at their Carn Brea shops from parts supplied by Slaughter, Bruning & Co. – no mean feat considering the very limited facilities at Carn Brea. Originally it had outside frames, but ran as an inside-framed engine after conversion. It was a poor steamer and far from reliable, being primarily employed as the Millbay Goods shunter. *Penwith* was an older engine, built for the WCR by Stothert & Slaughter in 1853. It was a 2–4–0, having inside frames after conversion, but unlike its companion, it was a very reliable engine and in consequence was usually Millbay's passenger shunter. That duty involved being shedded at Liskeard, working an early morning train to Plymouth, and returning to Liskeard with a late evening train. There was still a similar early morning and late evening working in 1902.

The remaining four engines came from the GWR in 1872. *Bulkeley, Fowler* and *Saunders* were 0–6–0 side tanks built at Swindon in 1865/6 – the only side tanks built by the GWR for use on the broad gauge – and were fitted with condensing gear for use when working over the Metropolitan Railway. When the Metropolitan converted to standard gauge in 1869, the condensing gear was removed from these engines, and three of the six were sold to the SDR. Of ungainly appearance, even for the broad gauge, it did little to help their looks when the SDR added short saddle tanks between the dome and the firebox! After 1876, the GWR rebuilt them as saddle tanks (as had already been done to the three engines not sold). The fourth engine, *Stromboli* (which was originally named *Juno*), was one of four 0–6–0 STs of the 'Banking' class, built at Swindon in 1852.

Between 1872 and 1875, a further 22 engines were built for the SDR by Avonside, and were designed to be easily convertible to the standard gauge. They comprised ten 0–6–0 STs for goods work, four more 4–4–0 STs for passenger duties, and eight 0–4–0 STs, of two different classes, for shunting. From 1892, nine of the goods and seven of the small shunting tanks were converted to the standard gauge.

The 0–6–0 STs had inside frames, straight footplating with closed-in wheel splashers, and were named *Buffalo, Elephant, Camel, Hercules, Dragon, Achilles, Dromedary, Emperor, Python* and *Vulcan*: once again, there was a mixture of natural history and classical mythology in the names, while *Emperor* presumably kept *King* and *Prince* company! *Hercules*, as GWR No.2163 was withdrawn in 1889, but the others were all converted – *Dromedary* being dealt with a month before the gauge conversion, in April 1892. As broad gauge engines, they had originally been given the number series 2160 to 2169 by the GWR. The nine converted survivors carried numbers from 1317 to 1325, though not in the same order.

The four 4–4–0 STs also had inside frames, with footplating outside the wheels and narrower fireboxes than previous engines of the type. They had a slightly less ungainly appearance than most other broad gauge engines, and the first two, *Leopard* and *Stag*, were unusual in having closed-in wheel splashers. *Lance* and *Osiris* were the last of the type to be built, but the distinction of being the last to be withdrawn was held by *Leopard* and *Stag* which survived until June 1893, being used as shunting engines for the condemned stock at Swindon.

The first three of the 0–4–0 Ts were well tanks, built in 1873, with inside frames and cylinders, and wheels 3'0" in diameter. *Weasel* (GWR No.2173) ceased work in June 1877 and was withdrawn in 1882 to become a portable engine of the Engineering Department. *Owl* and *Goat* (Nos.2172 and 2174) were withdrawn in 1889 and 1885 respectively, both being sold to Pearson & Son in 1890, after which they were used for working stone trains from a temporary quarry line near Ivybridge in connection with the doubling of the main line. In June 1893 they were bought back by the GWR and converted to standard gauge saddle tanks, running as Nos.1327 and 1328, the former being withdrawn in 1913 and the latter in 1910.

The other five engines, built in 1874, had short saddle tanks and *outside* cylinders – a feature shared only with Gooch's tank engines designed for the Metropolitan services. The wheels were of the same diameter as those on the well tanks built the previous year. They were named *Raven*, *Rook*, *Crow*, *Lark* and *Jay* – a unique achievement for the SDR of uniform naming! *Raven* was sold to the Torbay & Brixham Railway soon after 1876, returning to the GWR when that line was absorbed in 1883. All five were converted in 1892, being renumbered from Nos.2175–9 to Nos.1329–33. Most of their working lives, before being sold out of service between 1906 and 1910, were spent in the Millbay Docks at Plymouth. No.1330 returned to the GWR in 1924 when it was taken over from Messrs Powlesland

& Mason at Swansea, becoming No.925, being withdrawn in 1929.

Three engines were under construction at Newton Abbot when the amalgamation took place. They had been laid down in June and July 1875, most of the parts having been obtained from the Ince Forge Co. who had built the 2–4–0 ST *Prince* in 1871. They were to have been 2–4–0 STs and very similar to *Prince*. The work was transferred to Swindon and they eventually emerged as standard gauge side tanks bearing the numbers 1298–1300 instead of their intended names *Saturn*, *Jupiter* and *Mercury*.

With the exception of *Etna* (No.2132) all SDR engines retained their names when numbered by the GWR; *Etna*'s loss of name was due to that engine being fitted with a new saddle tank of B & ER origin. On conversion to the 'narrow' gauge however, all the ex-SDR engines lost their names.

SDR locomotives were painted dark green, with a black panel line having a thin white line on either side. Buffers and buffer beams were vermilion. Specifications for the engines built in 1859 stipulated that the engines be painted with four coats – boiler and wheels green, frame brown, picked out with red and black.

One further engine came into GWR stock from South Devon, though not from the SDR. This was an 0–4–0 well tank named *Queen*, the property of the Torbay & Brixham Railway who had purchased it in 1868 (hence the name *King* given to the Avonside engine for which they were unable to pay). It had been constructed by E. B. Wilson, being one of several engines built in 1852–53 for use on the formation of the Portland Breakwater. In 1870 it was mortgaged to the SDR, who also took over the second engine, *King*, in the following year. Although included in the SDR stock from July 1870, *Queen* continued to work on the Torbay and Brixham line – together with *Raven* purchased from the GWR in 1877 – until that line was absorbed on 1st January 1883. On that day, *Queen* was added to stock and also withdrawn – surely the shortest career of any GWR engine!

CHAPTER THREE

THE TWILIGHT OF THE BROAD GAUGE

On 1st February 1876 the GWR took possession of the South Devon Railway, and having taken over control of the neighbouring Bristol & Exeter the previous month, effectively doubled the length of its main line within this short period. The entire 246 miles between Paddington and Plymouth were now owned and worked by the company, which also worked the remaining 80 miles between Plymouth and Penzance. Although the Cornwall Railway remained an independent company, the GWR had a majority of members on its managing committee. The former SDR main line was later to become the best-known section on the GWR's system: postcards, posters, jig-saws and other publicity material all showed the 'Cornish Riviera' passing along the sea wall between Teignmouth and Dawlish, with either *Caerphilly Castle* or *King George V* at its head, depending upon the date of issue!

However, all this was far into the future when the company assumed responsibility for the lines west of Bristol. Nor were the problems of the incredible holiday traffic of the inter-war years likely to have entered into the minds or imagination of those involved with the day-to-day running of the service in the late 1870s. They were more concerned with the problems inherited from Brunel's genius: those sections of single line along the coast and between Rattery and Hemerdon, the curves and the gradients, and, most of all, the broad gauge itself. Although Brunel's gauge was not to disappear for another 16 years, the writing was on the wall. All that was left was the line from Paddington to Penzance, with sundry branches, while the frontier of the purely broad gauge lines had been pushed back as far west as Exeter. The former WCR line between Truro and Penzance was 'mixed' and the broad gauge rail was being added to the Launceston branch south of Lydford and to the main line between Tavistock Junction and Keyham, for the use of the LSWR. It was the twilight of the broad gauge.

The Torquay branch was being doubled, while a new station at Torquay had been promised by the SDR, and was to be provided by the GWR in the following year. Another new station, at North Road, Plymouth, intended primarily for the use of the LSWR, was originally to have been built of stone. However, delays in starting the work, and the impatience of the LSWR to have the station in use, resulted in the construction of a relatively inexpensive set of premises built of wood. There were Up and Down main line platforms on either side of the running lines, and it was not at all worthy of the town it served. Some improvements were made in later years, the refreshment rooms being opened in 1888.

The replacement of Brunel's 'baulk road', with its longitudinal sleepers, by cross-sleepered track, took place very slowly on the former SDR lines. The sections between St Thomas and Starcross, Newton Abbot and Torquay, were dealt with prior to 1892, and there was some new track at Dawlish station; Newton had been renamed Newton Abbot in 1877. Some of the broad gauge sleepers had extremely long lives, and some were still in use in the sidings behind Dainton signal box in the late 1940s, still in their original length and revealing where the broad gauge chairs had been fitted!

The major work of doubling the remaining single-line sections was not tackled for many years, though that through Teignmouth was doubled in July 1884. The old station at Teignmouth, which was of wood with an overall roof, was later replaced by much larger premises, the site of the old station, which was on a severe curve, being used for a goods station. The engineering work involved in the two remaining sections, the coastal tunnels near Dawlish, Marley Tunnel and the viaducts between Rattery and Hemerdon, was of such magnitude that the GWR had to allow the nuisance to continue.

The gradual substitution of semaphore signals in place of the old disc-and-crossbar type took place on the GWR during the 1860s, while fantail signals had been abolished between 1868 and 1874. However, the SDR did not follow suit, so that disc-and-crossbar signals were still to be found in the West of England in the 1890s. Both the SDR and the B & ER were fully equipped with block instruments; those on the SDR being of the single needle type, while the B & ER used Tyer's. In 1876 over 330 miles of double track on the GWR were still worked only by time intervals, and the last section, that between Wellington and Nantwich, did not disappear until 1891!

On 1st January 1883 the Torbay & Brixham's short line from Churston to Brixham was taken over. This was the only addition in South Devon to the broad gauge, but there were two new lines on the standard gauge. The little Teign Valley Railway, from Chudleigh Road to Ashton, was opened, after a most protracted gestation, on 9th October 1882; while the Princetown Railway, another single-line branch and built almost entirely on the course of the old Plymouth & Dartmoor Railway, was opened on 1st August 1883.

A major event of the latter days of the broad gauge occurred in March 1891, though it was neither part of the GWR's plans or to their liking. On 9th March came the great blizzard, the worst known in the West of England for many generations, which became part of local folklore. Much of the West Country was buried under several feet of snow, railway lines were blocked in numerous places and all traffic was stopped for several days. When the 3.00 p.m. express from Paddington (the 'Zulu'), due at Plymouth at 8.55 p.m., reached South Brent, it was unable to proceed any further. The passengers, who had left London on Monday afternoon, eventually reached Plymouth at midday on Friday!

A few weeks later, one end of Marley Tunnel appeared to be in danger of collapsing, and all traffic was stopped from

30th May to 4th June. The cause of the trouble was the construction of a second tunnel alongside, as part of the work required for the long overdue doubling of the main line. This had set an old landslide in motion, causing the wall of the old tunnel to bulge in a dangerous manner.

The amalgamation produced no startling changes or improvements in the train services, which were very similar to those during the early 1860s.

In June 1879 the first new express train for 17 years was introduced. This was the 'Zulu', running between Paddington and Plymouth at the same speeds as the 'Flying Dutchman' and carrying 1st and 2nd class passengers only. Its name was another unofficial bestowal on the part of the GWR staff, the Zulu War being in progress at that time.

March 1884 saw the Night Mail trains cease to be Limited, either in classes or in the number of passengers carried, and at the same time they were accelerated. The Down train now reached Bristol at 12.12 a.m., Exeter at 2.30 a.m., Plymouth at 4.27 a.m., and Penzance at 7.55 a.m. The Up service left Penzance at 5.00 p.m. (instead of 3.50 p.m.), Plymouth at 8.23 p.m., Exeter at 10.30 p.m., and Bristol at 12.45 a.m., arriving at Paddington at 4.00 a.m. From the same date, passengers were no longer carried between London and Bristol on the 8.10 p.m., a train which had run daily since 1855.

Being concerned by the success of the LSWR in the South Devon area, the GWR ordered an investigation to be undertaken, comparing the services of the two companies.

By 1884, it was clear that the GWR was losing traffic to the LSWR, with a 194-mile journey from London to Exeter (via Bristol), compared with the rival company's 171 miles. Further, the South Western's station at Queen Street was almost in the centre of the town, whereas St. Davids was about half a mile distant. The LSWR were considered to have the better train service, further enhanced by the fact that (from 1882) they conveyed third class passengers by all trains. The GWR, on the other hand, still ran the 11.45 a.m. and 3.00 p.m Paddington services (and the corresponding Up trains) for first and second class traffic only. In consequence, the LSWR carried over 19,000 bookings per year between London and Exeter, whilst the GWR's share was 7,600.

The LSWR had no independent line to Plymouth at the time, but ran over GWR tracks to and from 'Lidford Junction', a distance of 22¼ miles from Plymouth. They commenced running to and from Devonport on 18th May 1876, but upon the opening of North Road station on 28th March 1877 (joint with the GWR), commenced bookings from Plymouth itself. The LSW again had the edge on London traffic, with about 26,000 bookings per year to and from Plymouth as compared with the GWR's 23,000. As in the case of Exeter, the LSW conveyed the bulk of third class traffic, evident by the fact that they carried some 53% of the passengers for a 46% share of the total receipts.

In July 1887 a new express between Paddington and Plymouth was introduced in both directions for 3rd class passengers, who had until then no reasonable service between 9.00 a.m. and 5.00 p.m., and in consequence had travelled from Waterloo by the LSWR. Calling only at the same stations as the 'Flying Dutchman', it left Paddington at 1.00 p.m. and Plymouth at 12.00 noon, taking 6½ hours for the journey. It was at once named the 'Jubilee' by the staff. June 1889 saw the 'Zulu' downgraded to admit 3rd class passengers, while a

MAIN LINE SERVICES – OCTOBER 1880 (Abridged)

	Mail and Passenger		Local Goods (MX)	Goods		Fast Goods		Local Passenger	Passenger		Passenger	
Paddington		8/10					10/45					
Swindon	10/35	10/45				1.9	1.17					
Bristol	12.5	12.30			9/15	2.27	2.37					6.15
Exeter	2.40	2.50		1.35	2.0	5.4	5.15		..	7.5	8.32	8.40
Teignmouth	3.13	3.15	(4.45)	2.42	2.54	(5.49)			7.52	7.54	9.19	9.21
Newton Abbot	3.24	3.32	Kingsbridge Rd.	3.14	3.55	6.0	6.12	(9.0)	8.5	8.14	9.31	9.38
Ivybridge		(4.13)	5.20 X 5.25	6.10	6.20	7.16 X 7.21		Plympton	9.11	9.13	10.24	10.26
Plymouth	4.37	4.50	6.55	7.20		7.55		9.18	9.47		10.48	11.0
Penzance	8.10										2/53	

	Passenger		Local Goods (MX)	Passenger		Empty Plant (MO)	Passenger		Local Passenger	Fast Passenger	
Paddington					4.55			9.0			11.45
Swindon				5.30	5.0		10.50	10.55		1/12	1/27
Bristol	7.10		1.0	7.39 7.49	7.50 8.0		9.20 9.30			2/21	2/26
Exeter	10.48	10.55	6.20 7.30	11.50 11.58	12/50 1/0		2/10 2/20			4/0	4/10
Teignmouth	11.37	11.39	9.32 X 9.56	12/36 12/38	(1/35)		2/53 2/55			4/40	4/42
Newton Abbot	11.49	11.55	10.12 10.42	12/48 12/54	1/45 1/55		3/5 3/11		(5/25)	4/52	4/56
Ivybridge	12.54	12.56	1/17 1/24	1/43 1/45	(3/29)		4.0 4/2		Plympton	(5/35)	
Plymouth	1/27		2/0							6/0	6/10
Penzance				6/30			8/50			9/5	

	Passenger	Passenger	Fast Passenger		Passenger		Passenger (WO)	Fast Goods		Fast Passenger	
Paddington				3/0		10.30			5.55		5/0
Swindon	(to Liskeard)	4/27 4/37	1/0 1/30			10.0 11.10	6/50	7/0
Bristol		5/36 5/41	3/10 3/20		1/0 2/35	8/5	8/15
Exeter	(to St. Germans)	5/15	7/14 7/18	6/35 7/25		7/40 8/10	10/20 10/25
Teignmouth	6/0 6/2	7/40 7/42	8/6 8/8		(9/2)	10/51 10/55
Newton Abbot	6/12 6/18	7/51 7/55	8/18 8/23	(11/0 Plympton)	9/16 9/38	11/5 11/8
Ivybridge	6/2 X 6/4	7/12 X 7/14	(8/36)	9/20 X 9/22		(10/53)	(11/48)
Plymouth	6/35 6/40	7/50 8/0	9/0		10/0	11/17	11/30 2.0	12.15
Penzance	7/3 (St. G.)	9/5 (Lisk.)				to Falmouth	

	Goods							
Exeter	9/0							
Teignmouth	11/10 11/40							
Newton Abbot	11/53 12.25							
Ivybridge	(2.2)							
Plymouth	3.0 3.30							
Penzance	1/18							

	Local Goods	Local Goods	Passenger	Fast Passenger		Local Passenger	Passenger		Fast Passenger
Penzance				(7.25 Liskeard)					6.25
Plymouth	12.30	4.30	6.45	8.12 8.35		8.40	9.5	10.18 10.35
Ivybridge	3.0 3.5	5.19 X 5.21	7.20 X 7.22	(8.58)	(to Plympton)	9.40 9.42	11.2 11.4
Newton Abbot	(Kingsbridge Rd. 3.50)	7.30 7.55	8.15 8.24	9.39 9.44	8.54	10.35 10.43	11.44 11.50
Teignmouth	(8.10)	8.35 8.37	9.54 X 9.56		10.53 10.55	11.59 12/2
Exeter	9.0		9.25 9.45	10.75 10.50		11.40 11.50	12/40 12/50
Bristol		1/5 1/15	12/4 12/9		2/35	2/50 3/0
Swindon		2/35 2/42	1/8 1/18			4/5 4/10
Paddington		5/5	2/45			6/0

	Passenger	Passenger	Fast Passenger		Passenger		Passenger	Fast Goods		Local Passenger
Penzance				11.15		10.0				5/5
Plymouth	12/0	2/8	2/7 † 2/15	1/50 2/30		3/50	4/10	(to Plympton 5/18)
Ivybridge	12/37 12/39	(to North Rd)	(2/36)	3/1 3/3		4/28 4/30	(4/50)
Newton Abbot	1/29 1/35	† 2/11)	3/11 3/15	3/50 3/56		5/23 5/28	6/17 6/42
Teignmouth	1/45 1/47		3/24 3/27	4/6 4/8		5/38 5/41	(6/54)
Exeter	2/35 2/42		3/50 3/55	4/47 4/55		6/34 6/42	7/37 8/15
Bristol	6/30		5/29 5/34	6/50 7/0	10/10	12.5 1.0
Swindon			6/32 6/42	8/10 8/20		2.55 3.15
Paddington			8/10	10/20		6.45

	Perishables	Passenger	Night Mail	Market Goods	Fast Goods		Local Passenger (WO)	Goods	
Penzance	12/25		3/50	12/0				1/30
Plymouth	5/0 5/30	6/35	7/35 7/45	8/8 † 8/30	9/15		10/40	11/25 11/45
Ivybridge	(X 6/3)	7/11 X 7/13	8/13 8/15	9/14 X 9/23	(10/19)	(to Plympton	(12.36)
Newton Abbot	7/0 7/10	8/6 8/15	9/2 9/10	10/38 11/35	12.0 12.30	10/54)	2.15 3.10
Teignmouth	7/20 7/23	8/25 8/27	9/20 9/22	(11/50)	(12.44)		3.30 4.0
Exeter	8/0 8/10	9/15	10/2 10/12	12.35 1.0	2.5 2.30		6.15 6.45
Bristol	11/5 11/15		12.32 12.50	5.40	8.20		12/30
Swindon	12.30 12.35		2.10 2.22				
Paddington	3.5		4.35				

NOTES

X Train crosses another
WO Wednesdays only
† Plymouth (North Road)

year later the new 3rd class 'Cornishman' was introduced, this being the 10.05 a.m. Paddington to Penzance and the 11.15 a.m. Penzance to Paddington trains, which were accelerated. At long last, even the historic 'Flying Dutchman' had to surrender to the siege of the 3rd class, which it did in October.

The new 'Cornishman' omitted stops at Bath, Taunton and west of Exeter, easily outpacing both the 'Dutchman' and the 'Zulu'. Bristol was reached in 2½ hours (after the inevitable ten minute stop at Swindon in accordance with the terms of the lease of the Refreshment Rooms) and this was the first time this had been achieved since 1848! Exeter was reached in 4 hours 5 minutes, and Plymouth (North Road) in 5 hours 35 minutes, while Penzance, after 11 stops, was reached in 8 hours

A 'Rover' class 4–2–2 waiting at Exeter (St. David's) station with an Up passenger train during 1889. *Emperor* was another 'renewal' of an earlier 'Iron Duke' engine, entering traffic in 1880; a Bristol engine, she was probably working between Newton Abbot and her home town when photographed.

Collection R. C. Riley

42 minutes. The Up service, which was practically a first part of the 'Zulu' (still running at its old time from Plymouth), left Penzance at 11.15 a.m., North Road at 2.10 p.m., Exeter at 3.45 p.m. and Bristol at 5.18 p.m., to arrive at Paddington at 7.50 p.m. This was the first instance of Millbay being by-passed, as well as of non-stop running between Exeter and Plymouth. At the same time, June 1890, a fast broad gauge train was put on in each direction between Bristol and Plymouth, providing connections with the newly established 'West to North' and 'North to West' services via the Severn Tunnel, Hereford and Shrewsbury.

Following the amalgamation, little time was lost in sending both GWR and ex-B & ER engines to work in the West of England, and, as the changing of engines at Exeter was no longer necessary, through running was introduced between Bristol and Newton Abbot. Thus the famous 8 ft Singles became a familiar sight on the coastal section between Dawlish and Teignmouth. West of Newton the severe gradients and curves made it impractical to use the 'singles', so that Newton Abbot became the change-over point at which the 4—4—0 STs took over the trains.

Eight of the B & ER's original twenty 4–2–2 tender engines, smaller editions of Gooch's 'Iron Duke' class, survived to be taken over by the GWR and shared in the working of the Bristol to Newton section, the last of them being withdrawn in 1889. Three other 4–2–2s were of a very different design and appearance, having inside frames and bogies. They started life as 4–2–4 Ts, with 8 ft 10 in driving wheels (being 'renewals' of the legendary engines built by Rothwell's), four of which were built at Bristol in 1868 and 1873; they were thus almost brand new engines when taken over by the GWR. They became Nos.2001–4, but the first engine was involved in the Long Ashton accident on 27th July 1876 – and 'then there were three'. Converted to tender engines with 8 ft driving wheels, they became the first *inside* cylinder engines of that type in the country, No.2004 being renumbered 2001 when rebuilt. No.2003 was withdrawn in June 1884, but the other two survived until 1889 and 1890. At first they worked from Bristol, but in their later days they were at Newton Abbot.

The B & ER also bequeathed twenty-six 4–4–0 STs to the GWR, and some of these survived until the end of the broad gauge, working in South Devon and Cornwall. Ten 2–4–0

Activity at Totnes, 1892. An Up goods train, in the charge of a saddle tank engine, passing the camera with a largely-sheeted load, moving across onto the Up platform line to avoid a second train which is standing on the Up through road (the Ashburton branch train?). A passenger train can be seen departing from the Down platform behind a side-tank locomotive, probably a member of the 0—4—4T '3521' class. Yet another goods is waiting on the Down through line for the passenger to clear, with what appears to be one of the Armstrong 'convertible' six-coupled tanks at the head. Sawn timbers, partially-installed pointwork rails to the standard (or 'narrow') gauge and other clues point to an imminent change of gauge.

Collection Gerry Beale

tender engines, designed by the B & ER's Engineer, Pearson – who had once had the unenviable responsibility for supervising the SDR's 'Atmospheric' engines – were built at Bristol between 1870 and 1872. As GWR Nos. 2015–24, they were shedded mainly at Bristol and worked to Newton Abbot and, for a brief period, to Plymouth, No. 2017 being shedded there; however, its large wheels were not suitable for working over the gradients west of Newton Abbot.

The last of the original GWR 8 ft Singles of 1847–55 to remain in service, *Prometheus* (built in 1850), was withdrawn in 1887, but the 'Iron Duke' or 'Rover' class, built between 1871

at Newton Abbot and Totnes on banking duties up the Dainton and Rattery inclines. They were scrapped between 1884 and 1886.

An immediate consequence of the amalgamation was the altering to the broad gauge of ten 0–6–0 STs, Nos. 1228–37, which were being built at Swindon. A further 40 engines of this type, Nos. 1238–57 and 1561–80, were eventually altered, as were 20 of Armstrong's 'Standard Goods' 0–6–0s, Nos. 1196–1215. The latter were fitted with old broad gauge tenders while retaining their narrow, standard gauge cabs, which not only gave them a rather peculiar appearance, but also meant that

Armstrong 'Hawthorn' class 2–4–0 *Avonside*, built in 1865 by Slaughter Gruning & Co., was initially named *Slaughter* after her builders! Fortunately, that company changed its title to Avonside Engine Co., and the engine followed suit. Having originally worked in the Chippenham and Weymouth areas, *Avonside* made her way westwards, surviving until January 1892.
Collection R. C. Riley

and 1880, with a further three appearing as late as 1888, lasted until the end. A few of these, including *Iron Duke* and *Warlock*, were shedded at Newton Abbot. On one occasion *Lightning* was sent as pilot on a down train to Plymouth. 'She proved an indifferent help, and was sent back "light", but failed to work herself more than half-way up Hemerdon Bank, and the bank engine had to push her to the summit; this also occurring again at Dainton!'

The only surviving GWR 4–4–0 ST, *Horace*, was sent to finish its days in South Devon and Cornwall, but lasted only until 1880. Two 0–6–0 STs, similar to the SDR's *Stromboli*, named *Iago* and *Plato*, were also in the West Country. They had a daily duty in the early 1880s between Penzance and Plymouth on the Up Perishable (leaving Penzance at 12.30 p.m. and due at Plymouth at 5.10 p.m.), returning in the evening on the Down 'Flying Dutchman'. The only surviving member of the once numerous Gooch 0–6–0 goods engines, *Europa*, was shedded at Plymouth, and, most appropriately, this was the last broad gauge engine to leave there for Swindon, at 4.00 a.m. on Saturday, 21st May 1892.

Ten of Armstrong's 'Hawthorn' class 2–4–0s of 1865–6 were altered to tank engines in 1877 for service west of Exeter, having 5 ft coupled wheels instead of the original 6 ft diameter. In 1890: *Melling* and *Ostrich* were at Launceston, *Cerberus* at Ashburton, *Penn* at Moretonhampstead and *Hedley* at Kingswear, while in May 1892 *Bury* was involved in a collision at Buckfastleigh. Four of the tender engines of the class, *Avonside*, *Hawk*, *Wood* and *Dewrance* also went to South Devon, the last three being shedded at Plymouth from whence they often worked Ocean Mails to Bristol.

Three other engines which ended their days in South Devon were 0–6–0 STs from the former Vale of Neath Railway, absorbed in 1866. Rather unusually, they retained their original numbers (Nos. 12, 16 and 17). Their final years were spent

they were extremely draughty engines on which to work! They worked on the through goods services between London and Plymouth, while the tank engines were used on both passenger and goods duties, several having the coupling rods between the driving and trailing wheels removed to allow them to run more freely on passenger trains.

Other conversions were to Nos. 3501–10, which were 2–4–0 *side* tanks – a rare design for South Devon! Three of these, Nos. 3802, 3505 and 3508, were altered to tender engines in 1890 for the non-stop 'Cornishman' between Exeter and Plymouth, and Nos. 3501 and 3507 were altered a few months later. The last passenger tank engines for the broad gauge were Nos. 3541–60, designed by William Dean specially for service in the West Country and therefore built as 0–4–2 saddle tanks (twenty similar 'narrow gauge' engines, Nos. 3521–40, were built as side tanks). However, they were so unsteady that the last engine, No. 3560, was turned out as an 0–4–4T with short side and back tanks, the bogie having Mansell wooden centres to the wheels. Built in 1888–89, all were later altered to conform to No. 3560 – though the last two to be rebuilt, Nos. 3543 and 3547, never ran as such on the broad gauge. They had inside plate frames, and outside sandwich frames, the wheels on the broad gauge axles being outside both sets of frames.

The remaining eight Convertibles consisted of the first engines to be built of a new class of Singles, Nos. 3021–8, of the 2–2–2 type. Again, the wheels were outside the double frames. Built between April and August 1891, they were turned out as broad gauge engines to help the 'Iron Dukes' work the increasing passenger traffic during the last few months before the impending conversion. After May 1892 these engines were quickly converted to standard gauge, as were all the other Convertibles apart from one or two odd engines.

The long anticipated abolition of Brunel's magnificent 7'0$\frac{1}{4}$" gauge eventually took place in May 1892. Owing to the capital

Two views of Torquay in the final year of the broad gauge. The top view is looking north through the station towards Newton Abbot and shows the transoms of the track cut for conversion to narrow gauge. The lower view was taken from the north end, looking south, and shows the north signal box (which closed in 1910) of Saxby and Farmer origin and cross-sleepered broad gauge track. *L & GRP, courtesy David & Charles*

cost of converting the line (estimated in 1886 as being £128,698, though rails and other recovered materials would be worth no less than £146,979), and an estimated charge to revenue of £413,250 for the conversion and replacement of stock (against which it was proposed to save £39,000 annually on the transfer of goods and shunting), it had been postponed for several years. Sentiment also dictated that while Sir Daniel Gooch lived, the broad gauge remained. Even he realised that it was doomed, but was spared having to witness its demise as his death intervened in October 1889.

The need for quadrupling of the main line between Taplow and Didcot was the death-blow to the broad gauge. The wider trackbed required to accomodate extra broad or mixed gauge lines on this stretch would have caused undue engineering difficulties, and a four-track standard gauge format was agreed. It was also decided that the remaining broad and mixed gauge lines should be altered in May 1892. In February it was reported that preparations were well-advanced for the task, which was to be accomplished between the night of Friday, 20th May, and the following Monday morning. This was recommended by the newly-appointed Chief Engineer, Louis Trench, who had come to the GWR from the LNWR, the creation of Brunel's great rival and friend, Robert Stephenson. It was ironic that someone from that school should be responsible for the physical ending of Brunel's great creation.

By the end of April, all plans for traffic arrangements had been worked out and published, with a 55-page book of general instruction to the staff, issued by the General Manager, and a pamphlet for the public. Immediately prior to the crucial weekend, another 30-page book appeared; this contained local instructions from the Superintendents of the Plymouth, Exeter and Bristol Divisions.

No goods traffic for Cornwall was sent forward from Exeter after the night of Tuesday, 17th May, or for South Devon after 7.30 a.m. on the Wednesday. Down goods trains consisted only of engines and brake vans which were to bring all goods rolling stock out of Cornwall and South Devon. Traffic for Plymouth was not affected as the LSWR were to carry it over their line. The last broad gauge goods from London was the 10.25 p.m. express goods for Plymouth – for a long time the fastest goods train in the country and known to generations of GWR staff as the 'Tip'. Mails for Cornwall were conveyed by sea on the Saturday, there being no other railway into that county.

Thousands of workmen converged on Exeter from other parts of the GWR in readiness for the work of conversion, and were distributed along the entire line to Penzance, each gang of 20 men having about a mile of line to convert. Extra gangs were allocated to Newton Abbot, Plymouth, and other places where there were extensive sidings as well as running lines. Once the last broad gauge stock was removed, nothing prevented work being commenced in the goods yards, and at Brent the goods yard was completely changed over to standard gauge by the early evening of Friday, 20th May. All along the line, many hundreds of people with cherished memories of the broad gauge gathered to see the last trains go through. Many of the Up trains were formed of empty wagons and carriages which were being worked to Swindon for conversion or scrapping.

The last broad gauge train from Paddington to Penzance was the 10.15 a.m. 'Cornishman', which stopped at many additional stations; most appropriately it was headed by the Single *Great Western*. Both the 9.00 a.m. and the 11.45 a.m.

Looking south from Torquay station in May 1892.

L & GRP, courtesy David & Charles

'Flying Dutchman' ran no further than Plymouth on this day, and the very last broad gauge passenger train to leave Brunel's Paddington was the 5.00 p.m. to Plymouth. *Bulkeley* was in charge of the train to Bristol, and it was taken on to Newton Abbot by *Iron Duke*, returning for the last time to its home shed. That night the 9.00 p.m. Mail Train was standard gauge for the first time in its long history and reached Plymouth via the LSWR line from Exeter, as it also did on the Saturday and Sunday nights.

The Up trains ran as usual, the last broad gauge train being the Night Mail which arrived at Paddington 1½ hours late at about 5.30 a.m. behind *Bulkeley*. The empty passenger trains were sent to Swindon from Penzance or Plymouth as soon as they had finished their last journeys on Friday night, having been preceded by the goods wagons, though some of the latter were broken up or converted at Lostwithiel, Newton Abbot or Bridgwater. The last train of all left Penzance at 9.45 p.m. on Friday evening under the supervision, as far as Exeter, of the Chief Inspector of the Plymouth Division, who was charged with the responsibility of ensuring that all broad gauge stock had been sent away from each station, and that the last trains from the various branches had preceded him. After the Chief Inspector had issued a certificate that his was the last broad gauge train to travel over the line, the station master gave written permission to the Engineer's representative to take over that station and section of line.

The main work began at daybreak on Saturday in fine spring weather. Much work had been done in advance, with new point and crossing work set up on the spot, short rails provided at the curves, all transoms measured and marked, while every second one had been disconnected and cut to the new length. On the 36 miles of cross-sleepered track a third rail had already been laid. Many standard gauge engines had previously been sent from Swindon on broad gauge 'crocodile' trucks to Newton Abbot, Plymouth and the Cornish sheds. The work of conversion was tackled so quickly and smoothly that by the early afternoon some of these engines were out testing out sections of line; while by the evening a trial train was able to get through from Exeter to Plymouth! However, much work remained to be done on the Sunday, especially in the larger station yards.

Standard gauge carriages had also been sent down to the West of England. Those for Penzance and St Ives had travelled, like the engines, on 'crocodile' trucks. Three trains were sent over the LSWR's line to Laira sidings for Plymouth, Launceston and Liskeard, while Newton Abbot, Kingswear, Brixham, Moretonhampstead and Ashburton received their carriages by three special trains from Exeter, where a considerable amount of rolling stock and a number of engines had been stabled in readiness.

The whole of the regular service of passenger trains recommenced on the Monday, as planned, the goods trains beginning again on the Tuesday. Also on Tuesday, the vast army of workmen returned to their homes, dispersing over a wide area of the country. Doubtless, for the rest of their lives they told how they had helped to bury Brunel's broad gauge.

Gauge conversion in progress at Plymouth (Millbay) station during May 1892. The parapet of the Union Street bridge can be seen in the middle distance, with the tracks heading northwards towards Cornwall Junction (where the London and Penzance-bound lines diverged).

National Railway Museum, York

An Up passenger train at Ivybridge station with an interesting variety of vehicles in the formation. The engine itself appears to be a four-coupled design, possibly one of the 4—4—0 saddle tanks, and must surely have been near to its loading limit for the climb up Hemerdon and Dainton banks unaided. The eleven-bay viaduct was just over 250 yards in length, crossing 108 feet above the floor of the valley.

The main station building at Ivybridge, situated on the Up platform. This 'chalet' style of building could be found on many parts of the Great Western system, wherever Brunel and his associates had been involved in the construction. Doubling of the line at Ivybridge was carried out during 1893, when a new viaduct to accommodate two tracks was built alongside and to the south of the existing one. This also involved moving the trackwork through the station some yards to the south, and, as a consequence, the station building became 'stranded', being some way from the new platform edge. The original alignment can be seen in the previous photograph.

Photos: Lens of Sutton

The old and the new; Exeter (St. David's) station, c.1913, looking north. The first through station at Exeter (1844) was one of Brunel's 'one-sided' designs, with separate Up and Down stations positioned side by side on the east (Down) side of the line. Needless to say, this design imposed many operating difficulties, and in 1862 construction of a new station began. Opening in July 1864, it was of a more conventional style, possessing four-track access to platforms, which were covered by a very substantial train shed. The main station buildings, again situated on the Down side, presented a truly magnificent facade to the city. With the expansion of traffic during the first decade of the century, the station was again found wanting, and so in 1912 rebuilding was put in hand. This involved the removal of the train shed (the last portion of which can be seen at the far end of the station), and the construction of a new formation utilising canopies. This gave the GWR one Down through platform face (served by the main station buildings) and two Up (the left-hand island platform); the LSWR used the 'independent' centre island platform, and both companies were able to use the Down through line (not yet fully constructed in this view). In addition, the GWR had a bay at the north end of the long Down platform, being used mainly for the Exe Valley services. A 'Saint' class 4—6—0 (probably of the 'Court' series) is standing at the Down platform with an express.

National Railway Museum, York

CHAPTER FOUR

THE NEW ERA

The abolition of the broad gauge, with all its inconveniences, was not the final farewell to those reminders of Brunel's work which time had proved to be less than advantageous; there still remained the task of getting rid of the legacy of the 'Atmospheric Caper', the single-line sections on the main line. The $11\frac{1}{2}$ miles from Rattery to Hemerdon were the first to be tackled, a section which included the Marley Tunnel, five great viaducts, and the famous 'Cocked Hat' bridge at Wrangaton. A second single-line tunnel was bored beside the original at Marley, causing the trouble already related, whilst new masonry viaducts were built alongside the old wooden specimens. The 'Cocked Hat' bridge was replaced by a steel girder structure of quite ordinary design and appearance.

The new double line was opened in sections during 1893, the final section (over Blachford Viaduct to Cornwood) coming into use during November of that year. The piers of Brunel's original viaducts were left intact and remain to this day, providing a nesting place for jackdaws and other birds. Exactly a month after the main line improvements were finished, the long-awaited branch to Kingsbridge was opened from Brent. Kingsbridge Road station then reverted to its original name of Wrangaton, and the stage-coaches ceased to run to and from Kingsbridge.

Other new works undertaken during the 1890s were the provision of a new engine shed and repair shops at Newton Abbot, where the old SDR premises were outdated and far too small; the new facilities were opened in November 1893. The engine shed at Exeter, which dated from the rebuilding of the station in 1864, was enlarged, and the yard layout improved, during 1894. Two years later, Cockwood Viaduct (between Dawlish Warren and Starcross) was replaced by an embankment with two openings – fulfilling Brunel's original intention – and a new steel girder structure replaced the two bridges over the Exe to the west of St David's station. Two minor changes that occurred were the closure of Aller Junction signal box in 1895 and the Millbay ticket platform in 1896. Millbay itself was completely reconstructed and enlarged in 1900, creating what was almost a new station, while in the following year a new engine shed was opened at Laira to provide relief for the congested and overcrowded premises at Millbay.

During 1904 steam railmotors were introduced to the Exeter and Plymouth areas; these units provided services along the main line to Teignmouth, as well as over the newly opened Exeter Railway, which connected with the Teign Valley line. A station was opened at Dawlish Warren (initially called Warren Platform, it was replaced by new premises on a different site when the line was quadrupled), while water troughs were installed at Exminster in 1904. Further west, Bittaford Platform (between Wrangaton and Ivybridge) was opened in 1909; it was unusual in having a station master, albeit of the lowest grade.

The single-track section through the five tunnels in the cliffs between Dawlish and Teignmouth remained an operational bottleneck, especially during the summer months with the

An unidentified 'Star' class 4–6–0 departing from Exeter (St. David's) station with a rake of 'Dreadnought' coaches, probably forming the Down 'Riviera', c.1910. By the size of the nameplate, the engine would seem to be a member of the 'Knight' series, built in 1908.
Collection R. S. Carpenter

Exeter St. Thomas station was situated just under a mile to the west of St. David's, and, like the larger station, possessed a train shed; unlike St. David's, however, this structure lasted well into nationalisation. Despite being somewhat overshadowed by its more important neighbour, it was the terminating and mounting station for a steam railmotor service from and to Teignmouth before the Great War. The station was built in the centre of the 500 yard-long St. Thomas viaduct, and was the first SDR station (as such) from London. The station signal box can be seen at the far end of the opposite (Down) platform, with the 'Signal' and 'Telegraph' plates clearly visible. There could be a problem with the telegraph in the box, as the 'T' is showing its reverse (red on white) aspect. (1904)

National Railway Museum, York

The most important intermediate station between Newton Abbot and Plymouth, Totnes was the western limit of building works relating to Brunel's 'atmospheric' system of propulsion. The 'engine house', with its 'Italian campanile' chimney, can be seen to the left of the station; the building was to house the air pump, though it seems doubtful whether one was actually installed — the system certainly never reached Totnes. An unidentified 'Saint' is passing through on the Down Main with a westbound express. *Lens of Sutton*

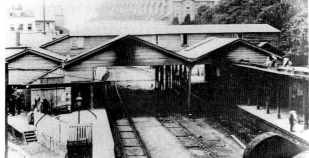

Teignmouth station — the original 'terminus' of the South Devon Railway system. The SDR station, pictured here, survived for over forty years before being rebuilt by the GWR; though rather primitive when compared with its successor, the wooden structure was not without charm. This view looks westwards (towards Newton Abbot), with the houses of Salisbury Terrace seen in the background. *Lens of Sutton*

Cornwood station, looking eastwards up the rising gradient towards Ivybridge, c.1914. The station, opened in 1852, was sandwiched between the lengthy Blatchford (309 yards) and Slade (275 yards) viaducts, and had latterly been provided with a footbridge, and a brick-built waiting shelter on the Down platform. *Lens of Sutton*

The village of Bittaford, some twelve miles east of Plymouth, was provided with a 'Platform' by the GWR during the early years of this century. The terminology was used to denote a station served by ordinary trains, and this required a longer platform (at least two coaches in length) than a 'Halte' (served only by railmotor or autotrain). Here a 'Bulldog' is struggling into the station with an eastbound stopping service, probably not long after the station opened.
Lens of Sutton

Steam railmotor No. 7 and a sister unit stand in Saltash station on a 'twin' working. The majority of suburban workings by the railmotors or autotrains in the Plymouth area ran between Saltash and Plympton, a distance of just over nine miles, with a typical journey time of forty minutes. Built in 1904, No. 7 spent her early years in the West Country, although by 1910 she was working in the Birmingham area; prior to her withdrawal, No. 7 worked from Bath, Bristol and Yatton. She entered Swindon Works in October 1914, emerging in due course as autotrailer No. 103.   *Lens of Sutton*

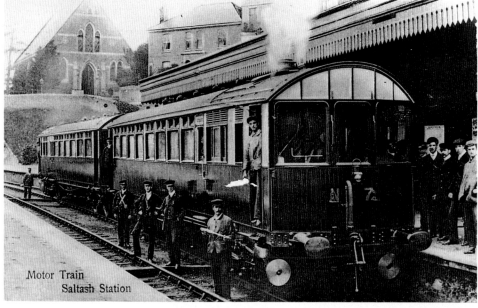

Motor Train
Saltash Station

increasing holiday traffic. A new sea wall was therefore built, and the tunnels enlarged in turn. Thanks to the liberal dimensions of Brunel's broad gauge tunnels, it was possible to use a movable steel-arched frame, 18 feet long, which allowed trains to run without any interruption. By October 1905, there was at last double track between Paddington and Plymouth, which would have existed from 1849 but for the wretched 'Atmospheric Caper'.

Considerable improvements were made at Plymouth in 1908 when North Road station was enlarged, while in 1911 a new marshalling yard was laid out at Newton Abbot on land reclaimed from the Hackney Marshes on the banks of the Teign. Another major work carried out was the complete reconstruction of St David's station at Exeter, which had long been inadequate for the volume of traffic it was called upon to

handle. The old station, with its great overall roof and stone walls, was almost completely swept away, and was replaced by the present well-known and spacious premises, between 1912 and 1914. Finally, during the Great War, the first stages of the creation of Tavistock Junction yard took place at Plymouth, where Up and Down loops, with eight Down and four Up sidings came into use in 1916.

After the gauge conversion of 1892, engine drivers had been instructed 'to run with great caution until the line is perfectly settled after the alteration'. However, there appears to have been an initial, and quite natural, inclination to show what could be done with the standard gauge, with the result that the Up 'Cornishman' (which had arrived in Plymouth before time) was four minutes early at Paddington on the first day of the restored running. Despite this initial burst of enthusiasm, there was consistent late running throughout June, and in July the schedule between Exeter and Penzance was altered to give between 20 and 30 minutes extra running time. A considerable amount of work had still to be done on the main line to bring it up to first-class standards after the great 'Conversion Weekend'.

Shortly after the conversion, a new express service was introduced between Paddington (11.25 a.m. departure) and Paignton, in a sense the first part of the Down 'Dutchman'. It comprised five 8-wheeled coaches, plus a pair for Ilfracombe. The stock returned as the 8.45 a.m. from Kingswear to Pad-

dington. Through carriages between Manchester, Liverpool and the West of England, something hitherto impossible, were also introduced. In November 1894 a midnight train from Paddington to the West was introduced, though this was 'balanced' by an express goods from Penzance and not by a corresponding Up passenger service!

No broad gauge corridor carriages or dining cars were ever built; indeed, such luxuries were unknown on the GWR prior to the 1890s. Soon after the introduction of the first corridor train between Paddington and Birkenhead in March 1892, similar services for Penzance and Torquay were commenced.

The station at Dawlish Warren (originally 'Warren Platform') seen in 1912, looking towards Exeter. Built in 1905, this station was replaced by a second in late 1912, erected a short distance to the north; it can be seen in the course of construction in the distance.
Lens of Sutton

The new station at Dawlish Warren opened on 23rd September 1912, with a four-track formation between the platforms. This pre-Great War photograph shows a 'Saint' on an Up local train formed of an Exeter/Plymouth Division 'B' set (6-wheel van, 6-wheel third, two 6-wheel composites, 8-wheel third and 6-wheel van), which operated many main line stopping trains in the area prior to and during World War I.
Chapman & Son

A 'Saint' class 4–6–0 approaching Starcross with a Down express one evening during 1908. The train is comprised mostly of local stock, though two or three coaches in the middle of the formation would appear to be through vehicles (with roofboards), possibly destined for the Torquay line.

Collection Paul Karau

Dawlish, in those halcyon years before the First World War. This Edwardian view shows a 'Badminton' 4—4—0 at the Down platform with a stopping train.
National Railway Museum, York

The western portal of Parsons tunnel c.1905, rebuilt in readiness for the doubling of the line carried out during the summer of that year. A 'Saint' class 4—6—0 is taking a Down express past the old signal box, moving onto the double track section along the sea wall. The movable wooden screens on the front elevation of the signal box could be raised to protect the windows from the effects of the sometimes wild seas of wintertime.
L & GRP, courtesy David & Charles

Just four miles to the east of Plymouth (North Road), Plympton station was situated at the foot of Hemerdon bank, which possessed gradients as fierce as 1 in 41. Having descended the bank, this double-headed train passing through the station, perhaps with a 'Bulldog' in the lead, seems to contain one or two vans. Plympton was the eastern extremity of the Plymouth main line suburban service, although the odd auto or steam railmotor did find its way further up the bank.

Collection J. E. Kite

An Up Ocean Mails express, behind an unidentified 'Saint' class engine, passing a short Down goods train in the charge of a Dean '2301' class 0–6–0 (probably the 'Pick-up') at the western approaches to Brent. The refuge siding on the right was converted into a loop during 1937, and its spur can be seen crossing the Brent Mill Viaduct with the main lines.

Coll. Graham Beare

As a consequence of this, the GWR was able to introduce the longest non-stop run in the world on 20th July 1896, by sending the first (Newquay) portion of the 'Cornishman' non-stop to Exeter via the Bristol relief line. This left Paddington at 10.30 a.m. (a portent of 'things to come'!), Exeter being reached at 2.15 p.m. At first only a feature of the summer months, it became an all-the-year round service in the Up direction in 1899, though there was no permanent Down service until 1902. The summer service of 1898 saw four 'coupled corridor trains' in use on West of England trains. These operated the 10.35 a.m. Paddington to Penzance, and the 11.30 a.m. to Kingswear; the balancing Up services were the 10.20 a.m. Penzance and 10.25 a.m. Kingswear. Each train consisted of five corridor vehicles, with additional non-corridor coaches serving other destinations also being conveyed. A further service, the 10.30 a.m. Paddington to Falmouth and Newquay (with the balancing 10.45 a.m. Falmouth/10.55 a.m. Newquay) was provided with 'lavatory stock'. Although no restaurant facilities were provided to the West Country at this time, a dining car did run on the 6.00 p.m. Paddington to Plymouth train, though only as far as Bristol.

During the winter service of 1898/9, there was one through train in each direction between the north and west of England. The Down service ran overnight, leaving Crewe at 1.20 a.m., conveying a van and an LNW Tri-Compo (possibly 6-wheel) between Liverpool and Penzance, a WCJS Composite between Glasgow and Plymouth, and a second Tri-Compo & Van (8-wheel) combination from Manchester to Penzance. The return service left Plymouth at 2.35 p.m., conveying the Manchester and Liverpool vehicles, whilst the Glasgow (WCJS) coach was attached to the following 12.00 noon Penzance to Paddington train, being detached at Bristol. All the vehicles then went forth as the 7.40 p.m. Bristol to Crewe.

Torbay vehicles were handled by a separate service; the 11.40 a.m. Crewe to Bristol conveyed an 8-wheel LNW Tri-Compo from Liverpool, and a GW Brake Tri-Compo from Birkenhead. Both vehicles were then attached to the 1.20 p.m. Paddington at Bristol, being detached at Newton Abbot for the final portion of their journeys to Kingswear. The return was made on the 8.30 a.m. Plymouth to Paddington express as far as Bristol, where they were attached to the 12.06 p.m. Weston-Super-Mare service to the north.

In May 1903 Exeter and Torquay were provided with restaurant car services on the 11.35 a.m. Paddington and 10.25 a.m. Kingswear trains. From 18th July the 10.40 a.m., first part of the 'Cornishman', brought Exeter within $3\frac{1}{2}$ hours of Paddington, with Plymouth being reached in 4 hours 50 minutes and Penzance in 7 hours 46 minutes; this train also conveyed a Dining Car as far as Exeter. The corresponding Up train left Penzance at 11.25 a.m., arriving in London at 7.00 p.m.

The first non-stop run between Plymouth and London had been made in the previous year, in connection with a visit of His Majesty, King Edward VII to the Naval College at Dartmouth. The Down journey provided the first non-stop run between Paddington and Kingswear (something rarely repeated). 'Atbara' class 4–4–0 No.3374, specially renamed *Britannia* for the occasion, was used for both journeys, which were made possible by new water troughs installed at Creech St Michael, north of Taunton.

The second non-stop journey, performed at record speed, took place on 14th July 1903, when the Duke and Duchess of Cornwall (later King George V and Queen Mary) travelled to Cornwall to stay at Tregothnan. A special first part of the 'Cornishman', which also carried some ordinary passengers, left Paddington at 10.40 a.m. and was due at North Road at

3.10 p.m. However, the arrival time was actually 2.33½ p.m.! The 245¾ miles were covered at an average speed of 63.4 mph, with a recorded maximum speed of 87.3 mph. The engine was one of Churchward's newest 4–4–0s, No.3433 *City of Bath*, with a train of five carriages weighing 130 tons. This was only a foretaste of the things to come.

The spring of 1904 saw the LSWR making a determined bid for traffic from the ocean liners which landed passengers and mail at Millbay Docks by tender, several very fast runs being made both by the GWR and their rivals. The rivalry cul-

20 minutes more than the 1890 'Cornishman' had taken to reach Exeter! The Up train left Penzance at 10.10 a.m. and Plymouth at 12.33 p.m., arriving at Paddington at 5.00 p.m. The normal load was seven carriages, five being clerestory-roofed stock, with a new elliptical-roofed 68 ft dining car, for Penzance, and a tri-composite carriage for Falmouth, detached at Truro.

The old 'Flying Dutchman', by this time a second-rate express, was retired to leave Paddington at 12.25 p.m. (having departed at 11.45 a.m. since 1862). It regained its old schedule

'Achilles' class 4–2–2 ('Dean Single') No. 3021 *Wigmore Castle* entering Exeter (St. David's) station with a Down train during the early years of the century. Originally constructed as a broad gauge 'convertible', she was modified to the 'narrow' gauge (as a 2–2–2) during the summer of 1892, and converted to a 'bogie' single a couple of years later. Allocated to Bristol and to Paddington during the 1900s, *Wigmore Castle* was probably working the express as far as Newton Abbot, where a 'Duke' or 'Bulldog' from Newton or Plymouth shed would take the train over. No. 3021 was withdrawn from service during 1909. Two LSWR locomotives stand on the engine spur on the left of the picture.

Collection R. S. Carpenter

minated in the 'record of records', established by the GWR on 9th May 1904. No.3440 *City of Truro*, with five vans containing 1,300 bags of mail, passed Exeter dead slow in 59 minutes from leaving Millbay Dock Gates (a distance of 52 miles, 73 chains) and reached Pylle Hill Junction, Bristol (75¼ miles from Exeter), 64 minutes and 17 seconds later. During the course of this run, the immortal first recorded speed of 100 mph was achieved down Wellington Bank. The latter part of the run, from Bristol to Paddington, with the load reduced from 140 tons to 120 tons, was made by the 7′8″ Single No.3065 *Duke of Connaught*, with the amazing time of 59 minutes 41 seconds for the 77¼ miles from Swindon (passed at walking pace) to Paddington.

July 1904 saw another record established for non-stop runs, which was to remain unsurpassed for nearly 25 years. It was made by the newly introduced 'Cornish Riviera Express', the most famous train in GWR history, which initially left Paddington at 10.10 a.m. and not at the later well-known 10.30 a.m. Plymouth was reached in 4 hours 25 minutes – only

by Plymouth, and reached Penzance at 8.30 p.m., half an hour earlier than in its palmy broad gauge days! After two years it departed later still, leaving Paddington at 1.00 p.m., with a 2-hour timing to Bristol, arriving in Plymouth at 6.30 p.m. and at Penzance at 9.40 p.m. Finally, in 1911, it was cut short at Bristol, and a new 1.30 p.m. (via Westbury) took its place. However, the Up 'Dutchman' still left Plymouth at the old time of 8.35 a.m., but reached Paddington 1½ hours earlier than its broad gauge ancestor. It was still leaving Plymouth at 8.30 a.m. over 30 years after the end of the GWR's existence – as an HST!

July 1906 saw the opening of the long awaited route via Westbury, reducing the distance to the West of England by almost 20 miles. The 'Cornish Riviera Express' ran throughout the year by the new route, leaving Paddington at a time which was to become synonymous with this most famous of GWR trains. The arrival time at North Road was 2.37 p.m. and at Penzance 5.05 p.m. In addition to carriages slipped at Westbury (for Weymouth) and a double slip at Taunton, for

Minehead and Ilfracombe, a third portion was released at Exeter for Kingsbridge (originally for Torquay). The main portions of the train were for Falmouth, St Ives and Penzance. The Up train still left Penzance at 10.00 a.m., but stopped at Exeter. The 'Limited' continued to run throughout the war years, leaving Paddington at 10.15 a.m., calling at Westbury, Taunton and Exeter. Slip carriages and restaurant cars disappeared from the GWR in general, and the 'Limited' in particular on 1st January 1917. With a stop at Newton Abbot, Penzance was not reached until 6.10 p.m. The pre-war timings were restored soon after the war ended.

Although the majority of trains between Paddington and the West of England used the new and shorter route, some continued to run via Bristol (in particular, the overnight services). The opening of a new line between Cheltenham and Honeybourne made possible a through service between Wolverhampton and Birmingham (Snow Hill) and the West of England, which was inaugurated in 1908.

The original service of nine or ten trains in each direction between Exeter and Plymouth had gradually been increased by the addition of a few trains from Bristol or Taunton. There were also one or two local trains between Newton Abbot and Totnes, and between Plymouth and Brent. In 1902 there were 11 trains from Exeter to Newton Abbot, three of which ran to Plymouth and two to Kingswear, and there were also three Newton Abbot to Plymouth trains. The Up service provided seven trains from Plymouth to Newton Abbot, five of which

ran through to Exeter, while one train ran from Kingswear to Exeter and seven from Newton Abbot to Exeter. There were two trains from Plymouth to Brent and back, leaving Brent at 8.15 a.m. and 8.50 p.m., neither of which connected with the Kingsbridge trains!

Teignmouth's service consisted of 17 Down trains and 15 Up; Dawlish had 14 in each direction; Totnes 12 Down and 11 Up; Brent 9 Down and 10 Up; and Ivybridge 10 Down and 11 Up. For many years the timetables indicated that certain trains from London stopped at Ivybridge 'to set down First Class passengers from London on notice being given to the Guard' – Ivybridge was the nearest station to the country residence of Lord Mildmay of Flete, a GWR Director!

The service on Sundays was much more limited; two trains ran in each direction between Exeter and Plymouth, and three each way between Exeter and Newton Abbot and between Newton Abbot and Plymouth. Teignmouth, Dawlish, Totnes and Brent had four trains in each direction; Brent's service included a return working from Plymouth, and there was a Sunday evening train from Plymouth to Ivybridge and back.

Several stopping trains ran to and from stations north of Exeter. The 7.00 a.m. from Bristol called at all stations to Newton Abbot (arr. 11.30 a.m.), as did the 3.48 p.m. from Taunton (Newton Abbot arr. 6.03 p.m.). The Up service included the 9.10 a.m. from Millbay, 'all stations' to Tiverton Junction (arr. 12.12 p.m.), which returned at 12.35 p.m. in similar fashion as far as Newton Abbot (arr. 2.15 p.m.).

Carrying her original round-top firebox, 'Duke' class 4–4–0 No. 3321 *Mercury* is shown here at Exeter St. David's, c.1905. It is believed that she was delivered when new (in June 1899) to the West Country, and was certainly at Newton Abbot throughout 1902. Early tests over the South Devon banks determined that the class could take '56 wheels' between Newton Abbot and Plymouth to schedule. By 1906, she was at Plymouth, remaining there probably until around 1913, when she received a Belpaire boiler at Swindon Factory. After modification, No. 3287 (as renumbered) spent a spell at Didcot, before moving west again, to Launceston, on 28th January 1914. *Mercury* remained in the West Country (mainly at Truro and Falmouth) until 1922, when on 10th March she arrived at Bristol (Bath Road) shed. Further moves were made to Swindon (1926), Gloucester and Cheltenham (1927), followed in 1932 by her last change of division, being transferred to the Cambrian section at Oswestry and Aberystwyth; she was withdrawn from service during the summer of 1949 from the latter shed. The lack of coupling rods, plus the fact that she is coupled to a goods brake van, suggests that she is off to the 'factory' (Swindon or possibly Newton Abbot) for attention. *Collection Gerry Beale*

Another 'all stations' train from Millbay was the 4.00 p.m. which continued from Taunton to Yeovil (arr. 9.56 p.m.). This was 'balanced' by the 5.10 p.m. from Swindon to Exeter (arr. 10.30 p.m.) via Westbury and Yeovil! Finally, the 5.15 p.m. from Millbay served the principal stations to Bath (arr. 11.23 p.m.). The Sunday service also provided some longer journeys, with the 6.45 a.m. and 3.40 p.m. trains from Bristol to Millbay (arr. 12.08 p.m. and 9.10 p.m.) while the 8.10 a.m.

Abbot. A number of the Singles moved away at this time to work on the Worcester and Wolverhampton services. Although the 2–4–0s of the '806' and '2201' classes were never used west of Exeter as main line engines, one or two, including No.823, were employed on local workings between Taunton or Exeter and Newton Abbot.

West of Newton Abbot smaller-wheeled engines were to be found, including the double-framed '3201' class 2–4–0s, some

A member of the '3521' class 0–4–4 tanks at Plymouth (North Road) station during the '90s. This engine, No. 3527, was one of the initial batch of twenty 'narrow gauge' examples of the class, being constructed as an 0–4–2T in 1887, and rebuilt as an 0–4–4T in 1892. After the abolition of the broad gauge, these engines were moved westwards to join their ex-broad gauge sisters on main line work. So poor were their riding qualities that the class was rebuilt as 4–4–0 tender engines, No. 3527 being so converted in 1900.

Collection R. C. Riley

from Penzance stopped at every station to Exeter, and most stations to Weston-super-Mare, where it terminated at 4.46 p.m., presumably too exhausted to complete the journey to Bristol!

In place of the 8 ft singles of the broad gauge, there appeared engines of great elegance and beauty – the Dean Bogie Singles. During the first few months of standard gauge working there were only 22 of these engines, all then being 2–2–2s – as were the eight which had run on the broad gauge and which were converted to standard gauge between May and August 1892. Responsible for the main duties between London, Bristol and Newton Abbot, engines of the class were shedded at all three places. In 1894 all were rebuilt with a leading bogie following the alarming derailment of No.3021 *Wigmore Castle* in Box Tunnel, while a new series, commencing with No.3021 *Achilles*, emerged from Swindon as 4–2–2s. In 1894, when there were forty in service, twenty were in steam daily – seven at Westbourne Park, eight at Bristol and five at Newton Abbot. Apart from a few which worked to Newport and Cardiff in the late 1890s (when all eighty engines of the class had been completed), the entire class was employed on the Bristol and West of England trains.

The first engines of the 4–4–0 'Badminton' class, which appeared in 1898, took over those trains which were becoming too heavy for the Singles, working to Exeter from Paddington and Bristol; they made only occasional visits to Newton Abbot. At the turn of the century, a number of trains changed engines at Exeter, a reversion to the pre-1876 practice, and this continued until the 1920s. Such trains were worked between Exeter and Plymouth by 'Dukes' and 'Bulldogs'. Most of the first 20 engines of the 'Atbara' class (built in 1900 and 1901) were at Bristol, and worked to Exeter and Newton Abbot as well as to Paddington; however, they were little used west of Newton

of which had worked on the broad gauge. With the conversion of the 2–4–0Ts Nos.3511–20 to tender engines, there were 25 of these. However, in 1895 the first 4–4–0s of the 'Duke' class appeared, a total of 60 being built up to 1899. These replaced the 2–4–0s by working all the important trains between Exeter and Penzance, and were shedded at Exeter, Newton Abbot, Plymouth and Penzance (although in 1901 no less than 18 were shedded at Westbourne Park in London). The 'Dukes' were supplanted within a few years by a small-wheeled version of the 'Atbaras', and about 50 out of the first 70 'Bulldogs' went to South Devon and Cornwall; they were to be associated with the South Devon gradients for over 50 years. The 'Dukes' joined the '3201' class 2–4–0s on local workings and on the Launceston branch.

There were also some sandwich-framed 4–4–0s of the '3521' class, rebuilt in 1899–1902 from the 0–4–4Ts which had been so prone to derailments. About half the class of 40 were sent to the West of England; some retained domed boilers, others were rebuilt with parallel domeless boilers. These were also used on such workings as the Launceston branch services. As tank engines, all had worked on the main line in Devon and Cornwall between 1892 and 1895, when the introduction of the 'Dukes' had seen them sent away to the West Midlands – to the great relief of the West Country enginemen!

Main line goods traffic was in the charge of 0–6–0s of the double-framed Armstrong 'Standard Goods' class (some of which had also worked on the broad gauge) and the inside-framed 'Dean Goods' class, one of which (No.2430) had been the first standard gauge engine to arrive at Penzance in May 1892. For the next 15 years the 'Dean Goods' were frequently used in South Devon. Larger, experimental goods engines, which appeared in the latter years of William Dean's tenure of office, also made their way down to South Devon. No.36, the

'31XX' class 2—6—2T No. 3132 at Exeter c.1912, one of two such engines allocated to that shed. One of their turns involved the 7.5 p.m. freight to Laira, conveying 80 wagons to Newton Abbot, and 42 beyond (with banking assistance).   *Collection P. Coutanche*

Following the 'Dukes' into the West Country came the 'Bulldogs', an ultimately more powerful design which initially worked alongside the 'Dukes', then eventually replaced them on the best services. Indeed, twenty of the 'Dukes' were rebuilt into 'Bulldogs' between 1902 and 1908, and the marriage of 'Duke' and 'Bulldog' components to produce the 32XX 'Dukedog' or 'Earl' class of 1936 serves to emphasise the 'relationship' between the two classes. No. 3282 *Maristowe* (an incorrect spelling — the name was subsequently adjusted to *Maristow*) started life in February 1897 as a 'Duke', but was rebuilt into a 'Bulldog' during 1907, in which form she is shown here at Newton Abbot, in 1908. As a 'Duke', she was allocated to Truro and Penzance during the early years of this century, and during 1903 was involved in a special working for company officials who were visiting all of the branch lines in Devon and Cornwall. On Sunday, 5th July, with her engineman, J. Nicholls, she ran from Penzance to Perranporth and back with the special. By 1906, she had moved eastwards to Exeter but, as a 'Bulldog', was at Plymouth in 1910, where she remained until the Great War. She carried the number 3309 with effect from December 1912, as part of the rationalisation scheme. During the conflict she moved to the Weymouth district, and on to Reading in May 1922. After four years at Hereford, and three at Gloucester, 3309 moved (in 1931) to spend her twilight years on the Wellington & Crewe line, being withdrawn in July 1934.   *Collection R. C. Riley*

In its early years the Kingsbridge branch was the province of four-coupled tanks. In 1902, '517' class 0—4—2T No. 534 started the year at the branch shed, working the line until early June, when the duty was taken over by 'Metro' 2—4—0T No. 470. In August, 'Metro' No. 1457 took over the working, being relieved by No. 1464 in September; this in turn handed over to No. 1448 in December. The latter 'Metro' had been specifically sent to Laira in August 1901 to work the Kingsbridge goods, though it clearly ended up working the passenger services from the branch shed too. In this early view, a 'Metro' has arrived at Kingsbridge with the branch train of 4/6-wheel stock.   *Lens of Sutton*

The Kingsbridge branch possessed some attractively-situated stations, running as it did for the most part in company with the River Avon, and sharing its wooded river valley. Avonwick was the first branch station, some 2½ miles to the south of Brent, and was most appealing in its location; in true Great Western tradition, however, it was an 'invigorating stroll' from the village after which it was named. Here an unidentified 'Metro' 2—4—0T pauses at the station with a Kingsbridge-bound train. As in the case of all the branch stations, the main buildings were attractively worked in stone to a common design.   *Lens of Sutton*

Plymouth Millbay c.1906, with 'Saint' 4—4—2 No. 182 and 0—4—0ST No. 1331 on shed. No. 182 was one of fourteen 'Atlantics' which appeared from Swindon between 1903 and 1905; she was completed in June 1905, received the name *Lalla Rookh* in September 1906, and was converted into a 4—6—0 in November 1912, the same year that she was renumbered to 2982. A Plymouth engine as new (July 1905), No. 182 spent most of her early years in the West Country. Sitting behind No. 182 in this view is the ex-SDR shunting tank, No. 1331. This locomotive began life as broad gauge engine *Crow* (built in 1874), receiving the GWR number 2177 upon amalgamation. Converted to the standard gauge in 1892, she was renumbered to 1331; in both forms, the engine spent most of her working life at Plymouth Docks, before being sold to Powlesland and Mason (Swansea) soon after this photograph was taken. *Collection Paul Karau*

first GWR 4–6–0, built in 1896 and resembling an elongated 'Duke', made at least one appearance at Exeter, while one of the 'Kruger' class 2–6–0s, No.2605, worked as far as Plymouth. Dean's final design for goods work, the well-known 'Aberdares' – a 2–6–0 version of the 'Bulldogs' – also appeared on through workings from South Wales, though at that time none were shedded in the West of England.

Exclusively a tank engine line, the SDR had no large turntables. This meant that the branch lines had to be worked by tank engines, though the Launceston line was an exception, as a larger turntable was installed there in 1899. The mainstay of such services were the little Wolverhampton-built '517' class 0–4–2Ts, which worked on the Moretonhampstead, Teign Valley, Brixham, Ashburton and Kingsbridge branches. The Swindon-built 'Metro' class 2–4–0Ts were also used on the Moretonhampstead and Kingsbridge lines, as well as being regular engines on the Torquay branch, No.3587 being shedded at Kingswear in 1901. 0–6–0 STs were also regularly used on passenger trains on the latter line, though they were mainly used for local goods and shunting duties. Several classes were represented, both double-framed and inside-framed, and mostly of Swindon origin, though there were also some of the small '850' and '1901' class engines built at Wolverhampton. Several ex-SDR engines which had been converted to standard gauge in 1892–94 continued to work in the area; *Taurus* (latterly No.1326) resumed working on such duties as the Ashburton and Brixham branches, and there were also Nos.1317–25 of the 'Buffalo' class, though at least three of these migrated to the Newport and Aberdare districts.

In exchange for the latter, several engines from the former Monmouthshire Railway, worked in the West of England at the turn of the century. Outside cylinder 0–6–0 side tanks Nos.1341 and 1343 worked there around the period 1900–2,

Another ex-SDR 0—4—0 tank, No. 1328 (ex *Goat*, No. 2174), seen here at Westbourne Park shed, near Paddington station.

both being withdrawn within a few years. There were also Nos.1346 and 1352, which had commenced life as double-framed 0–6–0 STs, but had been rebuilt in 1892 as 0–4–4 Ts. Their bogies had outside bearings, and their peculiar appearance was accentuated by having 4'1½" coupled wheels, little larger than those of the bogies, which were 3'8"! A third 0–4–4T, No.1309, paid occasional visits to Newton Abbot in the 1890s, though its regular working was on the Bridport branch with its sister engines Nos.1308 and 1310; these three were outside-framed saddle tanks, with inside-framed bogies. Finally, there were 4–4–0Ts Nos.1304 and 1307, with outside cylinders and 5'6" coupled wheels, part of a class of four built in 1870–74; both were withdrawn in 1905.

Soon after G.J. Churchward, that notable son of South Devon, commenced his epoch-making superintendency at Swindon, the 'Cities' became the premier main line engines,

Beneath the shadow of Brent Hill, an unidentified 'Bulldog' 4—4—0 is accelerating up the gradient away from Brent station, whose Up Home signal may be seen to the rear of the last coach on the train. Immediately behind the signal can be seen the buffer stop protecting the end of the Up Refuge Siding (which was converted into a loop during 1937). The train itself seems to be a mixture of six and eight-wheel stock, and was probably an Exeter—Plymouth working some time around 1905.

E. Pouteau

and had a monopoly of the most important trains between Paddington and the West of England. Some were shedded at Exeter and Newton Abbot, while *City of Birmingham* and *City of Exeter* were at Laira during 1904–5. *City of Truro* was the last to be shedded at Newton Abbot (until August 1913), though No.3709 *Quebec* remained at Exeter until 1915. However, the lovely Dean Singles could still be seen west of Exeter in 1906.

The pioneer passenger 4–6–0 No.100 (later named *William Dean*), the first of the new Standard express passenger engines,

'Queens' and 'Princesses' appeared between 1911 and 1914. In the latter year the allocation of each class to sheds in the South Devon area was:

2 cylinder 'Saints':   Laira 4, Newton Abbot 7, Exeter 5.
4 cylinder 'Stars':   Laira 13.

A final dozen 'Stars' (the 'Abbeys') appeared during 1922–3, by which time a considerable change in workings and allo-

'Saint' class 4–4–2 No. 172 *The Abbot* at Brent with an Up local train (c.1908) comprising an Exeter/Plymouth Division 'B' set of six-wheel (but including an eight-wheel third) stock. This engine was named *Quicksilver* until March 1907, and indeed may still be carrying those plates in this photograph. A Plymouth engine in 1906, *The Abbot* had moved to Exeter by 1910 and (as a 4–6–0, No. 2972) to Cardiff by 1914; in 1918 the engine was stationed at Wolverhampton, and at Bristol during 1922. After further allocations in the Newton Abbot, Newport, London, and Bristol Divisions, she was transferred to Cardiff in 1933 for her two remaining years in service.   *Lens of Sutton*

together with Nos.98, 171, and the French-built Compound Atlantic, No.102 *La France*, appeared on West of England expresses during 1903. In the following year they were joined by the first ten of the outside cylinder 4–4–0s of the 'County' class, which were used fairly regularly on the Plymouth trains for a year or two. The appearance from Swindon of further 4–6–0s and 4–4–2s (Nos.172–190), and the delivery of another two French Atlantics, Nos.103 and 104 (later named *President* and *Alliance*), meant that the 'Counties' were soon replaced, though they continued to work down to Plymouth for a number of years.

The 'Ladies' and 'Saints' built in 1906–7 were immediately drafted to the most important duties, and some were shedded in South Devon. The pioneer four-cylinder engine, No.40 *North Star*, which entered service in 1906, was at first almost exclusively employed on Paddington to Plymouth turns. Through running between Paddington and Plymouth in each direction was now a regular feature, and the practice of changing engines at Exeter or Newton Abbot gradually ceased. The 30 'Stars', 'Knights' and 'Kings' built by 1910 did not entirely replace the two-cylinder 'Saints', but 4–4–0s were rarely to be seen on the main West of England services. Further engines of both classes, the two-cylinder 'Courts' and the four-cylinder

cations was taking place. In 1921 there had been six 'Saints' and eight 'Stars' at Exeter, while Newton Abbot had only four 'Saints' and three 'Stars', and Laira had ten 'Stars'. In 1923 there were fifteen 'Stars' at Laira, nine at Newton Abbot (including Nos.4009 *Shooting Star*, 4031 *Queen Mary* and 4040 *Queen Boadicea*) and one at Exeter. By 1925, only a handful of 'Saints' were shedded in South Devon; Nos.2908 *Lady of Quality* and 2980 *Coeur de Lion* were at Newton Abbot, where their duties included working the precursor of the 'Torbay Express', while Exeter's seven engines included Nos.2906 *Lady of Lynn*, 2910 *Lady of Shalott*, 2917 *Saint Bernard*, 2937 *Clevedon Court* and 2978 *Kirkland*. Among the Exeter 'Saints' duties was the Down 'West of England Postal' to Penzance, returning next day on the corresponding Up train at 6.00 p.m., on which the engine worked right through to Paddington via Bristol!

Although, strictly speaking, confined to the main line between London and Bristol, Churchward's Pacific No.111 *The Great Bear* ventured as far as Newton Abbot on at least one occasion. Considerable difficulty was experienced in turning the engine; the tender had to be detached and turned separately, as was the case, a few years later, when the pioneer large 2–8–0 No.4700 made its first visit. Until 1926, Newton Abbot had only a 55 ft diameter turntable.

Rattery box was situated two miles to the east of Brent, at the top of the heavy gradients of the four-mile climb up from Totnes. Whilst the climb continued from Rattery, through Marley tunnel and Brent, to the summit at Wrangaton, the gradients were not as severe. An unidentified 'Duke' is shown here descending the bank tender-first after a banking duty, c.1904; a crossover was provided near the box to effect the passage of returning bank engines if circumstances permitted, otherwise they would be required to work through to Brent.

Collection R. C. Riley

Some 3½ miles to the south-east of Moretonhampstead lay the small station of Lustleigh, the first station out of the terminus; it consisted of just one through line, and a short siding to the rear of the platform. The train services provided did tend to vary over the years, with five each way daily (plus market day trains) up to the Great War, eight in the summer of 1922, and ten in 1934; there were eight return journeys through the station in the last year of the company. At the turn of the century, six-coupled tanks were in use on the line, mainly of the '1076' or 'Buffalo' class (of which No. 731 was allocated to Moretonhampstead shed during the 1901-1903 period). Newton also had members of the '850' and '1854' classes in some numbers, many of which may no doubt have found their way onto the line. In 1906, the 'Buffalo' class were still on the branch trains, though 'Metro' tanks were also appearing at Moretonhampstead shed.

Collection J. E. Kite

West of Plymouth, the 'Bulldogs' continued to be the principal main line engines until the appearance of the '4300' class 2–6–0s in 1911, after which the Moguls were employed in the West of England on a wide variety of duties. The 'Dukes' continued in South Devon as banking engines, though by 1921 only four remained, together with five 'Bulldogs'.

Also resident in the West Country were a few examples of the '31XX' class Prairie tanks; in 1913 these engines were used on goods traffic between Exeter and Laira, scheduled to take 80 wagons westbound to Newton Abbot, and 42 on to Laira (with assistance).

The 'Standard Goods' and 'Dean Goods' engines were still present on goods workings, as were the double-framed 0–6–0STs of the '1076' class. These classes were able to convey between 30 and 35 wagons westbound (assisted) over the banks. 'Deans' were to be found on such trains as the 9.40 p.m. Laira to Bristol during 1913, which carried coal empties destined for the Somerset coalfields (amongst others).

Express (vacuum) services at this time were in the hands of 4–4–2 or 4–6–0 locomotives, running between Laira and Paddington. 2–8–0 engines of the '28XX' class were to be seen on the 12.15 p.m. Penzance to Bristol goods from Laira, being able to convey 30 wagons (eastbound) over the South Devon banks unassisted, or 48 with banking power. They were also used on the 11.05 p.m. Bristol to Penzance as far as Laira. The Plymouth shed had one (No. 2846) allocated at this time. Limited use was also made of 2–6–0s, 4–4–0s and even 2–4–0s to cover some goods workings over the SDR sector.

In 1921 Laira had No.2815 and half-a-dozen of the 'ROD' class, but the only 2–8–0 at Newton Abbot was a 'ROD'. The double-framed 'Aberdare' 2–6–0s were still employed on Cardiff to Exeter coal trains in 1922, while engines shedded at Laira worked mineral traffic to and from St Blazey, others of the class being at Newton Abbot. Although four 'Dean Goods' were still at Exeter in 1921, with a fifth engine shedded at Newton Abbot, within a year or two only No.2483 remained at Exeter, working exclusively to Bristol. The 'Standard Goods' engines had disappeared from the area by 1921.

Another class which had been transferred away were the '3521' 4–4–0s, which had all gone by 1910; most had been transferred to the West Midlands, being replaced by 'Dukes' and the '4500' class 2–6–2Ts. The latter engines were to be found on the Moretonhampstead and Kingsbridge branches, as well as on the Kingswear line.

Buckfastleigh, with '517' class 0–4–2T No. 1466 in charge of a Totnes-bound service. The three-coach branch train of four-wheel Brake Third, Composite, Brake Third was complemented on market days by an extra Third. No. 1466 arrived in the West Country from the Marlborough branch in 1902, being allocated initially to Exeter; she spent a period between 1905 and 1907 on the Ashburton branch, before moving back to Exeter. No. 1466 may well have returned to the branch during the early 'twenties, at which time she was allocated to Newton, and might have appeared alongside sister engines Nos. 1440 and 571. Buckfastleigh was the only intermediate crossing place on the branch, and it was customary before the Great War for the branch passenger to cross the Newton Abbot goods there on each of the latter's journeys over the line. Latterly, only one crossing was necessary, except on Saturdays, when two were again made. *Lens of Sutton*

Teignmouth station, around the turn of the century, with Exeter '1854' class 0–6–0ST No. 1897 waiting on the Up Main, possibly for the signalled Down train to pass. The engine was built in July 1895 for goods and shunting work, on which duties she is pictured here. She was reboilered a number of times, and in November 1922 received pannier tanks as well. No. 1897 remained in the West Country at sheds between St. Blazey and Taunton until 1940, when she was transferred to Brecon. Her last move, to Cardiff East Dock, came in 1945; she was withdrawn from that shed in January 1949.

Collection R. S. Carpenter

All of the smaller-wheeled '4400' class, apart from two engines in South Wales, were in the West of England until 1925. Two of the class were generally at Princetown for the steeply graded line from Yelverton, whilst two were used on the Kingsbridge branch before the Great War.

Some branches, such as Ashburton, were still served by elderly 0–4–2Ts of the '517' class hauling a train of vintage four or six-wheeled carriages. A similar combination sufficed until the early 1900s for the Teign Valley line, and into the 1920s on the Brixham Branch.

The Kingswear Branch was often worked by 2–6–2Ts as, in addition to the '4500' class engines, there were some of the larger '3150' class tanks at Newton Abbot. Although mostly used for banking duties over Dainton and Rattery, the large 'prairies' also worked passenger trains on the branch, as the larger tender engines were prohibited from working beyond Paignton until the 'twenties. In 1921, Nos.4405 and 4542 were shedded at Kingswear. One or two large 2–6–2Ts were always at Laira for banking duties on the Hemerdon incline, while there was a brief trial in South Devon of one of the large-wheeled 'County Tank' class 4–4–2Ts, which was returned with polite thanks!

An earlier and more extensive trial was that of the '3600' class 2–4–2Ts, six of which (Nos.3601–4, 3608 and 3610) were in South Devon when newly built in 1902–3. Most of these worked between Exeter, Newton Abbot and Kingswear, though No.3601 was also observed at Plymouth (Millbay).

Shunting continued to be undertaken by a variety of 0–6–0Ts, both double and single-framed, some still with saddle tanks, and others rebuilt as Panniers. As well as differences in the size and shape of their bunkers, depending on whether they had been fitted at Swindon or Wolverhampton, there were one or two with a local, Newton Abbot variety. The '1661' class

double-framed engines, with larger wheels and deficient brake power, were as unpopular in South Devon as elsewhere, and the last of these left the area before 1918. Rather surprisingly, No.1694 of the class was one of the two banking engines shedded at Totnes in 1901, the other being No.1764 of the '1854' class.

Some of these 0–6–0Ts spent many years, or even their entire lives, in the same area. No.1897 of the '1854' class appears to have gone as a new engine to Millbay in 1895, and was there in 1901; it was working from Newton Abbot in the early 1900s, Truro and St. Blazey in 1914, and by 1921 was at Exeter. The engine spent the next eighteen years mostly at Laira and Exeter, before moving on to Brecon in 1940.

No. 2785 also spent a large portion of its life in the West Country. Having been allocated to sheds in the Bristol and Westbury district during its early years, it moved to the West Country during the Great War, being at Carn Brea when that shed closed in 1917. It then spent the remainder of its days alternating between St. Blazey and Newton Abbot, being withdrawn from the latter in April 1948.

Amongst the small Wolverhampton-built engines, No. 1930 was at Millbay in 1901, Newton Abbot, Helston and Penzance during the following year, Laira in 1914 and 1921, followed by a procession of West Country sheds between Bridgwater and Truro until its withdrawal in 1949.

Sister engine No. 1973 went to St. Blazey when built in 1890, and was still there in 1902, although it has worked on the Bodmin branch during that year. It was at Plymouth shed in 1914, St. Blazey again in 1921, with spells at Moorswater, St. Blazey, Exeter, Laira, Penzance and Taunton during the grouping period. It moved to Truro during 1947, from whence it was withdrawn in 1949.

As new in 1906, the '3101' (44XX) class 2—6—2 tanks were allocated to Princetown, Laira, and sheds to the west thereof (with the exception of the two engines in South Wales). Shortly afterwards, however, Laira engines were outstationed at Kingsbridge, in place of the four-coupled tanks which had worked the line since its opening in 1893; during 1910, Nos. 3102, 3103, 3104, 3108 and 3109 were variously allocated to Kingsbridge. In the top view, an unidentified engine is awaiting departure with the early morning mixed train from Brent station, whilst below, No. 3104 is at rest outside the western end of Brent goods shed. *Collection J. E. Kite*

The north (Up) end of Newton Abbot station, probably around 1920, showing 'Saint' class 4–6–0 No. 2978 *Kirkland* standing outside the train shed. This engine was allocated to Newton shed between 1918 and 1922, and is seen here on a coach formation headed by a 70ft 'Dreadnought' vehicle. It would seem as if the two ladies on the platform have arrived for a prolonged stay!

L & GRP, cty. David & Charles

CHAPTER FIVE

THE FINEST AND FINAL YEARS

The inter-war years saw the GWR at the height of its success and popularity, with South Devon as an essential ingredient in its appeal and fortunes. The still increasing holiday traffic meant that further improvements were made to expedite its movement during the 1920s and 1930s. Additional signal boxes were opened, increasing the number of sections between Exeter and Newton Abbot, and the junction at Aller was completely remodelled in 1925 to provide Up and Down main and relief lines in place of the separate Kingswear lines, involving the opening of a new signal box; the original had been closed 30 years previously.

Newton Abbot station, which dated from the 1860s, was the biggest obstacle to the frequent passage of trains. There were only three running lines through the station, each alongside a platform, only one of which could be used by Down trains. To the east of the station, two running lines had to suffice for main line traffic, the Moretonhampstead branch, and movements to and from Newton Abbot goods yard.

A thorough reconstruction and enlargement took place between 1925 and 1927, so that little remained of the old station. The new station had two long island platforms of sufficient length to permit two trains to stand at each face. Up and Down relief lines were connected to the outer platform lines by 'scissors' crossings half-way along the length of each platform. As a cross-over also connected the two running lines between the platforms, up to eight trains could use the station at the same time; however, owing to the GWR's emphasis on absolute safety in all aspects of train working, the full potential of the station was seldom exploited. A separate platform (Platform 9) with access only from the station forecourt, was provided for the Moretonhampstead and Teign Valley trains. The old Middle signal box was abolished, and the East and West boxes replaced by much larger structures. The station was formally re-opened by Lord Mildmay of Flete in April 1927. Two unusual features were a plaque in the entrance hall expressing the gratitude of the inhabitants of Newton Abbot

The rebuilt Newton Abbot station, on 1st August 1932, with what could be the 11.5 a.m. Paddington to Penzance train standing at the Down Main platform. The pilot engine is a Newton 'Bulldog', No. 3443 *Chaffinch*, at the head of an unidentified 'King'; on her own, the train engine could handle 360 tons (11/12 coaches) up the bank, and maintain the running schedule. Generally speaking, engines assisting 'Kings' were limited to the 'Blue' category (such as the 'Bulldog'), although 83XX and 93XX locomotives were also cleared. The banks of South Devon, however, were considered to be a special case, and *any* other 4—6—0 (except another 'King') was permitted to assist. On this particular occasion, the 'Bulldog' is obviously considered to be sufficient, as it was under most circumstances.

G. N. Southerden

A magnificenr view of Newton Abbot station, looking north (Up), in 1923. The station would seem to have been recently repainted, and has had the remaining glazing removed from the ends. The two roads through the train shed are signalled for two-way running, whilst the outer through platform (on the right) is for Down traffic only. Newton engine shed can be seen on the right, the structure being a straight road shed with a 'northlight' pattern roof.

National Railway Museum, York

Truly atmospheric views of the inside of the train shed, Newton Abbot, taken in 1924. All three look towards London, and show the considerable length of the structure.

National Railway Museum, York

A 1923 view of Newton Abbot station, north end, showing Newton Middle 'box on the left. The outer platform serving Down trains (to the left of the train shed) also had a covered road.
National Railway Museum, York

Newton Abbot station forecourt, 1923, with a delightful selection of road vehicles on display. Within three years, this scene had been swept away, and the building replaced by the three-storey brick-built structure which was considered to be more fitting to Newton Abbot as an important junction station.

National Railway Museum, York

This photo of Newton station was taken from the western approaches, c.1920. At this time, the four tracks heading westwards were grouped in pairs, with the Up and Down Plymouth to the west, and the Torbay lines to the east. On completion of the concurrent rebuilding of Aller Junction (one mile south of Newton), the lines were re-arranged to Up Main, Up Relief, Down Main and Down Relief respectively, with full connections at Aller to allow access to or from the Plymouth or Torbay lines. The old arrangements at the west end of the station clearly show the two 'through' Up/Down platform lines, with the Down through platform line to their right. The need for better running facilities at this increasingly busy junction station is apparent. The wagon repair shop can be seen to the right of centre, with the 'west' box on the left.   *L & GRP, cty. David & Charles*

79774. NEWTON ABBOT,   GREAT WESTERN STATION.

The new station building at Newton Abbot, probably shortly after the opening in 1927. This delightful building was a vast improvement over its predecessor, although perhaps not quite as convenient for passengers. Apart from the Moretonhampstead platform (situated to the left of and adjacent to the building), passengers could now only gain access to the platforms via a footbridge, this building being totally isolated. For London-bound passengers, this was a distinct disadvantage when compared with the platform arrangement of the old station. However, the vast improvement in facilities, including a spacious dining room, more than made up for any inconveniences.

Lens of Sutton

The two long island platform arrangement of the rebuilt station at Newton Abbot is evident in this photograph, taken on 4th May 1931 (looking towards Exeter). There were now six running lines through the station area, with an Up Through, an Up Main and Up Relief (left-hand platform), a Down Main and Relief (right-hand platform), and a Down Through; each of the Through lines avoided platforms. In addition, a bay platform was provided at the 'east' end of the station, next to the main building, for Moretonhampstead trains. The carriage sidings were situated to the right in this view, with the engine shed and works beyond them. On the Up Relief line, the station pilot (possibly a 'Duke'; Nos. 3272 and 3282 were both at Newton during 1931) appears to be 'tailing' an Up train. *L & GRP cty. David & Charles*

The Down platform line, Newton Abbot, October 1924, with Small 'Prairie' No. 4553 on a morning local service to the Torbay line. The leading two coaches (composite No. 6942, Dia. E98, and a van third) would probably have returned as the through Kingswear portion of a north-bound express, given the reversed roof-boards (possibly the 12.10 p.m. Kingswear, for Manchester, attached to the 1.0 p.m. Plymouth train at Exeter). The engine, built in 1915, was allocated to St. Blazey and Laira during her early years, moving up to Newton Abbot during 1923. She spent the years up to 1930 mostly at Newton, though with allocations to Kingsbridge and Exeter sheds too. After a short period at Moorswater and St. Blazey, she moved to South Wales in 1932, spending the great majority of her remaining GWR career at Whitland. *National Railway Museum, York*

At the 'west' (southern) end of the station, the tracks passed under the 'bow-girder' bridge carrying the main road to Torquay. The end of the Carriage & Wagon Works building can be seen on the left.   *National Railway Museum, York*

to the company, and the placing on the Down platform of the preserved broad gauge engine *Tiny*.

Improvements were also made to the engine shed and factory in 1914. One landmark from much earlier days remained, in the form of the lovely weather-vane over the engine shed, depicting a broad gauge engine. Laira engine sheds were also enlarged, a new building being provided in 1931 to complement the turntable shed. The need for such extra accommodation in Plymouth was demonstrated in 1924, when Millbay shed was closed and the engines were transferred to Laira; such was the resulting congestion and chaos, that Millbay had to be re-opened, and remained in limited use until Laira's new building was completed.

Major sea defence works were undertaken at Dawlish Warren, as erosion of the Warren was causing anxiety over the future safety of the main line between the station and Langstone Cliffs. Thousands of tons of rocks were dumped onto the beach, behind which a new stone platform was constructed, special sidings being laid down to give access to the site.

What would have been the greatest work of improvement was destined to remain unfulfilled. A new main line of 8½ miles on an inland route was planned between Dawlish Warren and Bishopsteignton, including a lengthy tunnel. This would have provided a faster route for trains not stopping at Dawlish or Teignmouth, as well as an alternative route in the event of problems with the sea walls and tunnels. The existing alternative route over the Teign Valley line was so restricted that only small tank engines could be used. An alternative and less expensive scheme was for the provision of a new station at Teignmouth, with quadruple track from there to Newton Abbot. Although land for the inland route was purchased by

the GWR, nothing had been done when war came in 1939, and the plan was abandoned.

With the publication of the summer timetables in 1924, regular interval services were introduced on all the GWR's main lines, and this resulted in considerable changes to the West of England services. Departures from Paddington were now at 5.30 a.m., 10.30 a.m., 1.30 p.m., 3.30 p.m., 4.30 p.m. and 6.30 p.m. Additional trains ran at 10.35 a.m. SO, 11.00 a.m. SO, 11.05 a.m., 12 noon, 12.05 p.m., 10.00 p.m. and 12 midnight, some of which (including both overnight trains) were routed via Bristol (as was the 5.30 a.m.). Sunday departures were at 10.30 a.m., 12.30 p.m., 2.30 p.m. and 4.30 p.m. The 5.30 a.m. via Bristol was of some interest from a locomotive point of view, as one of the few main line express duties still worked by a 'County' class 4–4–0 between Paddington and Bristol; beyond Bristol the train was worked by a 'Saint'.

The 1932 summer timetables gave the following services working to and from Paddington; the normal loading of these trains on weekdays and Sundays is also tabulated.

WEEKDAY SERVICES – PADDINGTON   Summer 1932

DOWN TRAINS

1.40 a.m. Paddington (via Lavington)

3 Coaches	Penzance
1 Bk Van	Penzance
1 Bk Van	North Rd.
1 Siphon G	Kingswear

(Plymouth due 6.5 a.m., Penzance 8.48 a.m.)

5.30 a.m. Paddington (via Bristol)

2 Bk Vans ‡	Penzance
4 Coaches	Penzance
1 Van	Plymouth
1 Siphon G	Plymouth
1 News Van	Kingswear
1 Siphon G	Paignton

(Plymouth due 12.26 p.m., Penzance 3.40 p.m.)

10.30 a.m. Paddington 'Cornish Riviera' (via Lavington)

7 Coaches (R.C.)	Penzance
1 Coach	St Ives
1 Coach	Falmouth
1 Coach	North Rd.

(Plymouth due 2.30 p.m., Penzance 4.50 p.m.)

11.5 a.m. Paddington (via Lavington)

6 Coaches (R.C.)	Penzance
3 Coaches	Newquay
2 Coaches	Kingsbridge

(Plymouth due 3.42 p.m., Penzance 6.40 p.m.)

1.30 p.m. Paddington (via Lavington)

5 Coaches (R.C.)	Penzance
2 Coaches	Newquay
2 Coaches	Kingswear

(Plymouth due 6.35 p.m., Penzance 9.30 p.m.)

3.30 p.m. Paddington (via Lavington)

3 Coaches	Truro
2 Coaches (R.C.)	North Rd.
2 Coaches	Paignton

(Plymouth due 8.8 p.m., Truro 9.1 p.m.)

4.30 p.m. Paddington (via Bristol)

5 Coaches (R.C.)	Plymouth
3 Coaches	Kingswear

(Plymouth due 10.24 p.m.)

6.30 p.m. Paddington (via Bristol)

1 Siphon G	Paignton
5 Coaches ‡	Plymouth
3 Coaches	Plymouth

(Plymouth due 12.45 a.m.)

9.50 p.m. Paddington (via Bristol)

1 Bk Van ‡	Penzance
1 Coach ‡	Penzance
1 Pcls Van	Penzance
6 Coaches	Penzance
(inc. 2 Sleepers)	
1 Siphon G	Newquay
3 Coaches	North Rd.

(Plymouth due 4.32 a.m., Penzance 7.40 a.m.)

'Duke' class 4—4—0 No. 3289 (formerly *St. Austell*) and 'Castle' No. 5007 *Rougemont Castle* swing westwards away from Aller Junction in 1930. As No. 3289 lost her nameplates during July 1930, the photograph was probably taken late summer, and in mid-afternoon. The train might be the 11.5 a.m. Paddington to Penzance, or perhaps the 10.40 a.m. Wolverhampton in view of the 'Castle' haulage. Both engines were from Laira shed.

R. Brookman

Totnes station, pictured on 1st June 1921, looking east. The covered platform roads are clearly seen in this photograph, with the station 'box on the Down platform.

L & GRP, cty. David & Charles

The station forecourt, Totnes, showing the Down side buildings and station signal box. The tower of the old atmospheric engine house dominates the scene, photographed in 1912.

L & GRP, cty. David & Charles

A '2721' class 0–6–0PT standing on the Up Main at Totnes with a local goods working, probably to Hackney yard. The engine head-lamp is not apparent but, being an Up working, this may have been positioned on the bunker. It is unlikely to have been the branch freight (10.10 a.m. Hackney to Ashburton) as the locomotive fell into the 'blue' category, far too heavy for the line; '2021' class engines were favoured for that task, followed by the '44XX'. The engine appears to be No. 2783, a member of a class long associated with both Laira and Newton Abbot sheds. *Lens of Sutton*

The goods shed at Totnes was situated at the east end of the Down platform, and is seen in this 1913 view, looking towards Newton Abbot. Ashburton Junction Signal Box is just visible to the left of the water tank, whilst the siding serving Totnes Quay started from the goods shed siding, beyond the bracket signal.   *L & GRP, cty. David & Charles*

Looking west through the rebuilt Totnes station towards Rattery Bank and Plymouth.   *Collection R. S. Carpenter*

The Totnes 'Butterwalk' photographed on a sunny afternoon in the late 1930s.   *M. F. Yarwood*

One of the glories of Totnes — predictably featured in GWR pictorial posters — was the arch spanning Fore Street, which marked the site of the former medieval East Gate. This lovely view, taken in the 1930s, shows this structure which was destroyed by fire in 1990.

M. F. Yarwood

The 'Western Beacon' (approx. 1000ft AMSL) dominates the skyline of this picture of a '43XX' class 2—6—0 bringing a Down goods across the viaduct and through Ivybridge station. The original SDR station building may be seen on the left, set well back from the platform edge.   *Lens of Sutton*

A Newton Abbot '3150', No. 3184, piloting an unidentified 'Castle' on a Down express, with about 100 yards to run to the eastern portal of Dainton tunnel, and the summit of the bank just beyond. The three-mile climb from Aller Junction involved gradients between 1 in 36 and 1 in 46, and was the inheritance from the 'Atmospheric' system proposed by Brunel. The '31XX' and '3150' classes of 2—6—2 tank were introduced to Newton for banking and passenger work during the Great War, and the latter class survived on such duties there until 1941.   *R. Brookman*

Mutley station, just 24 chains (about 500 metres) to the east of North Road, served the Plymouth suburb of the same name. It closed during the summer of 1939. The Southern Railway train seen departing from Mutley is about to pass under the bridge that separated the two stations. The Southern trains had a rather roundabout route out of Plymouth; leaving their Friary terminus heading eastwards, they joined the Sutton Harbour line to run north to Laira, then onto the GWR main line running westwards through Mutley to North Road. At this point, the train had travelled three miles, and was still only ¾ mile from Friary across the city! Just over ¼ mile to the west of North Road, the Southern train regained its own metals at Devonport Jct, and followed the GWR main line north-westwards, crossing under the eastern approaches to the Royal Albert Bridge, Saltash, before turning north and east to Okehampton and Exeter. Between Plymouth North Road and Exeter St. David's, the Southern line was only about six miles longer than the Great Western, although their fastest times were generally between 15 and 20 minutes slower than their Paddington-based competitors.   *G. N. Southerden*

12.00 m. Paddington (via Bristol)

2 Siphon G	North Rd.
2 Sleepers	North Rd.
1 Siphon G	Penzance
4 Coaches	Penzance

(Plymouth due 7.20 a.m., Penzance 10.56 a.m.)

In addition to its trio of 70 ft coaches from London, the 6.30 p.m. Paddington also conveyed a section of through coaches off the 4.7 p.m. Crewe to Bristol train. These comprised a pair of Brake Composites from Birkenhead and from Glasgow, each destined for Plymouth. These were followed by three LMS vehicles from Liverpool.

The 9.50 p.m. Paddington also carried 'foreign' vehicles, in the form of an LNER Full Brake and Brake Composite, the famous 'Aberdeen and Penzance' through service. These vehicles had reached Swindon on the 6.25 p.m. York train (via Banbury), which on Thursday and Friday nights formed a separate through train to Penzance.

UP TRAINS

9.0 p.m. Penzance (via Bristol)

1 Siphon G	from Paignton
1 Pcls Van	from North Rd.
2 Sleepers	from North Rd.
6 Coaches	from Penzance
(inc. 2 Sleepers)	
1 Siphon G	from Newquay

(Paddington due 7.10 a.m.)

Plymouth (North Road) station was opened in 1877, six years after Mutley, its neighbour, and 28 years after the Millbay terminus. The station was joint with the LSWR, and was 246 miles from Paddington (via Bristol); this distance was reduced by 20 miles when the 'Berks and Hants' line came into operation during 1906. The original station (of just two platforms) was replaced in 1908 by that shown in the photographs, both views showing the eastern (London) end of the station in the 'thirties. In essence, there were two stations side by side, each with two through platform lines (and three platform faces), separated by a 'middle' siding, used mainly for coach marshalling. In addition, each side had bay and loading bank lines. An extensive rebuilding scheme was finalised in 1935, work commencing during 1938, only to be halted by the war and was not resumed until the GWR had been nationalised. *C. L. Mowat and G. N. Southerden*

8.35 a.m. Plymouth (via Lavington)

3 Coaches	from Kingswear
5 Coaches (R.C.)	from Plymouth
1 Slip	from Plymouth
(for Reading)	

(Paddington due 1.15 p.m.)

9.15 a.m. Falmouth (via Lavington)

3 Coaches	from Exeter
2 Coaches	from Newquay
3 Coaches	from Falmouth
2 Coaches (R.C.)	from North Rd.
2 Coaches	from Kingsbridge
1 Slip	from Paignton
(for Reading)	

(Paddington due 4.30 p.m.)

10.0 a.m. Penzance 'Cornish Riviera' (via Lavington)

1 Coach	from North Rd.
1 Coach	from Falmouth
1 Coach	from St Ives
7 Coaches (R.C.)	from Penzance

(Paddington due 4.45 p.m.)

11.10 a.m. Penzance (via Lavington)

2 Coaches	from Paignton
3 Coaches	from Newquay
6 Coaches (R.C.)	from Penzance

(Paddington due 6.55 p.m.)

1.30 p.m. Penzance (via Lavington)

1 Bk Van ‡	from Penzance
5 Coaches (R.C.)	from Penzance
3 Coaches	from Paignton

(Paddington due 9.0 p.m.)

6.20 p.m. Plymouth (via Bristol)

1 Bk Van ‡	from Plymouth
1 Van	from Plymouth
1 Siphon G	from Plymouth
4 Coaches	from Plymouth
1 Siphon G	from Penzance

Whilst there were no 'slip' services as such west of Westbury or Yatton at this time, both the 8.35 a.m. Plymouth and 9.15 a.m. Falmouth trains conveyed such vehicles, both being slipped at Reading. Paddington-bound passengers occupying seats in those coaches would therefore need to change into the main body of the trains, or would be faced with an ominous silence when approaching Reading! Both slips were eventually dispatched to Paddington on local or semi-fast services, but the resulting delay was well over an hour in each case. The Slip Guard would, of course, ensure that such passengers did not remain in his vehicle.

SUNDAY SERVICES – PADDINGTON

DOWN TRAINS

12.30 a.m. Paddington (via Bristol)

1 Coach	North Rd.
2 Sleepers	North Rd.
4 Coaches	Penzance

(Plymouth due 7.36 a.m., Penzance 10.45 a.m.)

9.10 a.m. Paddington (via Bristol)

1 Van	Plymouth
6 Coaches	Plymouth

(Plymouth due 5.5 p.m.)

10.30 a.m. Paddington (via Lavington)

1 Coach	North Rd.
5 Coaches (R.C.)	Penzance
3 Coaches	Newquay

(Plymouth due 3.15 p.m., Penzance 5.45 p.m.)

2.30 p.m. Paddington (via Lavington)

4 Coaches	Plymouth
4 Coaches (R.C.)	Churston

(Plymouth due 7.58 p.m.)

4.30 p.m. Paddington (via Bristol)

6 Coaches (R.C.)	Plymouth
2 Coaches	Kingswear

(Plymouth due 10.27 p.m.)

9.50 p.m. Paddington (via Bristol)

1 Van	Penzance
6 Coaches	Penzance
(inc. 2 Sleepers)	
5 Coaches	North Rd.

(Plymouth due 4.32 a.m., Penzance 7.40 a.m.)

UP TRAINS

10.15 a.m. Plymouth (via Lavington)

3 Coaches	from Kingswear
5 Coaches (R.C.)	from Plymouth

(Paddington due 3.15 p.m.)

7.0 a.m. Plymouth (via Bristol)

1 Siphon G	from Plymouth
3 Coaches	from Plymouth
3 Coaches ‡(R.C.)	from Paignton

(Paddington due 3.35 p.m.)

9.45 a.m. Plymouth (via Bristol)

3 Coaches	from Paignton
4 Coaches (R.C.)	from Plymouth

(Paddington due 4.10 p.m.)

'Bulldog' class 4—4—0 No. 3401 *Vancouver* on station pilot duties at the carriage sidings behind the Up side of North Road station, during the mid-'30s. Like most 'Bulldogs', *Vancouver* had wandered over the years, being at Wolverhampton before the First World War, Cardiff in 1918, followed by ten years in the Bristol & Westbury areas. In 1932, she was allocated to Laira and, apart from a couple of years at Barnstaple, Taunton, and St. Blazey, remained there until nationalisation.

Dr. Ian C. Allen

10.50 a.m. Penzance (via Lavington)

3 Coaches	from Brixham
1 Coach	from North Rd.
5 Coaches (R.C.)	from Penzance

(Paddington due 7.5 p.m.)

12.25 p.m. Penzance (via Lavington)

3 Coaches	from Newquay
5 Coaches	from Penzance
2 Coaches ‡	from Penzance

(Paddington due 7.50 p.m.)

1.10 p.m. Plymouth (via Bristol)

| 4 Coaches | from Plymouth |

(Paddington due 8.10 p.m.)

5.5 p.m. Penzance (via Bristol)

| 4 Coaches | from Penzance |
| 3 Coaches ‡ | from Plymouth |

(Paddington due 3.5 a.m.)

9.0 p.m. Penzance (via Bristol)

1 Coach	from Penzance
2 Sleepers	from North Rd.
6 Coaches	from Penzance

(inc. 2 Sleepers)
(Paddington due 7.10 a.m.)

ABBREVIATIONS

‡	Vehicles to (or from) the Midlands or the North.
(R.C.)	Including (or comprising) a Restaurant Car or Dining Unit.
Bk Van	Passenger Brake Van
News Van	Newspaper Van
Pcls Van	Parcels Van

CROSS-COUNTRY SERVICES Summer 1932

Next in importance to the Paddington trains were those to and from the North of England, especially those via the Severn Tunnel. There were only two 'through' trains as such to Plymouth and beyond from this route, the 2.35 a.m. Shrewsbury, and the 10.32 a.m. Crewe. However, in addition to these, both the 1.10 p.m. and 4.7 p.m. Crewe trains conveyed through sections which were attached to or formed other trains destined for the far west. The two through trains were formed thus:

2.35 a.m. Shrewsbury

1 GW	Mail Van	Bristol	North Road
1 GW	Bk Van	Manchester	Plymouth
1 GW	Coach	Glasgow	Penzance
2 LMS	Coaches	Liverpool	Penzance
1 LMS	Bk Van	Liverpool	Penzance
2 LMS	Coaches	Manchester	Penzance
1 LMS	Bk Van	Manchester	Penzance
1 GW	Bk Van	Manchester	Penzance

A special note in the timetables stated 'Passengers can obtain breakfast at Bristol on giving notice to the Guard at Hereford'.

10.32 a.m. Crewe

1 GW	Coach	Birkenhead	Truro
3 GW	Coaches	Liverpool	Truro
1 GW	Coach	Liverpool	Newquay
1 LMS	Coach (R.C.)	Liverpool	North Rd.
1 LMS	Coach	Manchester	Paignton
2 GW	Coaches	Manchester	Paignton

The 1.10 p.m. Crewe to Taunton conveyed a number of vehicles that were destined for return workings to the North from Paignton, Plymouth and Penzance. Onwards from Taunton, these vehicles formed the 8.20 p.m. local train to Newton Abbot, and were conveyed to their final destinations the following morning.

8.20 p.m. Taunton

1 GW	Coach	Birkenhead	(Penzance)
3 LMS	Coaches	Liverpool	(Penzance)
1 GW	Coach (R.C.)	Liverpool	(North Rd.)
2 GW	Coaches	Manchester	(Paignton)

The through coaches on the 4.7 p.m. Crewe were conveyed onwards by the 6.30 p.m. Paddington from Bristol, as already discussed.

One rather curious service which conveyed stock eventually destined for the North was the 10.5 a.m. Bath to North Road; this consisted of vehicles from Manchester and Liverpool that had terminated at Bristol the previous evening. The stock was forwarded to Bath as the 8.30 a.m. local service from Temple Meads, to become the 10.5 a.m. departure.

10.5 a.m. Bath

2 GW	Coaches	(Liverpool)	North Rd.
2 LMS	Coaches	(Manchester)	North Rd.
1 LMS	Bk Van	(Manchester)	North Rd.
1 GW	Coach	(Bristol)	North Rd.
2 GW	Coaches	(Manchester)	Paignton
2 GW	Coaches	Wolverh'mpt'n	Kingswear

The stock destined for North Road continued through to Penzance later that afternoon, forming part of the 12.30 p.m. train to the North the following day. The two coaches at the rear were attached at Bristol from the 7.15 a.m. Wolverhampton to Weston-super-Mare train.

The main Wolverhampton and West Country service was the 10.40 a.m., running via the North Warwickshire line; this train departed from Bristol at 1.45 p.m., arriving at Plymouth at 4.55 p.m. and Penzance at 7.30 p.m.

10.40 a.m. Wolverhampton

6 Coaches (R.C.)	Penzance
2 Coaches	Newquay
3 Coaches	Kingswear

Direct communication between South Wales and the West Country was provided by the 9.45 a.m. Swansea, which conveyed through coaches to Plymouth on Fridays and Saturdays only.

9.45 a.m. Swansea

4 GW	Coaches	Paignton
4 GW	Coaches	Plymouth (FSO)
1 LMS	Bk Van	Penzance
1 LMS	Bk Van	Plymouth

The LMS Brake Vans originated from Carlisle and Leeds respectively, having been conveyed by the 3.50 a.m. Crewe 'Parcels' as far as Bristol, where they were subsequently attached to the 9.45 a.m. Swansea.

On Sundays, the regular 2.35 a.m. Shrewsbury train was joined by the 11.55 a.m. Crewe in serving the West, with through coaches from both Liverpool and Manchester to Plymouth (due 8.25 p.m.). The 'Wolverhampton' also ran, though the Restaurant Car portion now terminated at Paignton, with just a pair of coaches working through to Plymouth.

In the Up direction, through trains to the North of England (via the Severn Tunnel) abounded, with no less than five direct services being run on weekdays.

The earliest of these was the 8.45 a.m. Plymouth, followed throughout the day by the 7.45 a.m., 10.15 a.m., 12.30 p.m. and 5.5 p.m. departures from Penzance (departing from Plymouth at 10.30 a.m., 1.10 p.m., 3.55 p.m. and 8.0 p.m. respectively), providing a far more comprehensive service than was available in the Down direction. The trains were formed thus:

8.45 a.m. Plymouth

1 GW	Coach	Plymouth	Birkenhead
1 GW	Coach	Plymouth	Glasgow
3 LMS	Coaches	Plymouth	Liverpool
2 GW	Coaches	Paignton	Manchester

Dining facilities were attached to this train at Weston-super-Mare.

7.45 a.m. Penzance

2 GW	Coaches	Kingswear	Manchester
1 LMS	Coach	Kingswear	Manchester
1 LMS	Coach (R.C.)	North Road	Liverpool
3 LMS	Coaches	Penzance	Liverpool
1 GW	Coach	Penzance	Birkenhead
1 GW	Coach	Penzance	Wolverhampton
2 GW	Coaches	Kingswear	Wolverhampton

The three vehicles destined for Wolverhampton were detached at Bristol, being taken on by the 2.20 p.m. train thence. On Saturdays, the 7.45 a.m. Penzance became a Wolverhampton train, the North being served by just the three later trains.

10.15 a.m. Penzance

1 GW	Coach	North Road	Liverpool
1 GW	Coach	Newquay	Liverpool
3 GW	Coaches	Penzance	Liverpool
1 GW	Coach	Penzance	Birkenhead

In addition, a pair of coaches was attached at Exeter from the 12.30 p.m. Kingswear train, bound for Manchester.

The 12.30 p.m. Penzance was designated as a Mail Service, and conveyed a Post Office Car at the head of the train.

12.30 p.m. Penzance

1 GW	Mail Van (No. 838 or 840)	North Road	Bristol
1 GW	Coach	Penzance	Bristol
2 GW	Coaches	Penzance	Liverpool
1 LMS	Bk Van	Penzance	Manchester
2 LMS	Coaches	Penzance	Manchester
1 GW	Coach	Penzance	Glasgow
1 GW	Bk Van	Penzance	Sheffield

The last daily service to the North left Penzance at 5.5 p.m., with through coaches for both Liverpool and Manchester, with arrival times around 6.0 a.m. the following morning.

5.5 p.m. Penzance

1 LMS	Bk Van	Penzance	Manchester
2 LMS	Coaches	Penzance	Manchester
1 LMS	Bk Van	Penzance	Liverpool
2 LMS	Coaches	Penzance	Liverpool

'Duke' class 4—4—0 No. 3289 *St. Austell*, station pilot at North Road on 7th June 1930. This engine had a relatively short stay in the West Country, arriving at Laira during 1929 from Didcot, and departing for Swindon and Andover Junction in 1932. During that year, the last three 'Dukes' allocated to Devon sheds were transferred, finally breaking the link with the West Country that had endured since 1895. *St. Austell* lost her name about one month after this photograph, a victim of passenger confusion!

G. N. Southerden

The London end of North Road again, with a 'Duke' class 4—4—0 on an Up passenger train, 1913. Plymouth and Newton Abbot had 18 of the forty 'Dukes' between them at this time, and they were a common sight on passenger trains over the banks of South Devon. They were also used on the Launceston services, and this train could have been destined for either route.
L & GRP cty. David & Charles

Virtually all the 'North and West' trains carried portions to or from South Wales and the West Country to the north of Pontypool Road, and as a consequence were rather heavier on the northern portion of their journeys than they were on the South Devon section.

The balancing service to the 10.40 a.m. Wolverhampton train was the 10.45 a.m. departure from Penzance. In addition to the three portions detailed in the Down train, the 10.45 a.m. also conveyed the LNER coaches on the Aberdeen service.

10.45 a.m. Penzance

3	GW	Coaches	Paignton	Wolverhampton
2	GW	Coaches	Newquay	Wolverhampton
5	GW	Coaches (R.C.)	Penzance	Wolverhampton
1	LNE	Coach	Penzance	Aberdeen
1	LNE	Bk Van	Penzance	Edinburgh

The Paignton coaches were attached to the train at Exeter in this instance, whilst the LNER vehicles were detached at Taunton. On Fridays and Saturdays, the latter portion consisted of four LNE vehicles, plus a GW Brake Compo to Glasgow (also via the Great Central route).

On Sundays, only a late train conveyed through coaches to the North via the Severn Tunnel (although connections were available to trains from Torbay earlier in the day). The service in question was the 5.5 p.m. Penzance to Paddington, which conveyed three LMS vehicles between North Road (8.0 p.m. departure) and Manchester.

The 12.25 p.m. Penzance to Paddington train carried the pair of coaches destined for Wolverhampton on Sundays. These were detached at Exeter, and attached to the 3.40 p.m. train from Paignton for the remainder of their journey.

Summer Fridays and Saturdays brought a tremendous increase in the services to and from Paddington, the North of England, South Wales and the West Midlands, and a number of trains were shown as being 'Holiday Ticket Trains'.

Only one of the nine local trains between Exeter and Newton Abbot continued to Plymouth, though several ran through to either Paignton or Kingswear. However, four of the fourteen trains from Newton Abbot to Exeter commenced at Plymouth, while the remaining ten came from the Kingswear Branch. The local service between Newton Abbot and Plymouth consisted of

six Down trains (one from Exeter) and nine Up trains (four continuing to Exeter).

There were also a small number of 'intermediate' workings to wayside stations by local trains. Amongst these were services to Dawlish Warren from Exeter, and to Totnes from Newton Abbot, each with their balancing trains.

Teignmouth now had 22 Down and 20 Up trains, while Dawlish had 17 Down and 20 Up, both stations having additional trains on Saturdays. Totnes was served by 10 Down and 12 Up trains, Brent having 9 Down and 11 Up; again, both stations had extra trains on Saturdays. There were no longer any Plymouth to Ivybridge or Brent local trains.

On Sundays there was only one Exeter and Plymouth train in each direction, with three Down and four Up trains between Newton Abbot and Plymouth. However, there were no less than 12 Down trains between Exeter and Newton Abbot, nine of which ran forward over the Kingswear Branch, three of these terminating at Brixham! Of the ten Up trains, all except one (from Plymouth) came from the Kingswear Branch, and three commenced from Brixham! Although Teignmouth and Dawlish both enjoyed a Sunday service almost as good as that on weekdays, Totnes had only seven Down and eight Up trains, while Brent had four Down trains and five Up. One late evening train terminated at Teignmouth, returning shortly afterwards to Newton Abbot.

On weekdays, there were two Taunton to Kingswear trains; the 12 noon served all stations except St Thomas and Exminster, arriving at Kingswear at 3.05 p.m., while the 8.20 p.m. stopped at every station to Kingswear (arr. 11.40 p.m.). The 4.25 p.m. from Millbay called at all stations to Taunton (arr. 8.06), as did the 6.40 p.m. from Kingswear (Taunton arr. 9.42 p.m.). On Saturdays the 12.10 p.m. Paddington to Plymouth, a six-coach 'Luncheon and Tea Car Train' as far as Newton Abbot, stopped at every station from Exeter (except Exminster) and took the place of the weekday 4.20 p.m. Newton Abbot to Millbay.

On Sundays, the 6.45 a.m. 'North of England to Plymouth Express' from Bristol omitted only Exminster and Mutley after leaving Exeter(!), arriving at Millbay at 12.10 p.m. This was exactly the same service and timing as in 1902, except that it now took two minutes longer! The 7.00 a.m. Millbay to Paddington (arr. 3.55 p.m.) stopped at ten stations in addition

'Castles' had appeared on West Country services in the autumn of 1923 with the introduction of No. 4073, and by the following spring, ten of the class were at work. It was not until May 1925, however, that Laira shed received its first allocation, in the form of Nos. 4084 to 4088; by the time No. 5041 *Tiverton Castle* arrived at the shed 'as new' from Swindon Factory in July 1935, there were twelve other 'Castles' in residence. Apart from short periods of loan to other West Country sheds, No. 5041 remained a Laira engine throughout her GWR career. Whilst the 'Kings' now handled the heaviest of the trains, 'Castles' still had some of the London services, as well as many of the through trains to the Midlands and the North.

D. B. Hart

to Newton Abbot and Exeter before reaching Taunton at 10.15 a.m.; while the 6.45 p.m. Paignton to Taunton (arr. 9.23 p.m.) missed out only five stations.

Most of the local services at this time were operated by 3 or 4 coach sets (sometimes corridor stock), with a small number run by 'balancing' main line stock sets.

Within six months of the final three 'Stars' emerging from Swindon, No.4073 *Caerphilly Castle* made its debut on the 'Cornish Riviera Express' in August 1923, followed later that year by No.4074 *Caldicot Castle*. The first eleven 'Castles' were all shedded at Old Oak Common, No.4084 *Aberystwyth Castle* being the first received by Laira in May 1925. The next four engines, Nos.4085 *Berkeley Castle*, 4086 *Builth Castle*, 4087 *Cardigan Castle* and 4089 *Dartmouth Castle* were also sent to Laira during the summer of that year. Old Oak Common had the next six, Laira's turn coming again with Nos.4095 *Harlech Castle* and 4096 *Highclere Castle* in July 1926. The first of the class to be shedded at Newton Abbot was No.5003 *Lulworth Castle* in 1927, followed later that year by Nos.5011 *Tintagel Castle* and 5012 *Berry Pomeroy Castle*. In the meantime, Laira had received Nos.5004 *Llanstephan Castle*, 5007 *Rougemont Castle*, 5008 *Raglan*

Castle and 5009 *Shrewsbury Castle*. By this time, some of the earlier engines had changed sheds, with 4075 *Cardiff Castle* and 4080 *Powderham Castle* moving to Laira.

1927 also saw the advent of the mighty 'Kings', which immediately took over the premier workings such as the Up and Down 'Cornish Riviera Express'. Laira was allocated the third engine built, No.6002 *King William IV* and then had all the engines with 'even numbers' up to 6010, followed by Nos.6016 *King Edward V* and 6018 *King Henry VI* – the latter always regarded as probably the best of the class. The interesting sequence of 'even numbers' in South Devon was maintained by Nos.6012 *King Edward VI* and 6014 *King Henry VII* being sent to Newton Abbot, and by 6020 *King Henry IV*, 6022 *King Edward III* and 6024 *King Edward I* (of the 1930 batch) all going to Laira; however, something went 'adrift' when Newton Abbot received No.6023 *King Edward II*! Although one or two of the 'Kings' changed sheds within the Division, the numbers remained more or less the same.

A surprising event was the allocation of 'Kings' to Exeter for short periods; No.6001 was there for August 1930 (having spent June at Reading). Received from Old Oak Common, it

A superb study of Exeter St. David's, c.1929, with Laira 'King' 4–6–0 No. 6006 *King George I* standing at the Down platform with an express, possibly the 1.30 p.m. Paddington to Penzance. The vehicles visible behind the engine are 70ft steel-panelled stock; this length of coach was extensively used on the Penzance portions of daily trains at this time. *King George I* was allocated to Laira when new, in March 1928, and was transferred to Stafford Road shed, Wolverhampton, in September 1930; she remained there until withdrawal in February 1962. The 'Kings' had charge of the 'Riviera', 'Torbay', and three or four other principal London trains in each direction during the late 'twenties, plus some less prestigious 'balancing' trips.

Collection R. C. Riley

Exeter St. David's c.1915 (looking north), on completion of the rebuilding; the photograph was probably taken from the top of the oil gas depôt – the old 'Atmospheric' railway pump house. It shows the new station in all its glory, a considerable improvement over its predecessor. From the left, the passenger running lines are: Up Relief (with a station pilot, '45XX' class 2–6–2 tank, engaged in shunting), Up Main, Up Middle (LSWR), Down Main (through) and the Down Main platform. The near two lines (running diagonally across the bottom left of the photograph) are the Up and Down Goods running lines, which ran around the western edge of the goods yard (seen in the distance) before rejoining the main lines to the north of the station. The two LSWR lines, although designated Up and Down Middle, were, in operational terms, Down and Up respectively, owing to the peculiarities of 'South Western' routes in the district; Plymouth-bound services departed in the Up direction, London-bound in the Down. Curiously, this situation was mirrored at Plymouth (North Road).

National Railway Museum, York

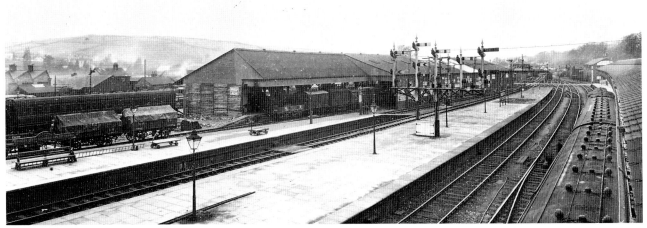

Exeter St. David's (north end), looking towards London (c.1914), and showing the substantial goods shed. The structure was some 400ft in length, with external offices situated at its northern end. Access was provided by the crossing seen just off the ends of the long platforms, which passed between the goods shed and the new Exeter Middle Signal Box. The length of the Up island platform was limited by the proximity of the goods shed, although some adjustments were made to the latter at a later date to allow a northerly extension.
National Railway Museum, York

A South Western 'G6' 0—6—0T from Exmouth Junction shed passing beneath the luggage and parcels bridge, situated at the northern end of the station buildings at St. David's; a separate passenger footbridge was provided in the centre of the station complex. The brick building to the right of the picture is the Divisional Superintendent's office, housing the senior officers of the Exeter traffic district and their staffs. The locomotive organisation was separate, being based at Newton Abbot (and covering sheds between Bridgwater and Penzance). Behind the office is the Exe Valley bay, and loading bank. The old 'Middle' signal box can just be seen in the middle distance, situated immediately beyond the road crossing, and between the Up and Down main lines. The old goods shed can also be seen to the left of and beyond the box.
National Railway Museum, York

The 3.26 p.m. Down Exe Valley train from Dulverton entering the Bay platform at the north end of Exeter St. David's station on 30th August 1930. The ex-LSWR 'G6' 0–6–0T on the left is ready for banking duties on Southern Railway trains to Exeter Queen Street.

G. N. Southerden

WARD & Cº

GUANO, OILCAKE CORN SALT & ARTIFICIAL MANURE STORES LIME COAL & TILE YARD

Looking down through the station from the east end on 11th June 1921.

L & GRP, courtesy David & Charles

'517' class No. 1162 at Exeter St. David's on 30th August 1930.

G. N. Southerden

Exeter St. David's (south end) c.1932, looking south (Down) from the Up Main platform, with the West Signal Box in the centre of the picture. The GWR main line passes to the right of the signal box, converging to double track for the crossing of the River Exe, immediately beyond the 'box; the Southern line to Queen Street (Central from 1933) and Waterloo diverges to the left, climbing sharply. The London & South Western Railway reached St. David's on its way westwards in February 1862, at a time when the Bristol & Exeter was still using the separate Up and Down stations. This new line had forced the issue, and rebuilding was put in hand, with the new St. David's station opened in July 1864.

C. L. Mowat

The south end of St. David's station, Exeter, looking in the direction of London, c.1932, with a pannier tank preparing to back from the Up Relief platform onto the Up Main, perhaps having collected empty gas tanks from the rear of an Up train; the tanks were replenished at the adjacent oil gas depot. The Up Southern train at the Down Middle platform is behind what may be a 4–4–0 (K10/L11?), awaiting departure for Queen Street, up the 1 in 37 bank between the two stations; the headcode seems to indicate an Exeter to Exmouth Junction train. Alongside the nearby Down Main platform is an unidentified 'King' with an express for Torbay or the West. *C. L. Mowat*

Another view of the West box, at the southern approaches to the station, taken from a train standing at the Up Main platform. The wooden structure to the left is the carriage shed ('South Devon Sidings'), providing an ideal advertising space! A porter making his way along the barrow crossing towards the Up GW platform, meets an ice cream vendor, with a prominent 'Stop Me and Buy One' sign on the front of his cart. The bracket signal controlled movements from the Up Middle (Down SR) platform in the Down direction, the starting signal being for a departure on the GWR Down Main.

Collection W. G. Rear

Contrast in styles; a Maunsell 'N' class 2—6—0 piloting a Down Southern train, is shown alongside an unidentified 'Castle' 4—6—0 of Lot 234 (Nos 4093-9; 5000-12) on an Up working, at the north end of Exeter St David's. The single headlamp on the 'Castle' may indicate that it has just joined the train as a light engine; if so, the service might be the 3.55 p.m. Exeter to Paddington (via Bristol), on 27th August 1932. The Southern engine is carrying the headcode of an Exeter to Ilfracombe service.

G. N. Southerden

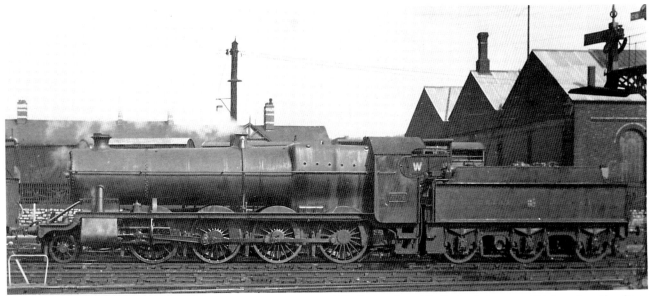

Churchward '47XX' class 2–8–0 No. 4706 at Newton Abbot c.1930. Designed specifically for fast vacuum-fitted services, the class initially (1923) operated on freights between London and Wolverhampton, Bristol, and Plymouth, with Laira receiving its locomotive (No. 4707) in April of that year. Exeter acquired No. 4706 during 1928, and, apart from spells at Old Oak, Newton, and Laira, this engine remained at Exeter until nationalisation. By 1928, Bristol had lost its '47XX' allocation (No. 4706 had been at St. Philip's Marsh), and there were two return services each night between London and Wolverhampton, and the West Country. No. 4706 was employed on an Up train from Exeter, returning the following night on the 11.35 p.m. Paddington to Newton Abbot, alternating with an Old Oak engine; Laira and Old Oak similarly operated a nightly service in each direction between London and Plymouth. The normal maximum loading of these trains was 70 wagons.   *Collection R. C. Riley*

returned there in September, being replaced by No.6025 (then only two months old), which itself returned to Old Oak Common at the end of November. At the same time, No.6026 was at Reading, while in May, No.6013 had been at Taunton. These allocations appear to have been made to ensure 'standby' cover in case of a failure on 'The Limited'.

In January 1932, the allocation of express engines in South Devon was:

'Kings' – Laira 7, Newton Abbot 3.
'Castles' – Laira 7, Newton Abbot 9.
'Stars' – Exeter 5.

These figures were amended by the requirements for the summer service, whilst a further four 'Castles' were allocated to Laira, and one to Newton – all new, straight from Swindon Factory.

Although one or two 'Stars' returned to Newton Abbot in later years, only 4012 *Knight of the Thistle* spent any time at Laira, during the early years of the Second World War. No 'Saints' were ever again shedded in the West of England, though they continued to appear fairly regularly on workings from other sheds, especially Bristol Bath Road. From 1928, the 'Halls' were in charge of many trains previously worked by Moguls, the first 14 'Halls' being at either Laira, Truro or Penzance. However, the Moguls did a considerable amount of main line work, resulting in the weight distribution being altered to produce the 83XX series, and in 1934 South Devon and Cornwall had 33 out of the 65 modified engines, and only one of the unaltered examples.

From 1936 onwards, withdrawn engines of the '4300' class were replaced by the 'Granges'. The first two, Nos.6800 *Arlington Grange* and 6801 *Aylburton Grange*, were sent to Penzance and

Laira respectively (Penzance also receiving Nos.6808 *Beenham Grange*), while Exeter had Nos.6813 *Eastbury Grange*, 6814 *Enborne Grange*, 6822 *Manton Grange* and 6825 *Llanvair Grange*, whilst Nos.6827 *Llanfrechfa Grange*, 6829 *Burmington Grange* and 6837 *Forthampton Grange* were at Truro. The new engines worked on a wide variety of passenger and goods duties in South Devon and Cornwall.

By 1932 only a handful of 'Dukes' remained in the West of England (3272 at Newton, 3284 and 3289 at Laira), the majority having been sent to work on the former Cambrian Railways lines in Central Wales. The dozen 'Bulldogs' remaining in the area were used for assisting trains over the South Devon banks, or as station pilots at Exeter and Newton Abbot.

By 1938, the only 'Star' remaining in South Devon was No.4056 *Princess Margaret* at Newton Abbot. The express passenger allocations were:

'Kings' – Laira 8, Newton Abbot 3.
'Castles' – Laira 9, Newton Abbot 11, Exeter 7, Penzance 2.

Penzance had a dozen 'Halls'; there were six at Truro, nine at Laira and three at Newton Abbot.

Up to 1934 both Laira and Newton had some of the 'ROD' class 2–8–0s, as well as one or two of the '2800' class; thereafter, each shed maintained a small number of the latter class.

Two of the magnificent mixed traffic 2–8–0s of the '4700' class were shedded locally, being employed almost exclusively on night-time fast fitted freights, though also appearing on occasions on holiday trains during the summer months. No.4707 went to Laira as a new engine in April 1923, remaining at that shed until 1931, when it was replaced by 4705; this in turn was replaced by 4704 in 1933. No.4703 then arrived during 1935, to assume the duties until nationalisation. During

An official photograph of Exeter's locomotive facilities taken in 1921, showing the 'north light' pattern shed with offices, turntable, and coal stage. The lifting shop was situated on the side of the shed, beyond the offices, whilst the sand dryer (with chimney) can be seen between the offices and the turntable. At this time, Exeter was host to engines of the '517' class 0–4–2T (auto and passenger services), '850', '1076' and '1854' classes of 0–6–0T (passenger, local goods and shunting), together with small numbers of '2301' (Dean Goods) and '43XX' class 2–6–0s for the longer goods turns. As far as is known, Exeter did not receive one of the familiar '45XX' class 2–6–2 tanks until 22nd June 1922. For main line passenger services, six 'Saints' and five or six 'Stars' were provided during the period up to the Grouping. Taken from the Up Relief platform, this view shows some of the vast array of pointwork in this congested location. The nearest group of sidings served the goods shed and carriage shoot, whilst the line immediately beyond the near bracket signal connected to the goods yard. Between the water crane and the further bracket signal ran the Down and Up goods lines respectively, with the engine shed trackwork beyond.

National Railway Museum, York

Exeter St. David's, south end, c.1935, with an unidentified '30XX' (ROD) class 2—8—0 at the head of an 'H' class goods train on the Down goods running line. This train probably originated in South Wales, consisting as it does entirely of coal wagons! The 'RODs' were a familiar sight in the West Country between 1927 and 1935, when one or two examples were shedded at Exeter, Newton, and Laira; Exeter retained the last of these (No. 3031) until 1936, when it left for Oxford shed. Unassisted, these engines could handle thirty loaded coal wagons between Taunton and Exeter (limited by Wellington bank), 83 from Exeter to Newton Abbot, and 16 between Newton and Plymouth (limited by Dainton bank).

G. N. Southerden

A pristine '2301' Dean Goods class 0–6–0 No. 2483, with Belpaire boiler and top feed fitted during 1907. Built in 1896, she was allocated to Newton Abbot and Exeter during 1902, to Laira in 1906, subsequently residing variously at those three sheds until 1932. She was at Exeter in 1914, working mainly to and from Bristol, with regular forays into South Wales. After a brief spell at Taunton in 1923/3, No. 2483 moved to Central Wales, where she ended her days.
Collection
R. S. Carpenter

the grouping period, Exeter had 4706 (from 1928 until the end of the GWR's existence), with 4707 putting in an appearance in its place for three years during the late 'thirties.

The last 'Standard Goods' 0–6–0 to work in South Devon was No.436, withdrawn from Exeter in 1930 (having gone there in the 1920s after a period when none of the class was in South Devon), while the last 'Dean Goods', No.2483, left Exeter during 1932. However, 'Deans' still appeared occasionally, their most frequent visits in later years being on a Sunday fish train from Swindon to Newton Abbot. The local 'Aberdares' were transferred away from Laira and Exeter sheds during 1934, being replaced on the South Wales to Exeter coal trains by the new '7200' class 2–8–2 Ts, rebuilt from 2–8–0 Ts of the '4200' and '5200' classes. One of the 2–8–0 Ts was shedded at Laira from new in September 1924 (No.5243), whilst a second was allocated to Truro (No.5244); both moved on to South Wales the following year and were not replaced. The class re-appeared in 1928, with a pair allocated to St. Blazey to work china clay traffic to Fowey and Plymouth. Nos. 4215 and 4298, the regular engines for many years, occasionally appeared at Newton Abbot for attention in the factory (after which they sometimes worked goods trains to Kingswear!); both engines reached St. Blazey in the early 'thirties, remaining until after Nationalisation. Otherwise appearances by the class were most infrequent.

In 1929, following a redistribution of weight and renumbering into the 51XX series, the '3100' class 2–6–2 Ts disappeared from South Devon. Two of the new '5101' class, Nos.4109 and 4117, were at Newton Abbot in 1938. No.8108 of the '8100' class was sent to Newton Abbot in 1939 when newly rebuilt from No.5133, but was transferred away during the early years of the war. For banking duties, Newton Abbot had five of the larger '3150' class engines in 1938, and two of the class were at Laira.

The smaller '4500' class engines continued to be the 'mainstay' on many of the branch lines and on local workings. In 1938 there were ten at Newton Abbot, thirteen at Laira and three at Exeter. They had a monopoly of the Launceston trains; passenger and goods workings were in the charge of two of the

'1361' class No. 1364 for shunting at Plymouth Millbay Docks.
W. Potter

class. The Moretonhampstead line was served by them for many years, and they regularly worked on the Kingswear Branch, including banking between Torquay and Torre on Summer Saturdays. The entire class of eleven engines of the '4400' series was to be found on West of England branches between 1925 and 1931, but by the mid-1930s only five remained – two at Laira for the Princetown Branch, one at Exeter for the City Basin goods lines, another at Newton Abbot for the Ashburton goods and a fifth at Penzance.

Exeter shed was host to a pair of steam railmotors throughout the 'twenties and early 'thirties; the last unit left in 1935. In the early 'twenties, they were used on main line services between Exeter, Dawlish Warren and Teignmouth, and on the Exe and Teign Valley branches.

By the late 'twenties, auto train services were being introduced in the South Devon area, with Ashburton, Brixham and the Teign Valley lines being worked by such units (shown in the timetables as 'Rail Motor Car, one class only'). These distinctive trains also worked between Newton Abbot and Bovey on the Moretonhampstead Branch, which was entirely auto-worked on Sundays. From 1932, the aged '517' class 0–4–2 Ts were replaced by the new '4800' class engines, and by 1938 almost one fifth of the class was in South Devon, four

Exminster station, five miles south of Exeter St. David's, on Sunday, 13th March 1932, with an unidentified 'Star' 4—6—0 approaching on a Down stopping train, possibly the 4.15 p.m. Exeter to Brixham; the 'Star' would probably come off at Newton Abbot together with the leading van. Exminster station was rebuilt during the 'twenties and 'thirties; the Down side (which the 'Star' is entering) was completed in 1924, though the Up platform was less than a year old at the time of the photograph. The original station was double track, with the Up platform situated against the station master's house on the left of the picture; the modifications at this time provided two extra platform lines (loops), making both platforms into islands.

G. N. Southerden

being at Newton Abbot and no less than ten at Exeter. From the 1890s some of the 'Metro' class 2–4–0 Ts had always been shedded at Newton Abbot, and No.3590 was there until 1940, moving on to Exeter for a further three-year spell. Another member of the class, No.3582, left Newton in 1945 for St. Blazey.

Until the arrival of the first of the '5700' class Panniers, the older engines of the '1854' and '2721' classes remained responsible for local goods and shunting work, though there were also one or two of the Wolverhampton-built '645' class. By 1938 they were out-numbered by the new engines, of which No.7761 (Exeter) and 8719 (Newton Abbot) appear to have been the first to arrive, during 1931; Laira seemingly did not receive one until 1934 (No.7715, ex-St. Blazey). The last of the double-framed engines, No.1650 of the '1076' class, was withdrawn from Newton Abbot in March 1938. Laira and Exeter still retained a few of the small '1901' and '2021' classes for lines with weight restrictions, and there were two of the new, 'yellow'-route engines of the '7400' class, No.7422 at Laira, and No.7427 at Newton Abbot, where it was used on station pilot duties. The only other shunting engines were the five saddle tanks of the '1361' class employed in Millbay Docks and at Newton Abbot Wagon Works.

The outbreak of war in September 1939 brought an immediate increase in freight traffic, which continued throughout the war years, though express passenger services were considerably reduced. When the expected air onslaught did not materialise, many trains were gradually reinstated. The 'Cornish Riviera Express' at first travelled via Bath and Bristol, leaving Pad-dington at its usual time, but combining the functions of the 10.00 a.m. (Bristol), 10.30 a.m., 11.00 a.m. (Penzance), 11.15 a.m. (Weston-super-Mare) and 12.00 noon ('Torbay Express') trains! The Torquay part was formed into a separate 10.40 a.m. service a little later. The 'Limited' was one of only four trains in the country to carry its name throughout the war years; it ran non-stop to Exeter, but the only through carriages were for Penzance, additional carriages for Plymouth being attached to the rear of the train. Plymouth was not reached until 3.25 p.m. and Penzance at 6.25 p.m. The Up train left Penzance at 9.30 a.m., Plymouth at 12.30 p.m. and Exeter at 1.55 p.m., reaching Paddington at 5.30 p.m.

'The Devonian' between Bradford and the Torquay line, and all services between Wolverhampton and the West of England were withdrawn for the duration of the war. Services between the West of England and the North of England via the Severn Tunnel were not reduced, due to the vital link they provided between the ports of Plymouth and Liverpool. However, there were no longer any through coaches between Scotland and the West of England, nor to and from Birkenhead. All of those services which had been withdrawn were reinstated during 1946, with the exception of the Birkenhead coaches.

A new Down loop was provided on the main line to the west of Aller Junction, together with new crossovers and a spur for banking engines, the work being completed in 1941. The following year there were alterations and extensions at Exmin-ster, with the Down refuge siding being converted into a loop and three new loop sidings provided. Additional sidings were also constructed at Hackney Yard and Tavistock Junction.

War-time co-operation between the GWR and the Southern Railway included the construction, in March 1941, of a spur linking their lines at St Budeaux, Plymouth, which was used for emergency working on numerous occasions during the next four years.

Plymouth suffered severe bombing during the war, with great damage to numerous railway installations, and many wagons and some carriages were burnt out or destroyed. At Keyham, No.4911 *Bowden Hall* was completely destroyed by a bomb. Newton Abbot suffered a daylight bombing attack in August 1940, when an attempt was made to destroy the bridge carrying the Torquay Road over the main lines. The target was missed by a matter of yards, but much of the shed yard was rendered unusable, and several engines were badly damaged. 0–6–0 PT No.2785 suffered such damage that its withdrawal was proposed. However, it was later repaired, and survived to shunt Hackney Yard for several more years.

The tremendous increase in freight traffic eventually affected even the Kingsbridge branch and, during the latter months of war, ambulance trains were running over such unlikely routes as the Teign Valley line and the Moretonhampstead Branch. There were also numerous troop trains and other special workings in connection with services personnel and, in the early days, there were the various evacuation specials bringing children into South Devon from London and Bristol.

Among the unusual locomotives which appeared in South Devon were LMS '8F' class 2–8–0s, eighty of which had been built at Swindon. Laira, Newton Abbot and Exeter each had one or more of these, and there was even one at Penzance, probably the only eight-coupled tender engine ever shedded in Cornwall. During 1943–44, US Army 2–8–0s were loaned to the GWR prior to being sent to Europe after 'D Day', and some of these worked from Newton Abbot and Laira. Earlier in the war, when a number of Southern engines were on loan, 'N15X' class 4–6–0 No.2329 *Stephenson* was shedded at Exeter, working to Newton Abbot and Kingswear. Southern engines and carriages regularly worked on stopping trains between Exeter, Newton Abbot and Plymouth – the 11.15 a.m. from Exeter and the 2.20 p.m. and 4.30 p.m. from Plymouth. The 'N' class 2–6–0s were normally used, though the 'U' class Moguls also occasionally appeared. Similar workings by GWR Moguls took place over the SR route via Okehampton. These workings ensured that enginemen were familiar with both routes in the event of any emergency.

The most unlikely engines to appear in South Devon were LNER inside-cylinder 4–6–0s of the 'B12' class, which were

'Twixt cliffs and sea'; a '2301' class 0–6–0 at Dawlish with a Down goods. The photograph would appear to have been taken around late morning, so the Dean's train could therefore have been the 9.0 a.m. Exeter to Newton pick-up goods, scheduled to perform work at Dawlish between 11.10 and 11.30 a.m. during the inter-war period. The cramped goods facilities can be seen, with a goods shed siding, a mileage/loading bank siding, plus the short spurs associated with the wagon turntable (just visible in front of the wagons in the end-loading dock). It all seems so inadequate for a town such as Dawlish, yet it was all that the available space would allow. *B. Chapman*

One of the earlier (1927/8) batch of 'Kings' heading a Down express out of the 513-yard Parsons Tunnel, c.1930, having negotiated the mile-long stretch of five bores. It is about to pass the site of Parson's Tunnel Signal Box, opened in 1934 to provide another useful section on the busier days. Curiously, there had originally been a box in this location before, having been closed in 1905 when the line through the tunnels was doubled. The train itself could be the 5.30 a.m. Paddington to Penzance (via Bristol), due at Parsons's around 11.0 a.m., which was scheduled to convey two vans from the north at the head of the train.

Dr. Ian C. Allen

Having passed through the short Clerk's Tunnel, 'Hall' class 4–6–0 No. 4906 *Bradfield Hall* is approaching the eastern end of Parson's Tunnel with a mid-morning Down local train from Exeter, c.1930. This engine, built in January 1929, was allocated to Truro when new, moving to Penzance a few months later. During 1930, she moved away to Old Oak Common, followed by allocations to Chester, Swindon, and Westbury, before returning to Truro in 1935; No. 4906 thereafter spent the remainder of her GWR career at Truro and Penzance sheds. The four-coach train is a familiar formation in this district, being known as an 'M' set. Dawlish can be seen in the right background, and the station can just be seen on the shoreline to the right of the town.   *Dr. Ian C. Allen*

used on ambulance trains over the Teign Valley line from Exeter to Heathfield, and thence over the Moretonhampstead Branch; the GWR's Manor House Hotel, outside Moretonhampstead, had become an army hospital. Their low axle-loading enabled these engines to work over many routes barred to other engines of their size.

Alterations in duties and workings took place almost daily, especially during the periods of severe bombing at Plymouth; a number of engines were dispersed to other sheds, several 'Kings' being allocated to Exeter. The latter shed no longer had any 'Granges'; Nos.6813 *Eastbury Grange*, 6814 *Enborne Grange* and 6822 *Manton Grange* were at Newton Abbot, as was No.6829 *Burmington Grange* from Truro, while No.6825 *Llanvair Grange* had moved to Penzance, where there were now four of the class (including No.6801 *Aylburton Grange*, formerly at Laira). Those at Newton Abbot joined the 'Bulldogs' in assisting trains over the South Devon banks, and they also worked on passenger and freight traffic, both on the main line and over the Kingswear branch.

The large '3150' class 2–6–2 Ts at Newton Abbot were all replaced by engines of the '5100' or '5101' classes, though two remained at Laira. The '6100' class engines Nos.6100, 6107, and 6146, formerly in the London area, were sent down to South Devon and shedded at Newton Abbot for two or three

years. They worked on the Kingswear line, and also shared in banking duties on the Dainton and Rattery inclines. Three of the powerful 2–8–2 Ts, Nos.7208, 7221 and 7222, were also sent to Newton Abbot during the war years and were used on banking duties, as well as on working coal trains from Kingswear to Newton Abbot. They were replaced by Nos.7200, 7220 and 7250 during 1946–7.

1945 saw the introduction of the new 'County' class 4–6–0s, and the second engine, No.1001 (later *County of Bucks*), was allocated to Newton Abbot, being joined there a few months later by No.1018 (named *County of Leicester* within a few weeks). Laira received Nos.1004 (*County of Somerset*), 1006 (*County of Cornwall*) and 1009 (*County of Carmarthen*). No.1020 *County of Monmouth* went to Exeter, Nos.1019 *County of Merioneth* and 1022 *County of Northampton* to Penzance, and No.1023 *County of Oxford* was sent to Truro, no doubt to the amazement of the shed staff! Others regularly worked down from Old Oak Common and Bristol (Bath Road), and a Stafford Road 'County' was often used on the restored Wolverhampton to Penzance service, a Penzance 'County' working the train west of Newton Abbot, and on the Up service (non-stop from Plymouth) as far as Exeter.

Two of the post-war 'Castles', Nos.5098 *Clifford Castle* and 7000 *Viscount Portal*, were sent to Exeter and Newton Abbot

The official photograph of the Down 'Cornish Riviera Limited', seen behind 'King' class 4–6–0 No. 6002 *King William IV* at Teignmouth. The train has left the sea wall, passed through the station, and now hugs the northern bank of the River Teign on the five mile run inland to Newton Abbot, where she would cross the river. Apart from three short spells at Exeter during the early part of the war, *King William IV* was a permanent resident of Laira shed, Plymouth, during Great Western days. The coaches are, of course, the new 'Centenary' stock, and the photograph shows the summer 1935 formation of the service. The first seven coaches (Van Third, 2 Thirds, Third Dining Saloon, Kitchen First Diner, Composite, and Van Third) are destined for Penzance, and are followed by a Third and Brake Composite for St. Ives; the final vehicle is another Brake Compo, bound for Falmouth (Saturdays excepted) or St. Ives (Saturdays only). A truly classic train in every sense.

National Railway Museum, York

respectively. The former engine was always reckoned to be one of the best of the class, while the latter was employed almost exclusively on the 'double home' duty to Shrewsbury with the Liverpool and Manchester through trains.

The war-time increase of heavy freight engines allocated to Laira and Newton Abbot continued in the post-war years when Laira had several '2800' class 2–8–0s, including a number of the oil-burning engines (renumbered into the 48XX series) as well as some ex-War Department 'Austerity' engines, others being sent to Newton Abbot. Although there were no longer any of the '2800' class at Newton Abbot, there were two at Exeter. 0–6–0 tender classes had never been plentiful to the west of Taunton, although Exeter did have a Collett Goods (No.2255) for three years in the early 'thirties. No.2230, of the same class, arrived at Exeter during late 1940 for a short spell, returning again in 1945.

Among the older engines withdrawn after the war had ended, were several 'Bulldogs', including the doyen of the class, No.3313 *Jupiter*, and No.3373 *Sir Watkin Wynn*, both of which had been at Newton Abbot. A number of the older 0–6–0 PTs were also withdrawn, some spending many months 'dumped' out of use at the rear of Newton Abbot factory. Another casualty was one of Newton Abbot's long line of 'Metro' tanks, No.3590; the last 'Metro' left Newton in 1945 for St. Blazey (No.3582).

Post-war summers saw a restoration of extra weekend holiday trains to and from Paddington, the North of England, the Midlands and South Wales. Some traditional services, such as the Wolverhampton and Penzance through train (with TC for Kingswear) and 'The Devonian', also re-appeared, though 'The Devonian' ran only during the summer. The disastrous

winter weather of 1946–47, coupled with a critical shortage of coal, led to the withdrawal of many trains re-introduced a few months previously, but by the summer of 1947 the number of extra holiday trains had almost reached the level of the 1930s.

The weekday services for the South Devon area during the summer of 1947 was:

WEEKDAY SERVICES – PADDINGTON – Summer 1947

DOWN TRAINS

5.30 a.m. Paddington (via Bristol)

6 Coaches	Penzance
2 Bk Vans	Penzance
1 Van ‡	Penzance
1 Bk Van ‡	Penzance

(Plymouth arr. 12.45 p.m., Penzance 4.25 p.m.)
‡ The Vans originated from Nottingham and Sheffield respectively, both routed via Banbury.

10.30 a.m. Paddington 'Cornish Riviera' (via Lavington)

9 Coaches (R.C.)	Penzance
3 Coaches	North Road

(Plymouth N/Rd. arr. 3.10 p.m., Penzance 5.35 p.m.)

1.30 p.m. Paddington (via Lavington)

8 Coaches (R.C.)	Penzance
5 Coaches	Kingswear

(Plymouth arr. 6.55 p.m., Penzance 9.50 p.m.)

Another familiar locomotive type to West Country metals was the 'Grange' class, a member of which is shown here at the Up platform at Paignton station in July 1946. No. 6808 *Beenham Grange* was delivered as new to Penzance in October 1936; she spent the early war years at Exeter and Newton Abbot, returning to Penzance during 1943, where she stayed for the remainder of her GWR service. Here, she is being utilised for the Saturdays Only 10.0 a.m. Paignton to Cardiff express, which clearly included LMS stock; this was by no means unusual during this period, and 'cosmopolitan' trains of stock belonging to two or more of the companies were frequently noted!

W. Potter

The Bell: 'King' class 4–6–0 No. 6000 *King George V* at Exeter shed, probably c.1946/7. As well as the inscribed bell, No. 6000 carried two medallions on the cabside, mounted above the numberplate; this meant that, unusually, the 'double red' route discs of the class were placed below that plate, as may be seen. The tractive effort of the 'Kings' (40,300 lbs) was such that they exceeded the lettering scheme for classification, and were termed 'special'; they did not therefore carry a letter within the route disc, as was generally the case. By the time of this study, she was stationed at Laira, having been an Old Oak engine up to the outbreak of war. She did, however, spend prolonged periods at Exeter shed between 1939 and 1942, before her transfer to Laira.

R. C. Riley

'County' Class 4—6—0 No. 1018 *County of Leicester* pausing at Exeter St. David's station with a Down express, c.1947. By this time, these engines were rostered on similar duties to the 'Castles', having previously been scheduled on 'King' turns too. *R. C. Riley*

5.0 p.m. Paddington (via Bristol)

8 Coaches (R.C.)	North Road
5 Coaches	Paignton

(Plymouth arr. 11.14 p.m.)

6.30 p.m. Paddington (via Bristol)

4 Coaches	North Road
3 Coaches ‡	North Road
1 Coach (R.C.)	North Road

(Plymouth arr. 12.34 a.m.)

‡ LMS stock, from Manchester, attached at Bristol; the following Restaurant Car (running 'light') was attached at the same venue.

9.50 p.m. Paddington (via Bristol)

11 Coaches	Penzance
2 Coaches	North Road

(Plymouth arr. 5.30 a.m., Penzance 8.20 a.m.)

The Penzance portion included a First Class Sleeper.

11.50 p.m. Paddington (via Bristol)

1 Siphon G	North Road
2 Coaches	North Road
(inc. First Sleeper)	
7 Coaches	Penzance
1 Siphon G	Penzance

(Plymouth arr. 7.25 a.m., Penzance 11.0 a.m.)

UP TRAINS

8.40 p.m. Penzance (11.55 p.m. Plymouth, via Bristol)

3 Coaches	from North Road
(inc. First Sleeper)	
8 Coaches	from Penzance
(inc. two First Sleepers)	
1 Siphon G	from Penzance

(due Paddington 7.30 a.m.)

8.30 a.m. Plymouth (via Lavington)

5 Coaches	from Paignton
5 Coaches (R.C.)	from North Road
1 Slip	from North Road

(due Paddington 1.44 p.m.)

The Slip Coach was worked into Reading

8.0 a.m. Penzance (11.10 a.m. Plymouth, via Lavington)

5 Coaches (R.C.)	from North Road
7 Coaches	from Penzance

(due Paddington 4.37 p.m.)

9.45 a.m. Penzance 'Cornish Riviera' (12.20 p.m. Plymouth, via Lavington)

3 Coaches	from North Road
9 Coaches (R.C.)	from Penzance

(due Paddington 5.0 p.m.)

11.5 a.m. Penzance (1.55 p.m. Plymouth, via Lavington)

5 Coaches	from Kingswear
8 Coaches (R.C.)	from Penzance

(due Paddington 7.20 p.m.)

SUNDAYS – DOWN TRAINS

10.30 a.m. Paddington (via Lavington)

9 Coaches (R.C.)	Penzance
3 Coaches	North Road

(Plymouth arr. 3.35 p.m., Penzance 6.17 p.m.)

11.0 a.m. Paddington (via Lavington)

7 Coaches (R.C.)	North Road
5 Coaches	Kingswear

(Plymouth arr. 4.35 p.m.)

'Saint' class 4–6–0 No. 2931 *Arlington Court*, every inch a thoroughbred, standing alongside the Down Main platform at Exeter St. David's on Saturday, 13th September 1947. Her train is a relief portion of the 11.5 a.m. Paddington to Penzance, which may have been routed via Bristol, as she was a Bath Road engine at this time. No. 2931 was a familiar sight in Exeter during the years up to 1920, being shedded variously at Laira, Newton, and Exeter during that decade. Thereafter she went all over the place, being shedded at Cardiff, Swansea, Weymouth, Gloucester, Worcester, Hereford, Chester, Tyseley and Swindon before being transferred to Bath Road during 1941.

R. C. Riley

4.30 p.m. Paddington (via Bristol)

9 Coaches (R.C.)	North Road
5 Coaches	Paignton

(Plymouth arr. 11.50 p.m.)

9.50 p.m. Paddington

7 Coaches	Penzance
(inc. First Sleeper)	
6 Coaches	North Road

(Plymouth arr. 5.30 a.m., Penzance 8.20 a.m.)

11.50 p.m. Paddington

4 Coaches	North Road
(inc. First Sleeper)	
7 Coaches	Penzance

SUNDAYS – UP TRAINS

7.5 a.m. Plymouth (via Bristol)

4 Coaches	from North Road
4 Coaches ‡	from North Road

(due Paddington 3.50 p.m.)

‡ The rear coaches were destined for Liverpool, forwarded on the 12.35 p.m. Bristol train.

9.30 a.m. Plymouth (via Bristol)

6 Coaches	from Kingswear
8 Coaches (R.C.)	from North Road

(due Paddington 4.35 p.m.)

9.45 a.m. Penzance (12.20 p.m. Plymouth, via Lavington)

3 Coaches	from North Road
9 Coaches (R.C.)	from Penzance

(due Paddington 5.20 p.m.)

12.15 p.m. Penzance (3.0 p.m. Plymouth, via Lavington)

3 Coaches	from North Road
9 Coaches (R.C.)	from Penzance

(due Paddington 8.35 p.m.)

1.20 a.m. Plymouth (via Bristol)

7 Coaches	from North Road

(due Paddington 8.45 p.m.)

4.45 p.m. Penzance (8.5 p.m. Plymouth, via Bristol)

5 Coaches ‡	from North Road
1 Bk Van ‡	from North Road
6 Coaches	from Penzance
1 Bk Van	from Penzance
2 Coaches	from North Road

(due Paddington 3.29 a.m.)

9.30 p.m. Truro (Relief) (11.42 p.m. Plymouth, via Lavington)

7 Coaches	from Truro

(due Paddington 5.5 a.m.)

8.40 p.m. (11.55 p.m. Plymouth, via Bristol)

3 Coaches	from North Road
(inc. First Sleeper)	
9 Coaches	from Penzance
(inc. 3 First Sleepers)	

(due Paddington 7.30 a.m.)

Through services between the North of England (via Severn Tunnel) and the Midlands (via North Warwickshire line) were similar in number to their pre-war counterparts, though with detail differences;

CROSS COUNTRY SERVICES – Summer 1947

DOWN TRAINS

12.30 a.m. Manchester (6.45 a.m. Bristol)

5 GW	Coaches	Manchester	Penzance
1 LMS	Brake Van	Manchester	Penzance
1 GW	Brake Van	Manchester	Penzance
1 LMS	Brake Van	Manchester	Penzance
1 LMS	Brake Van	Liverpool	Penzance
3 LMS	Coaches	Glasgow	Penzance
1 GW	Van	Birkenhead	Penzance

(North Road arr. 10.45 a.m., Penzance 1.40 p.m.)

9.10 a.m. Manchester (2.5 p.m. Bristol)

8 LMS	Coaches	Manchester	North Road
4 GW	Coaches	Bristol	N. Abbot

(North Road arr. 6.27 p.m.)

9.15 a.m. Liverpool (3.35 p.m. Bristol)

6 GW	Coaches	Liverpool	Penzance
3 LMS	Coaches	Liverpool	Kingswear

(North Road arr. 7.25 p.m., Penzance 10.30 p.m.)

12.15 p.m. Manchester (6.5 p.m. Bristol)

3 LMS‡	Coaches (R.C.)	Manchester	North Road
5 LMS	Coaches	Manchester	North Road
2 LMS	Coaches	Manchester	N. Abbot

‡ LMS & GW vehicles alternating

(North Road arr. 10.10 p.m.)

The arrangements of Down trains from the North was much more positive than pre-war, with all four services running through, rather than working locally to their destinations (as was the case of two of the trains in 1932) from Bristol.

The 'Wolverhampton' was re-instated, although it had lost its Newquay portion.

10.40 a.m. Wolverhampton (1.45 p.m. Bristol)

8	Coaches (R.C.)	Wolverhampton	Penzance
4	Coaches	Wolverhampton	Kingswear

(North Road arr. 5.0 p.m., Penzance 7.40 p.m.)

In addition to the cross-country services, there were two fast trains in each direction between Bristol and Plymouth. The first Down service was the 6.30 a.m. Bristol, conveying 7 coaches to North Road (due 10.22 a.m.); this train formed a relief to the following 12.30 a.m. Manchester.

The other Down train was the familiar 10.2 a.m. Bath.

10.2 a.m. Bath (10.30 a.m. Bristol)

6	Coaches	Bath	North Road
4	Coaches	Bath	Kingswear

Unlike its pre-war counterpart, this train consisted of a standard 6-coach set ('K' set), rather than a mixture of vehicles from the North of England.

The daily service from Cardiff to Plymouth also ran, although there was no balancing train as such in the opposite direction; the coaches returned to South Wales on local workings.

11.30 a.m. Cardiff (12.55 p.m. Bristol)

6	Coaches	Cardiff	North Road
6	Coaches	Bristol	Paignton

The 'Up' services during the summer of 1947 were as follows:

8.45 a.m. Plymouth

5	LMS	Coaches	North Road	Liverpool
3	LMS‡	Coaches (R.C.)	North Road	Manchester
5	LMS	Coaches	Paignton	Manchester

(‡ LMS and GW vehicles alternating)

10.5 a.m. Penzance (1.0 p.m. Plymouth)

3	LMS	Coaches	North Road	Liverpool
5	LMS	Coaches	Penzance	Liverpool
1	LMS	Bk Van	Penzance	Manchester

12.0 noon Penzance (3.45 p.m. Plymouth)

3	LMS	Coaches	North Road	Liverpool
3	GW	Coaches	Penzance	Liverpool
1	GW	Siphon G	Penzance	Liverpool
3	GW	Coaches	Penzance	Liverpool
1	LMS	Brake Van	Penzance	Manchester
1	GW	Van	Penzance	Leeds
1	GW	Brake Van	Penzance	Sheffield

A truly 'mixed' train, both in ownership and vehicle types. The Sheffield Van was routed via Banbury and the LNE line.

4.45 p.m. Penzance (8.7 p.m. Plymouth)

1	LMS	Brake Van	Penzance	Manchester
5	GW	Coaches	Penzance	Manchester
1	GW	Brake Van	Penzance	Manchester
1	LMS	Brake Van	North Road	Manchester
3	LMS	Coaches	North Road	Manchester
1	LMS	Van	North Road	Sheffield

In this instance, the rearmost Van was destined for Sheffield LMS, running via the Midland route.

The Up 'Wolverhampton' had again lost the Newquay portion of its pre-war counterpart.

10.40 a.m. Penzance (1.35 p.m. Plymouth N/Rd)

4	Coaches	Paignton	Wolverhampton
8	Coaches (R.C.)	Penzance	Wolverhampton

The two through trains to Bristol were similar to their 'Down' balancing services:

7.40 a.m. Penzance (10.30 a.m. Plymouth N/Rd)

7	Coaches	Penzance	Bristol
4	Coaches	Kingswear	Bristol

The other service, 6.15 p.m. from North Road, was the return working of the 6-coach set that operated westwards as the 10.2 a.m. Bath that morning.

CROSS COUNTRY SERVICES – SUNDAYS

There were two trains in each direction connecting the North of England with the West Country. In the Down direction, both services were through, viz:

1.40 a.m. Crewe (7.0 a.m. Bristol)

1	LMS	Brake Van	Glasgow	North Road
3	LMS	Coaches	Glasgow	North Road
5	GW	Coaches	Manchester	North Road
1	LMS	Brake Van	Liverpool	North Road

(North Road arr. 11.51 a.m.)

10.40 a.m. Liverpool (5.45 p.m. Bristol)

5	LMS	Coaches	Liverpool	North Road
3	LMS	Coaches	Manchester	North Road

(North Road arr. 9.40 p.m.)

In the Up direction, both services to the North were attached to London-bound trains as far as Bristol. The 7.5 a.m. Plymouth (North Road) carried 4 GW coaches for Liverpool at the rear, these being conveyed onwards by the 12.35 p.m. Bristol. Later in the day, the 4.45 p.m. Penzance train attached 5 coaches and 1 brake van (GW stock) at North Road; the Monday morning (12.3 a.m.) Bristol service carried them through to their destination, Manchester. This latter train departed from North Road at 8.5 p.m.

The Exeter to Newton Abbot local service (weekday) consisted of eleven trains, with an additional two Saturday only. Only one of these ran through to Plymouth, the remainder continued over the Kingswear Branch or terminated at Newton. The Up service had 15 trains, 11 being from Kingswear or Newton and the other four from Plymouth. There were six trains from Newton Abbot to Plymouth (one being from Exeter), and eight from Plymouth to Newton Abbot (including three to Exeter). Teignmouth was served by 22 Down and 20 Up trains, while Dawlish had 18 Down trains and 20 Up, both having extra trains on Saturdays. Totnes had

Dainton summit, with just a few yards of level track beyond the signal box before the drop to Aller Junction. This picture shows a 'Hall' class 4—6—0 piloting a 'Castle' on an Up train over the last section of the 1 in 40 reverse gradient on the five mile climb from Totnes, to be confronted with a similar forward gradient beyond the tunnel at the start of the descent towards Newton Abbot. The steepest gradients occurred for about two miles on either side of the summit.

R. C. Riley

Dainton tunnel and signal box on 1st June 1921. *L & GRP cty. David & Charles*

15 Down and 14 Up trains, while Brent had 10 Down and 10 Up trains. There was an early morning return working between Newton Abbot and Totnes by an auto-train (which continued to Moretonhampstead), the only time a '4800' class 0–4–2 T and trailers regularly ventured over Dainton Summit!

There were several long-distance stopping trains. The 7.40 a.m. from Newton Abbot worked through to Penzance (arr. 11.00 a.m.), while the 9.15 p.m. from Taunton terminated at Newton Abbot at 11.12 p.m. The 6.30 a.m. Newton Abbot to Bristol (arr. 10.08 a.m.) called at all stations to Weston-super-Mare, except Brean Road Halt, the 7.00 a.m. Kingswear to Cardiff (arr. 12.39 p.m.) called at all stations to Exeter, ran non-stop to Taunton, and then served the more important stations to Bristol (arr. 11.02 a.m.). One of the three Plymouth

From the earliest days of co-operation between the SDR and Great Western, milk traffic had formed an important part of revenue-earning activities. An early afternoon train from Penzance conveying 'perishables' was running daily to London before the turn of the century, and probably carried milk too. It was not until World War II, however, that a milk train as such began to run from the West Country on a regular basis, and this left Penzance at 6.20 p.m. with vehicles for Wood Lane and Kensington. By 1946, this had been joined by a second train, departing from Penzance at 12.35 p.m., again for Kensington. The successor to this latter train is seen on 29th June 1957 at Dainton Summit, in the hands of 'Hall' class 4–6–0 No. 6986 *Rydal Hall* and 28XX class 2–8–0 No. 3832. In addition to the six tanks and Passenger Brake Van (for churn traffic and the guard), a 'Cordon' gas tank wagon is attached, possibly destined for the gas depot at Exeter, or perhaps Swindon. The mirror over the Up line enabled the signalman to inspect Up trains to ensure the tail lamp was in place if they were concealed by a Down, vital in such a location with the risk of trains dividing on the imposing banks.
R. C. Riley

'14XX' No. 1408 passing Laira with an Up auto-train, with the locomotive depot on the left. The carriage sidings on the right accommodated the auto-trailers used on the intensive suburban service around Plymouth, the track layout of which enabled the auto-engines to be marshalled in the centre of the four-coach trains used on the rush hour services. The boarded track in the foreground allowed the horse-drawn wagon of the Lee Moor Tramway to cross the GWR main line on the level.

R. E. Vincent

Laira locomotive depot coaling stage with a 'Castle', a 'King' and an unidentified '57XX' 0—6—0PT receiving attention in the yard on 27th June 1960. *W. Potter*

to Exeter trains was provided by the 7.30 a.m. from Truro (Exeter arr. 11.47 a.m.); while the 5.15 p.m. Newton Abbot to Bristol (arr. 9.51 p.m.) called at all stations except Long Ashton. In addition, the 1.22 p.m. Crewe train (12.15 p.m. Manchester) called at all stations between Newton and North Road.

On Sundays, six local trains ran from Exeter to Newton Abbot; one continued to Plymouth and the remainder went forward over the Kingswear branch. There were seven trains from Newton Abbot to Exeter, five from the Kingswear line and the other two from Plymouth. There were two Newton Abbot to Plymouth trains as well as the one from Exeter, but the only trains from Plymouth were the two for Exeter. Teignmouth had 14 Down and 10 Up trains; Dawlish 13 Down and 8 Up; Totnes 9 Down and 5 Up; and Brent 5 Down and 3 Up trains.

The early morning train from Bristol (ex-Crewe) called at the majority of stations between Taunton and Plymouth that

were open on Sundays. Similarly, the 9.30 a.m. Plymouth to Paddington train served all stations to Newton Abbot (Wrangaton was closed on Sundays). Two trains from Kingswear called at all stations to Taunton, the 5.00 p.m. to Bristol (arr. 10.00 p.m.) and the 8.15 p.m. which terminated there at 10.08 p.m.

When the GWR ceased to exist, at the end of 1947, a number of major works remained unaccomplished, including the provision of adequate station facilities at North Road (which had never been intended to serve as the principal station for Plymouth, though it now found itself in that position). There were also plans for a greatly enlarged station at Paignton, with adequate carriage sidings and locomotive facilities, and for the alternative main line from Dawlish Warren to Bishopsteignton. However, compared with the situation inherited in 1876, the company had good reason to be satisfied with its record of progress, not least in the achievements of its finest and final years.

Brixham harbour (c.1925), with a quayside meeting in progress. Was it a fish auction or, in view of the waiting charabancs, a Sunday outing? The station was situated behind the buildings at the top right-hand corner of the photograph.

National Railway Museum, York

CHAPTER SIX

DARTMOUTH AND TORBAY

On 18th December 1848, the SDR opened its first branch line, from Newton to Torquay. Those responsible must have been relieved that, at long last, the line was built and opened, the five previous proposals having been abortive!

As early as 1832, the Torquay, Newton & Ashburton Railway was mooted, followed by proposals to build a line from Newton to Torquay 'in order to facilitate intercourse between Newton and that port'. Next was Brunel's original

Lords. It was not until November 1848 that permanent rails were laid as far as Kingskerswell, by which time the station at Torre was almost complete. Although an extension of the line to the centre of Torquay was proposed, the Directors stated that it would be postponed 'until the conditional prospects of the Company were in such a state as to warrant further outlay'.

The line to Torre (known until 1859 as Torquay) was opened with the usual celebrations, the first train being worked by the

A 'Buffalo' ('1076' class) tank No. 1148 piloting an unidentified 'Star' at Aller Junction on a Torbay branch local train, c.1932. The 'Star' would almost certainly be running to Paignton to take over a mid-morning Up service; there being no turning facilities, the engines were positioned tender first for their 'outbound' trip. The immaculate 'Buffalo' is very much an Exeter engine, moving there during 1921 for a continuous allocation of fourteen years; she was withdrawn in July 1934.   *W. Potter*

proposal for the Plymouth to Exeter which would have taken it close to Torquay, while in October 1844 a further survey was made for a line from Aller to Torquay which was to terminate at the harbour.

The fifth proposal, made in September 1845, was the most unexpected (and, as far as the SDR was concerned, the most unwelcome). The Dartmouth, Torbay & North Devon Junction Railway was to build a line from both Dartmouth and Brixham, to run northwards along the course of the Teign, through Chudleigh and Moretonhampstead, to join the projected Cornwall & North Devon Central Railway 'which would give a direct line to Exeter' to join the 'narrow gauge' railway which would link Exeter with Salisbury and London. Had this come to pass, the Torbay resorts might have been served by through trains from Waterloo, and not from Paddington!

However, on 28th August 1846 the Royal Assent was given to a branch line 'from Aller to a certain field in the manor of Tormohun' (Torre), although the extension of the line to Paignton and Dartmouth had been blocked by the House of

GWR engine *Taurus*. It consisted of nine 1st class and fifteen 2nd class carriages, 200 people being carried; the six-mile journey took 13 minutes. Brunel was among the passengers, and the banners at the station included salutes to 'Brunel and the Broad Gauge'. Goods traffic did not commence until 6th October 1849.

From Aller Junction the line rises on a gradient of 1 in 107 to 1 in 112 for about three miles through Kingskerswell, after which there is nearly half a mile of 1 in 71 down to Torre station. There was a large goods yard and shed at the station, which became the centre for all goods traffic in the Torquay district. Initially there was also some sort of engine shed or servicing point, possibly adjacent to the south end of the Down platform, where a turntable and sidings still existed at the end of the last century. A separate train shed was erected at Newton, making three distinct stations there; there was no junction at Aller, and the Plymouth and Torquay lines ran into Newton independently.

Proposals for extension to Torquay (Livermead) and on to Brixham (with the building of a quay for the landing of fish

Kingskerswell station, seen in the years before the Great War, looking towards Newton Abbot. This station, 1¼ miles from Aller Junction, was opened in 1853, some five years after the branch commenced operations. The broad gauge origins of the station are apparent in the track spacing, with a 'ten foot' way rather than the normal 'six foot' being used. In the distance, a Down local train of four/six-wheel stock in the charge of a saddle tank can be seen running up the gradient into the station. The main station building (on the extreme left) was a two-storey structure, with the upper floor fronting onto the road across the bridge, forming the station entrance; the road also served for the crossing between platforms as there was no separate footbridge. *Collection J. E. Kite*

from Brixham) were made, and powers obtained, but no action was taken. However, Kingskerswell station was opened in 1853, the event being signalled by the firing of a cannon! Considerable dissatisfaction was being expressed at this time concerning the delivery of parcels by the railway, which was said to be 'less efficient than when the Stage Waggons ran'. In the same year, the Dartmouth, Torbay & South Devon Extension Railway was proposed, to build a line to a terminus in Brixham and another to the Higher Ferry on the Kingswear side of the Dart; although the survey had been undertaken by Brunel, nothing came of it, nor of a final attempt in the following year to extend the line to the Western Quay, near the Strand.

Finally, in 1857, the Dartmouth & Torbay Railway Company was formed to build a line from the SDR terminus to the east bank of the Dart, and to use a steam ferry to reach Dartmouth. The Royal Assent was given on 27th July, and on 1st January 1858 the first sod was cut with due ceremony. By building the new Torquay station near Torre Abbey, the Directors concluded that most passengers would use it in preference to Torre; fortunately they were correct in their conclusion, as this saved the line from bankruptcy! The line descended from Torre on a gradient of 1 in 55, which meant that trains starting from Torquay were faced with an immediate climb for a mile to Torre, followed by another climb of about half a mile at 1 in 71.

The first train ran to the new Torquay station in 1859; the line was opened to Paignton in August of that year, to Brixham Road (later Churston) in 1861, and finally completed to Kings-

wear in 1864. At one time it had been proposed to make the terminus at Greenway, with a view to a subsequent crossing of the river and the building of a line down the western side of the Dart to Dartmouth. Such a line might well have altered the course of that celebrated borough's history, and saved it from slow decay; however, owing to opposition by a local landowner, the Kingswear route was taken instead. A large hotel was built at Kingswear in the hope that the terminus would become a landing-place for some of the Atlantic passenger traffic, but this proved to be an idle dream.

The branch trains running on Tuesday, 3rd July 1866, were varied in composition. For example, the 7.23 a.m. Kingswear departed with 1 first class coach, 1 second, 2 third class, and a van; at Torquay a carriage truck and a horse-box were added. The 11.30 a.m. Paignton comprised 2 first class, 1 second, and a van, whilst the 1.18 p.m. from Kingswear conveyed 1 first, 2 second, 1 third, and a van.

In 1873 the Dartmouth & Torbay directors promised the Local Board that they would build a new station at Torquay which would replace 'the unpretentious little structure which had done duty for many years'. However, the company was nearing the end of its existence, and it was the GWR who would eventually put the work in hand; the old station, which was nearer to Paignton, was demolished in 1878. The line had been doubled as far as Kingskerswell by 1876, and to the new Torquay station by 1882. From 1855 the branch line between Newton and Aller had also served as the Down main line to Plymouth, but in 1874 a new independent single line was

The original terminus of the branch from Newton Abbot, Torre (then named 'Torquay') served as the station for that town until 1859, when the line was extended to Paignton. During that year, Torquay station (proper) opened, and the old terminus was renamed 'Torre'. The spacing between the platforms is very wide, though not wide enough to take three broad gauge tracks, as was the case at Torquay. From the station there was a one-mile climb at 1 in 71 towards Kingskerswell and Newton, an incline that provided no little excitement in the early days!

Lens of Sutton

Torre was the goods station for the Torquay district, the latter station having no freight-handling facilities other than loading docks. A fairly substantial goods shed was provided (seen to the right of the water crane), whilst mileage and coal sidings were situated on the Up side, behind the tall signal box. In addition, there were a number of short dock sidings at the southern end of the station, behind the Down platform. Torre station also served the adjacent districts of Babbacombe and St. Marychurch (which were included on the station nameboard), as well as other northern and central parts of the town. This post-war view was taken looking north towards Newton Abbot.

Collection W. G. Rear

Glorious Devon

Torquay station, looking north, c.1925 with '45XX' class 'Prairie' No. 4553 leaving the Down platform with a local train of typically unmatched stock! During that year, the platforms at this end of the station had been extended, in the case of the Down platform necessitating the removal of a bay. From this time, the station had just two short sidings within a bay situated behind the Up platform at the north end. The centre road was used mostly for storage of stock, in this case coal wagons (probably destined for the Gas House, situated about a mile down the line, towards Paignton). No. 4553 spent her early years at St. Blazey and Laira, moving up to Newton Abbot during 1923. She remained in the area until 1930, when a transfer back to Moorswater and St. Blazey was effected. This was followed in 1932 by a move to South Wales, where she saw out the Great Western, having spent many of those years at Whitland shed.

A. C. Roberts

NORTH SANDS, PAIGNTON

SOUTH SANDS, PAIGNTON

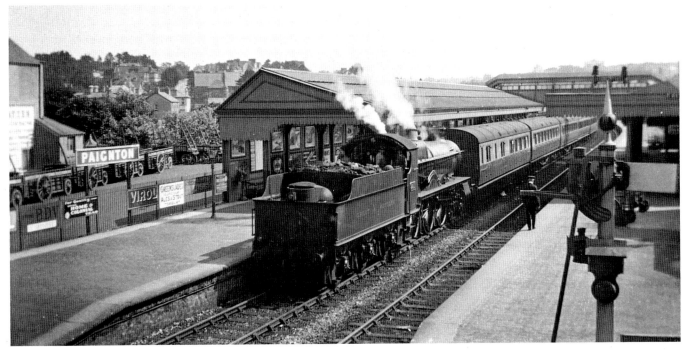

'Saint' class 4—6—0 No. 2911 *Saint Agatha* standing at the Down platform at Paignton station on 12th June 1927. The 'D' headlamps on her tender were the code for an 'empty coaching stock' train, which she had probably brought up from Goodrington Yard. *Saint Agatha* was a Cardiff engine at that time, and may have been working home with a Sunday excursion, the coaches having paper labels on their windows.   *Collection R. S. Carpenter*

Paignton goods yard, seen on 23rd September 1922.   *National Railway Museum, York*

An Up local passenger train coasting down the gradient between Churston and Goodrington during July 1946, with 'Bulldog' class 4–4–0 No. 3341 *Blasius* in charge. This engine was the first 'Bulldog' to be built with straight frames, in May 1900; she also carries the combined name and numberplate (oval) on the cabside. Originally numbered 3353, she spent her early years at Plymouth, though had been re-allocated to Swansea by 1910. Further transfers within South Wales followed, before a move was made to the London Division in 1926, being stationed mainly at Reading. After a three-year allocation to Carmarthen during 1936–9, and a brief visit to Wolverhampton (Oxley), she was transferred to Newton Abbot during 1940. *Blasius* remained there until Nationalisation, being withdrawn from Exeter in November 1949. Her main duties at Newton during the 'forties were local passenger and banking/pilot turns.   *W. Potter*

laid for the Torquay trains. The line between Torquay and Paignton has 20 bridges, a short tunnel at Livermead, and a viaduct – all in three miles – so it was not surprising that it remained single-track for another 30 years! When doubled during 1908–10, the tunnel was removed, and the viaduct was replaced by an embankment.

Until 1862 Paignton appears to have lacked a goods shed, and the station yard held only 25 wagons. Nor did the company provide a waiting room for passengers; the local inhabitants, understandably, had little regard for their station, and there was agitation for 'a better station as at Torquay'. Similar demands were still being made in this century, after the platforms had been lengthened and a waiting room provided.

Furthermore, the train service was also the subject of complaint; in 1883 it was stated that only four trains a day left for London, two of these being 1st and 2nd class only, whilst on the others there were 'lots of open thirds with scarce a foot warmer'.

Dreams of a new route to Plymouth still came to the surface, as in April 1894 when the Totnes, Paignton & Torquay Railway Bill was before the House, but was not passed. As late as 1925, a deputation met Sir Felix Pole, the GWR's General Manager, concerning a railway through the South Hams to Plymouth. Even after the Second World War rumours abounded concerning a proposed new line from Paignton to Totnes, avoiding Dainton incline, for main line trains!

Early in 1903 a landslip 'between the Gasworks and the Tunnel' resulted in the line being laid further inland. The single track between Torquay and Paignton had always caused delays; it was stated that those returning from Moretonhampstead and the Chudleigh line on summer evenings had to wait for 62 minutes at Torquay station! This was interesting evidence of the practice of Torbay residents spending 'days out' in the Teign Valley. When the work was taken in hand, a new Up line was built, commencing from Paignton, and extensive alterations were made at Torquay, where the platforms were lengthened and the old North Signal Box was taken out of use (it was still intact 50 years later, and it was not unknown for tomatoes to be grown inside it!). A new signal box was opened at Gas House Sidings when the double line reached that point.

In 1911 Preston Platform was opened, but remained in use only until about 1916. Its opening coincided with the withdrawal of the GWR's bus service between Torquay and Paignton when the tramway was extended to the latter town; the trams appear to have won! Curiously, it remained in the Working Timetables until at least 1922, though not, of course, in public editions.

Not until 1930 was anything done about the matter of Paignton's goods facilities, when a new goods station was opened at Goodrington, the line having been doubled as far as the level-crossing in 1928. Goodrington Sands Halt was opened at about this time, and passenger facilities at Paignton were improved by platform extensions, and the opening of Park Sidings – five long carriage sidings. A locomotive siding was provided to the south of the station on the Down side, but there

Churston station was opened in March 1861, though under the name of 'Brixham Road'; with the completion of the railway to Brixham in 1868, the new junction station was renamed 'Churston', after the nearby village of Churston Ferrers. It was situated at the summit of fairly steep two-mile climbs from both the Goodrington and Kingswear directions, though the station itself was on reasonably level ground. The platform serving the Brixham branch was situated at the far (northern) end of the station, and was in the form of a 'semi-open' bay; it was long enough to take a locomotive and two bogie coaches, which would amply cover the normal needs of the branch. There was a loading dock on the opposite side of the running lines from this platform, whilst the goods shed was situated beyond the road bridge on the south side of the branch line. *Lens of Sutton*

'45XX' ('4575' series) 2—6—2T No. 4591, standing at the Down platform at Churston c.1936. This locomotive was a fleeting visitor to the Newton area, arriving in 1934 and leaving some three years later. During her stay, she was the 'Moretonhampstead engine', though would obviously have found employment on other local services at times. Here, she heads what is almost certainly the 5.15 p.m. Newton Abbot to Kingswear train, conveying through vehicles off the 10.32 a.m. Crewe to Plymouth service. The leading Composite (No. 6179) carries 'Torquay, Bristol, Shrewsbury and Manchester (London Road)' headboards, and is followed by a Van Third. These would be accompanied by another Compo and Van Third, also from Manchester. These two pairs of coaches would leave Kingswear the following morning on the 10.30 a.m. to Newton (attached there to the 7.45 a.m. Penzance, destined for Manchester) and the 6.40 a.m. (through train to Crewe) respectively. *Collection W. G. Rear*

The Kingswear line was almost unique in being the only branch (apart from Millbay) able to accommodate 'Kings' and '47XXs'. Here, one of the latter class, No. 4705, is crossing the Broadsands viaduct with the 3.15 p.m. (Sundays) Newton Abbot to Kingswear service on 19th September 1954. Whilst these engines were built for fast vacuum freights, they were frequently used on local passenger trains for filling-in or positioning purposes; No. 4705 will probably work an evening Up 'vacuum' back to London, and is 'warming up' on the local. They were also used on express passenger trains when circumstances dictated, and their regular turn on those occasions (if they had been temporarily displaced) might have been worked by a 'Hall' with a reduced load.

P. F. Bowles

Broadsands viaduct again, with 'King' class 4–6–0 No. 6028 *King George VI* at the head of the Up 'Torbay Express', the 11.25 a.m. from Kingswear. The ten-coach summer formation shown here included a Restaurant Car; during the winter months, the dining facilities were retained, although the train was normally reduced to eight vehicles. Extra coaches were added to the tail at Paignton on Saturdays during the holiday season, although not in the case of this train, which was photographed on Monday, 26th July 1948. No. 6028 (*King Henry II* until 1937) was one of the five 'Kings' allocated to Newton Abbot at this time, and they traditionally shared the 'Torbay' duty with Old Oak Common engines.   *W. Potter*

was no turntable. The absence of the latter, together with inadequate berthing facilities for empty carriage stock, required tender engines either to continue to Kingswear for turning, or to return tender-first to Newton Abbot, in either case hauling empty trains whose movements were a major contribution to the congestion and delays experienced on Saturdays during the summer months.

Plans published in 1935 showed that a five-platform station was proposed for Paignton (where many trains terminated or commenced) with the replacement of the level crossing at Goodrington by a bridge, and the provision of more carriage sidings and locomotive servicing facilities. Nothing was done, however, apart from the replacement of the old Roundham Bridge by a steel structure in March 1939.

Beyond Goodrington the line remained single track, with only a passing loop at Churston Station (the junction for the Brixham branch). Until 1913 access to the Brixham branch was by a trailing cross-over from the Up line into the very short terminal bay, but this was then replaced by a direct connection from the branch to the Down line, again by a trailing point.

The most impressive feature of the single-line section was the lofty, 148 yd-long Hookhills Viaduct near Broadsands, which precluded serious consideration being given to the doubling of the line. There was also a tunnel, 495 yards long, near Greenway, whose excavation through hard limestone was a difficult task. Much of the excavated material was used in the construction of the ten-arched Maypool Viaduct near the southern end of the tunnel. Nearer to Kingswear, the line had originally been carried over two small inlets from the River Dart by means of two short wooden viaducts, the Noss and Longwood. The line was replaced at this point by a deviation further inland in May 1923. Even after this work was carried out, it was some years before large tender engines were allowed to work beyond Paignton.

The original Kingswear station had a short platform with a bay behind, the latter providing access (by a trailing point) to a single-road engine shed. There was a ticket platform about a quarter-mile north of the station. In addition to a goods shed and sidings, there was access by means of a small wagon turntable to a landing stage on the river bank (later removed). The Dart Estuary was formerly a bunkering station for steamships, and coal was transhipped from the railway at Kingswear to bunkering vessels moored in the river. This traffic ceased as vessels changed to oil firing, and the role of Kingswear was reversed; it became a discharging point for coastal colliers whose cargoes were hauled by rail to the Torquay Gasworks

The sweeping Greenway (or Maypool) viaduct, just over 150 yards in length, situated immediately to the south of Greenway tunnel. Kingswear station was just over two miles distant, the descent to which involved gradients of around 1 in 60.

L & GRP
cty. David & Charles

The original line to Kingswear, opened in 1864, had kept quite close to the Dart in order to effect the descent from Greenway tunnel, and had crossed the two creeks at Noss (1¼ miles to the north of the station) by means of timber viaducts; the northerly structure of the pair was the Longwood viaduct, 200 yards in length, seen here in the early 'twenties. In 1923, a deviation was opened at this site, whereby the line was re-routed inland by some 200 yards to round the creeks by an embankment, rather than rebuild the viaducts (the condition of which were causing some concern); the resultant section, 'Noss Curve', was of a fairly sharp radius. The beginning of the earthworks for the deviation may be seen in the bottom right-hand corner of the picture. The cruiser is probably the *Stettin* of the Imperial German Navy. As part of the High Seas Fleet, she was at Jutland in 1916 and was laid up following the Armistice in 1918. In 1920 she was assigned to Britain for scrap as part of the war reparations scheme, the work possibly carried out by Philip & Son at the Noss shipyard.

L & GRP, courtesy David & Charles

The southerly viaduct of the pair was Noss, slightly shorter in length than its partner, Longwood, though again built of timber. The line bisected the properties of Philip & Son (marine engineers); after the completion of the deviation line in 1923, this company benefited both by the removal of the line as seen, and also (in 1929) by the provision of a private siding to serve the premises, connected to the main line at a junction just to the north of Kingswear Crossing (later Britannia Halt). The shipping anchored upstream in the deep, sheltered waters of the Dart may have been laid up as a result of the trade depression following the Great War.

L & GRP, courtesy David & Charles

The station throat at Kingswear, c.1923, with the station 'box prominent. The lines curving to the left on the embankment became single as they approached Waterhead viaduct, in order to cross the timber-built spans which provided access to Waterhead Creek (seen in the background). The timber structure may just be seen beyond the bracket signal at the left-hand edge of the picture; this was replaced in the latter 'twenties by a steel span with double-track capacity. The provision of the new viaduct at Waterhead permitted the use of larger locomotives (hitherto banned to the south of Churston), and 4–6–0s appeared on trains alongside the '43XX' 2–6–0s, 'Dukes' and 'Bulldogs' which had up to that time worked the heavier services.   *L & GRP, cty. David & Charles*

or Newton Abbot Power Station. From Kingswear to Churston much of the three miles is on a rising of 1 in 66, with 1 in 100 through the Greenway Tunnel, so that coal trains often required banking assistance.

Kingswear station was extensively rebuilt and enlarged during the late 1920s, the engine shed having been closed on 14th July 1924, and later demolished as part of the improvement made, the whole scheme being completed by May 1929. An earlier improvement was the installation of a 55 ft turntable and additional carriage sidings between 1900 and 1905 (the original turntable, situated immediately in front of the engine shed had been of the SDR's usual miniscule diameter).

Although Kingswear was the physical terminus of the branch, the timetables always showed the line as ending at Dartmouth, on the far side of the River Dart. No rails ever reached that town, but it did possess a station which was served by a steam ferry from Kingswear, and such was the importance of Dartmouth's traffic in connection with the Royal Naval College, that for many years its station master was of a higher grade than his 'opposite number' at Kingswear!

The original terminus of the Torquay branch, Torre, was little affected by all the alterations, and the station remained in much the same condition throughout its GWR ownership. Alterations were confined to the layout of the goods depot, notably the removal of the turntable behind the Down

platform. For many years the station name-boards bore the legend 'Torre for St Marychurch and Babbacombe' (there being a direct tram, and later bus, route). A prominent feature was the very tall signal box at the north end of the Up platform, the height being dictated by the need for signalmen to be able to see trains coming up the 1 in 55 incline from Torquay.

The steep gradient facing trains leaving Torquay for Torre, followed by another half-mile climb after that station, limited the weight allowed to be taken by engines on Up trains, even by the 'Kings'. The well-filled holiday trains on Summer Saturdays were therefore banked from Torquay through Torre (where none of them stopped) to the advance starter signal at Shiphay Bridge. Either 0–6–0 PTs or '4500' class 2–6–2 Ts were normally employed on this duty. Tank engines working over the branch normally faced chimney-first on Down trains, returning bunker-first to Newton Abbot, and this was the usual practice for the banking engines. The central siding at Torquay station used by the banking engines was reached by trailing points off both Up and Down lines; in addition, there was a facing cross-over at the Up end, and a trailing cross-over at the Down end of the station.

The original train service to Torre was of six Down and five Up trains, with a reduced service on Sundays. Coaches from Paignton, Brixham and Dartmouth met the Bristol Mail and the London trains. The SDR improved its services for a short

A view of Kingswear station, taken from the adjacent Churston road on 5th June 1921. Beyond the old travelling steam cranes can be seen the jetty, on which rails were laid, with access via a wagon turntable situated at the junction of the jetty and quay, and served by the furthest of the three goods sidings. Halfway along the jetty (at the point at which the bend occurs) was another wagon turntable, with a small lighthouse (showing red/white) adjacent to it. The jetty and quay handled the extensive inbound coal traffic, much of it destined for the Torbay area (including Torquay gasworks). Passenger crossing facilities to and from Dartmouth were provided by a ferry service, which used a pontoon landing stage situated behind the station train shed.   *L & GRP, cty. David & Charles*

'Small Prairie' No. 2182 at Kingswear station, c.1910; built in March 1909, this engine was sent to Newton Abbot when new, where it operated on both the Moretonhampstead and Kingswear lines, in addition to turns on the main line. Renumbered to 4521 in December 1912, she was transferred westwards to St. Blazey, but returned to Newton during the Great War. The engine alternated between St. Blazey, Plymouth and Newton (with spells at Kingsbridge) until 1926, when she was moved to Old Oak Common for carriage pilot duties. She did, however, return to the West Country for a seven year stay during the 'thirties. The engine shed (closed in 1924) is to the right of the engine, with watering and coaling facilities adjacent. The cattle pens can be seen at the end of the siding to the left of the shed, whilst an 0–6–0ST stands on the turntable road behind the 'Prairie'. At this time, 0–6–0 tanks operated most of the goods trains on the Kingswear line, although the 'Prairies' did have the odd turn. Until the years just before the turn of the century, the engine shed marked the station limits in that direction, with Waterhead creek immediately beyond it.   *HMRS*

'King' class 4–6–0 No. 6018 *King Henry VI* bringing the Down 'Torbay Express' into Kingswear station (due 4.9 p.m.), c.1932. The seven-coach train is the winter (September to early July) formation of the service, and included a pair of dining vehicles. The public footbridge crossing the line was provided to connect the Churston road with the river bank, and a footpath ran beside the railway at least as far as the Hoodown sidings (seen in the middle distance). The extent of land reclamation required to provide space for the turntable and adjacent sidings can be seen here; the right-hand edge of the original embankment extended from the existing viaduct, around the back of the signal box, to meet the bank at the right-hand edge of the photograph approximately underneath the footbridge. The platform at that time was considerably shorter than that shown in the photograph, and would not have been visible in this view.

Collection W. G. Rear

Collett 'Hall' class 4—6—0 No. 4943 *Marrington Hall* passing the signal box and entering the main platform at Kingswear with a mid-afternoon local train, c.1936. No. 4943 was built in 1929, and spent a short period during 1936/7 at Newton shed, during which time she was recorded on this service. After similar spells at Truro and Penzance sheds, she returned to Old Oak Common, her first home. The coach formation on the service is an 'E' set (Brake Compo, Lav. Third, Van Third) which, with the four-coach 'M' set, formed the backbone of main line stopping services in the Exeter and Plymouth Divisions during the 'thirties. *Collection W. G. Rear*

A striking portrait of Newton Abbot 'King' No. 6018 *King Henry VI* at Kingswear, c.1932; apart from a six-month allocation to Laira when new, No. 6018 spent her entire Great Western career at Newton Abbot, and was therefore no stranger to the Kingswear line. The 'Kings' were used on the 'Torbay Express' (alternating with Old Oak engines), and were certainly required on that service during the holiday season, when regular loads of 14 or 15 coaches were run (8 to Kingswear, the balance to Paignton). *Collection W. G. Rear*

The 'Torquay Pullman' was one of the shortest-lived of Great Western services; inaugurated on Monday, 8th July 1929, it ran only until the end of the following year's summer schedule (September 1930). 'Kings' and 'Castles' from Newton shed were used on this service, and No. 6018 *King Henry VI* from that shed is seen on arrival at Torquay with the Down train, the 11.0 a.m. Paddington. The return train departed from Paignton at 4.30 p.m.   *Lens of Sutton*

time in the early 1850s, but after 1852 most alterations were for the worse. The service to Torquay was reduced in 1855, and again early in the next year, most of the evening trains being withdrawn. 'Surely the Directors will not be so blind to their own interest as to allow this crying evil to continue' commented a mystified local paper. However, when the celebrated 'Flying Dutchman' was introduced by the GWR and SDR in March 1862, it ran to and from Torquay, though after September 1864 it was transferred to Plymouth.

Although in 1883 only four trains daily left Paignton for London, others connected with the main line services. The services in 1877 were:

WEEKDAYS
Down

Torquay	8.39 10.01 12.09 1.46 3.42 5.11 6.32 8.46 11.20
Kingswear	9.10 10.31 12.38 2.18 4.09 5.37 — 9.15 11.53
Dartmouth	9.20 10.55 1.00 2.50 4.20 5.46 — 9.25 —

Up

Dartmouth	7.00 — 9.35 10.30 12.35 2.30 4.27 7.50
Kingswear	7.13 — 9.48 10.45 12.50 2.43 4.40 8.05
Torquay	7.42 9.20 10.15 11.15 1.30 3.11 5.10 8.34

Sundays
Down

Torquay	8.49 11.06 8.24
Kingswear	9.17 11.34 8.52

Up

Kingswear	7.30 1.20 7.05
Torquay	7.57 1.47 7.32

There was no service for Dartmouth on Sundays.

In 1891 Torquay was brought within five hours from Paddington by through coaches off the 'Flying Dutchman' which

were run non-stop from Exeter in advance of the Plymouth portion. The abolition of the broad gauge was followed by the introduction of a new express, practically a first part of the 'Flying Dutchman' to and from Torbay. This train left Paddington at 11.25 a.m., twenty minutes ahead of the 'Dutchman', with five through coaches for Paignton. The balancing Up service left Kingswear at 8.45 a.m. Other through coaches left Paddington for Kingswear on the 9.00 a.m., 1.15, 3.00 and 5.00 p.m. departures, returning as the 10.45, 11.57 a.m., 2.20 and 4.00 p.m. from Kingswear; two coaches, or two coaches and a van normally sufficed. The first corridor train between Paddington and Torquay made its appearance in 1893, at the same time as that to and from Penzance.

In 1902 the great majority of local trains ran between Newton Abbot and Kingswear, only a handful running to and from Exeter or beyond. The most important through service was the 11.30 a.m. from Paddington, the 'Torquay Corridor Express', which ran non-stop from Exeter to Torquay (arr. 4.28 p.m.). The Up service consisted of through coaches leaving Kingswear at 10.25 a.m., which were attached the 10.30 a.m. from Plymouth, the 'Plymouth, Torquay and Exeter Corridor Express'. There were also through coaches on the 10.00 p.m. from Paddington, which terminated at Torquay at 4.05 a.m.; there were also TCs to Kingswear on the 7.25 a.m., 9.00 a.m. and 6.00 p.m. trains from Paddington. The Up service had TCs from Kingswear at 8.30 a.m. (for the 8.30 a.m. 'Flying Dutchman' from Plymouth), 2.20 p.m. (attached to the 2.15 p.m. from Plymouth) and an overnight service at 8.25 p.m. (attached to the 4.50 p.m. from Penzance).

On Sundays there was the overnight 10.00 p.m. TC from Paddington, and a counterpart to the 'Torquay Corridor Express', leaving Paddington at 9.20 a.m. and terminating at Paignton at 5.50 p.m. (having stopped at all stations from Exeter). The only Up service to run beyond Newton Abbot was the 6.35 p.m. from Kingswear, 'all stations' to Exeter. On weekdays there were two Exeter to Kingswear trains, and one from Kingswear to Exeter.

TORQUAY AND DARTMOUTH BRANCH.
Analysis of Services, 1902.

	WEEKDAYS		SUNDAYS	
	No. of Trains	First/Last arrivals	No. of Trains	First/Last arrivals
DOWN				
Torquay	20	4.05 a.m. 12.17 a.m.	6	4.05 a.m. 8.27 p.m.
Paignton	19	7.41 a.m. 12.27 a.m.	5	9.24 a.m. 8.35 p.m.
Churston*	14	7.50 a.m. 12.36 a.m.	3	9.33 a.m. 8.27 p.m.
Kingswear	12	8.00 a.m. 12.47 a.m.	3	9.44 a.m. 8.38 p.m.
Dartmouth	11	8.25 a.m. 11.35 p.m.		No service.
UP				
Dartmouth	12	6.45 a.m. 10.45 p.m.		No service.
Kingswear	12	6.55 a.m. 11.00 p.m.	3	7.50 a.m. 6.35 p.m.
Churston*	14	7.08 a.m. 11.12 p.m.	3	8.02 a.m. 6.48 p.m.
Paignton	19	7.16 a.m. 11.20 p.m.	5	8.10 a.m. 8.45 p.m.
Torquay	19	7.23 a.m. 11.26 p.m.	5	8.16 a.m. 8.55 p.m.

* Two trains terminated at Churston and two commenced from there. Kingskerswell's service was 12 Down and 15 Up trains. Sundays 4 Down and 4 Up. Torre's service was the same as that for Paignton.

The opening of the new route via Westbury in 1906 reduced the journey time between Paddington and Torquay by nearly an hour. Whereas in 1900 the fastest time had been 4 hours 50 minutes, by 1912 it was 3 hours 35 minutes. The successor to the old 11.35 a.m. 'Torquay Corridor Express' left Paddington at 11.50 a.m. (changed to 12 noon just prior to the Great War); through coaches for Ilfracombe were slipped at Taunton and the train reached Exeter at 2.50 p.m. This was one of the services on which a restaurant car was provided. The Up service left Torquay at 11.00 a.m. and there was a lengthy wait at Newton Abbot for the arrival of through coaches from Plymouth; despite a fast run from Exeter in 185 minutes, Paddington was not reached until 3.10 p.m. While the Down train was 67 minutes quicker than when it travelled via Bristol, the Up train took only 25 minutes less. During the 1920s this train received the name 'Torbay Express' (though at first it was 'The Torbay Limited').

In addition to these trains, a second through service was running during the years leading up to the Great War; this left Paddington at 9.00 a.m. for Kingswear, running via Bristol, with a five-coach portion (corridor) for Torbay. The balancing train departed from Paignton at 12.11 p.m., again running via Bristol. Further through coaches were provided on the 10.30 a.m. 'Limited' (a slip, dropped at Exeter, conveyed onwards by the 1.42 p.m. to Kingswear), and by the 1.30, 3.30, 4.15 and 6.30 p.m. departures from Paddington. In the Up

direction, through coaches departed from Kingswear at 8.30 a.m., 2.20 and 3.51 p.m. The 12.11 p.m. Paignton also conveyed the slip vehicle to Exeter, where it was attached to the Up 'Limited'.

After the First World War, the through trains from Paddington at 9.15 a.m. and 12.00 a.m. (both with dining cars) were running again, although the only 'direct' Up service was the 11.30 a.m. Kingswear. The stock of the 9.15 a.m. Paddington returned as the 11.28 a.m. Churston (less dining car), being attached to the 9.50 a.m. Truro at Exeter. Further Down through coaches left Paddington on the 2.00, 4.15 (for Kingswear) and 6.00 p.m. (for Paignton) trains. These returned from Kingswear at 8.20 a.m., from Paignton at 2.15 p.m. and Kingswear (with dining car) at 3.50 p.m.

Through coaches between Bradford (Midland) and Paignton had commenced c.1905, although it was not until the post-Great War period that a through train as such began to run on a daily basis. By 1922, the five-coach train (GW and Midland stock alternating) departed from Paignton at 9.25 a.m. and Bradford at 10.12 a.m. The northbound service left Bristol at 12.20 p.m., suitably strengthened, with a restaurant car attached. Southbound, the dining facilities were removed at Bristol, and the five-coach portion attached to the 11.42 a.m. Crewe train; the section was detached at Newton to form the 6.48 p.m. departure for Torquay (7.03 p.m.) and Paignton (7.12 p.m.)

The Torbay branch also saw through vehicles from and to Manchester, Birmingham, and Wolverhampton during 1922.

Local trains on the line were mostly 6-wheel 'M' sets (6 coaches), although a small number of bogie vehicles were in use.

A new and short-lived venture which commenced in July 1929 was the 'Torquay Pullman', which left Paddington at 11.00 a.m. and ran non-stop to Newton Abbot, Torquay being reached at 2.40 p.m. It returned from Paignton at 4.30 p.m., with a non-stop run from Torquay (dep. 4.40 p.m.) to Paddington. The eight carriages had an interior decor of green and blue, with sand-coloured Wilton carpets; however, it was not a success, and on its inaugural run on 8th July it carried only 24 passengers! It was later combined with a Kingsbridge portion (attached and detached at Exeter), composed of ordinary stock, but was withdrawn within a few months.

By 1932 the services had increased considerably, especially in the summer months. Most noticeable was the number of local trains running to and from Exeter or beyond, and there was a greatly increased Sunday service. There were 10 stopping trains from Exeter, as well as the 12 noon and 8.20 p.m. from Taunton to Kingswear (arr. 3.05 p.m. and 11.40 p.m. respectively).

As has already been noted, the branch saw a small number of through trains to and from Paddington and the North, plus a greater number of through coaches. The through train service (and the local services conveying through coaches) for the summer of 1932 was as follows:

THROUGH SERVICES – WEEKDAYS
DOWN TRAINS
1.0 p.m. Newton

2	GW	Coaches	Bath	Paignton	(10.5 a.m. Bath)
2	GW	Coaches	Wol'h'ton	Kingswear	(10.5 a.m. Bath)

9.0 a.m. Paddington

3 GW	Coaches	Paddington	Kingswear

9.45 a.m. Swansea

4 GW	Coaches	Swansea	Paignton
1 GW	Coach	Bristol	Paignton

12.0 noon Paddington

9 GW	Coaches	Paddington	Kingswear
	(R.C.)		

4.6 p.m. Newton

3 GW	Coaches	Wol'h'ton	Kingswear	(10.40 a.m. Wolverhampton)

5.20 p.m. Newton

1 LMS	Coach	Manchester	Paignton	(10.32 a.m. Crewe)
2 GW	Coaches	Manchester	Paignton	(10.32 a.m. Crewe)

5.49 p.m. Newton

2 GW	Coaches	Paddington	Kingswear	(1.30 p.m. Paddington)

10.12 a.m. Bradford

2 GW	Coaches	Bristol	Kingswear
2 GW	Coaches	Bradford	Kingswear
3 LMS	Coaches	Bradford	Kingswear
	(R.C.)		
2 GW	Coaches	Bradford	Kingswear

7.23 p.m. Newton

2 GW	Coaches	Paddington	Paignton	(3.30 p.m. Paddington)

9.24 p.m. Newton

3 GW	Coaches	Paddington	Kingswear	(4.30 p.m. Paddington)

The services shown in brackets are those trains by which the through coaches arrived at Newton Abbot.

The Up local service provided nine trains to Exeter, the 7.50 a.m. from Kingswear continuing to Bristol, and the 6.40 p.m. from Kingswear being 'all stations' to Taunton (arr. 9.42 p.m.).

The through services were as follows:

UP TRAINS

7.7 a.m. Kingswear

4 GW	Coaches	Kingswear	Swansea
3 GW	Coaches	Kingswear	Bristol

8.15 a.m. Kingswear to Exeter

3 GW	Coaches	Kingswear	Paddington	(8.35 a.m. Plymouth)
2 GW	Coaches	Paignton	Manchester	(8.45 a.m. Plymouth)

9.5 a.m. Kingswear

2 GW	Coaches	Kingswear	Bradford
3 LMS	Coaches	Kingswear	Bradford
	(R.C)		
2 GW	Coaches	Kingswear	Bradford

10.30 a.m. Kingswear

2 GW	Coaches	Kingswear	Manchester	(7.45 a.m. Penzance)
1 LMS	Coaches	Kingswer	Manchester	(7.45 a.m. Penzance)
2 GW	Coaches	Kingswear	Wol'h'ton	(7.45 a.m. Penzance)

11.20 p.m. Kingswear

9 GW	Coaches	Kingswear	Paddington
	(R.C.)		

12.20 p.m. Paignton

1 GW	Slip	Paignton	Reading	(9.15 a.m. Falmouth)

12.30 p.m. Kingswear

2 GW	Coaches	Kingswear	Manchester	(10.15 a.m. Penzance)

1.35 p.m. Paignton

3 GW	Coaches	Paignton	Wol'h'ton	(10.45 a.m. Penzance)

2.25 p.m. Paignton

2 GW	Coaches	Paignton	Paddington	(11.10 a.m. Penzance)

4.30 p.m. Paignton

3 GW	Coaches	Paignton	Paddington	(1.30 p.m. Penzance)

The trains shown in brackets are the forwarding services from Newton Abbot (or Exeter) for the through coaches.

On Sundays there were nine local trains from Exeter, three of which ran to Brixham.

The through services were thus:

THROUGH SERVICES – SUNDAYS

DOWN TRAINS

12.0 noon Paddington

9 GW	Coaches	Paddington	Kingswear
	(R.C)		

10.50 a.m. Wolverhampton

6 GW	Coaches	Wol'h'ton	Paignton
	(R.C.)		

A small Prairie, '45XX' class No. 4561 of Exeter shed at the Brixham branch platform, Churston, c.1935. During the week, services were operated by 'Metro' 2–4–0T or '517' class 0–4–2T engines and an autocoach (or two at peak times), with the new Collett '48XX' class appearing during 1936. However, on Sundays during the 'twenties and 'thirties, three and four-coach trains appeared on the branch, headed by '45XX' tanks, despite the fact that the branch platform at Churston could not accommodate a train of that length! Be that as it may, this practice continued for many years, and it is reasonable to assume, therefore, that this photograph was taken on a Sunday.

Lens of Sutton

7.7 p.m. Newton

| 4 | GW | Coaches (R.C.) | Paddington | Churston | (2.30 p.m. Paddington) |

9.30 p.m. Newton

| 2 | GW | Coaches | Paddington | Kingswear | (4.30 p.m. Paddington) |

Eight stopping trains ran to Exeter, and another terminated at Teignmouth at 10.28 p.m., two of the Exeter trains being from Brixham.

The Up through services were very comprehensive when compared with the Down trains, with services to the North as well as to Wolverhampton and Paddington.

UP TRAINS

7.35 a.m. Paignton

| 3 | | Coaches (R.C.) | Paignton | Manchester | (7.0 a.m. Plymouth) |

10.20 a.m. Paignton

| 3 | GW | Coaches | Paignton | Paddington | (9.45 a.m. Plymouth) |

10.20 a.m. Kingswear

| 3 | GW | Coaches | Kingswear | Paddington | (10.15 a.m. Plymouth) |

11.25 a.m. Paignton

| 3 | LMS | Coaches | Paignton | Liverpool | |
| 9 | LMS | Coaches (R.C.) | Paignton | Manchester | |

11.55 a.m. Paignton

1	LMS	Van	Paignton	Nottingham	
1	LMS	Van	Paignton	Bradford	
1	LMS	Coaches	Paignton	Sheffield	
6	LMS	Coaches (R.C.)	Paignton	Derby	

1.50 p.m. Brixham

| 3 | GW | Coaches | Brixham | Paddington | (10.50 a.m. Penzance) |

2.40 p.m. Kingswear

| 8 | GW | Coaches (R.C.) | Kingswear | Paddington | |

3.40 p.m. Paignton

| 6 | GW | Coaches (R.C.) | Paignton | Wol'h'ton | |

4.55 p.m. Paignton

| 11 | GW | Coaches | Paignton | Paddington | |

The two LMS trains (11.25 and 11.55 a.m. Paignton) were both return workings of 'Saturdays Only' services from Manchester and Nottingham respectively.

An ingenious set of diagrams were used for the Brixham branch on Sundays. On weekdays this was a 'self-contained' line, operated by a '517' class 0–4–2 T and auto-trailer, but on Sundays it was worked by normal stock and a '4500' class 2–6–2 T from Exeter or Newton Abbot, there being through trains between Exeter and Brixham! The workings from Exeter were at 10.50 a.m., 2.05 p.m. and 4.15 p.m., and each engine and train worked two return journeys over the branch before returning to Newton Abbot (arr. 2.40 p.m.) or Exeter (arr.

6.53 p.m. and 9.00 p.m.). The fourth diagram was worked from Newton Abbot, commencing at 7.07 p.m. with TCs from the 2.30 p.m. Paddington to Plymouth (RC to Churston), which gave Brixham a Sundays only through service from Paddington! Reaching Brixham at 8.27 p.m., the train left again at 8.35 p.m. (the last train on the branch) and arrived back at Newton Abbot at 9.21 p.m.

In 1939 the 'Torbay Express' (calling at Exeter at 2.49 p.m.) was due at Torquay at 3.30 p.m. – the fastest time ever operated between Paddington and Torquay. The Up train was allowed a little longer, not being due at Paddington until 3.35 p.m. During the summer months it ran non-stop in each direction on Saturdays.

The 'Torbay Express', 'The Devonian' and the Wolverhampton through services were withdrawn for the duration of World War Two. The 'Torbay Express' was restored, with its old 12 noon departure time, in July 1946; suspended during the following winter owing to fuel cuts, it was restored again

A late afternoon auto service from the Moretonhampstead line alongside the branch platform at Newton Abbot on 9th September 1933. The driving trailer is one of the so-called 'Clifton Downs' vehicles, built originally in the summer of 1898 as a Brake Third, and subsequently converted to an auto coach; No. 3331, shown in the photograph, was so modified during the summer of 1913. Many of the driving trailers were paired with a non-driving trailer, and No. 3331 normally ran in company with Auto Third No. 3275; both were withdrawn from service at Swindon on 2nd November 1946. The line to the right of the trailer is the Up Through, with the Up Main platform beyond it. The buildings on the left of the picture are stores, beyond which the Moretonhampstead branch diverged to the left.

G. N. Southerden

Saltern Cove is situated to the east of Goodrington village, just over half a mile to the south of Goodrington Sands Halt; here, 'Castle' class 4–6–0 No. 5071 *Spitfire* is passing this secluded spot with a mid-afternoon local passenger train in July 1946. Delivered as new to Newton Abbot in July 1938, No. 5071 (then named *Clifford Castle*) remained at that shed until the mid-'fifties, being renamed *Spitfire* in September 1940, at a time when the country needed all the 'Spitfires' it could lay its hands on! By 1946, Newton shed was home to no less than twenty large passenger engines, having five 'Kings', fourteen 'Castles' and a 'Star', in addition to half a dozen other 4–6–0s of the 'Hall', 'Grange' and 'County' classes.   *W. Potter*

in 1947. 'The Devonian' also re-appeared in the summer of 1946, but with an earlier departure from Bradford (9.30 a.m.) and a later arrival time at Paignton (7.20 p.m.). It was also extended to run to and from Kingswear (dep. 9.05 a.m.); there was no service during the winters of 1946 and 1947. The through service between Wolverhampton and the Torbay resorts was also restored, with the traditional departure time of 10.40 a.m. from Wolverhampton. The Kingswear coaches, detached at Newton Abbot, arrived at Torquay at 4.28 p.m. and at Kingswear at 4.55 p.m. However, the Up service started from *Paignton* at 1.35 p.m., the through vehicles being attached to the Penzance train at Exeter. The Sunday service (summer months only) took considerably longer, the Down train leaving Wolverhampton at 10.10 a.m. and arriving at Torquay at 4.47 p.m., while the Up train did not leave Paignton until 2.55 p.m.

Although in 1947 there were about the same number of local trains to and from Exeter as in 1932, the service as a whole had been reduced. Some interesting workings were those performed by the Moretonhampstead and Newton Abbot auto-trains, with through running between both Totnes and Paignton to Moretonhampstead, a resurrection of pre-war practice. The 7.00 a.m. from Kingswear ran to Bristol (as the 7.50 a.m. had done in 1932), but then continued to Cardiff; there was no corresponding service from either Cardiff or Bristol. During the summer months there were two through trains on Sundays from Taunton (9.00 a.m. to Kingswear and 7.20 p.m. to Paignton). The Up trains included the 5.10 p.m. from Kingswear to Avonmouth(!) and the 7.30 p.m. Good-

rington to Taunton. Both these continued to run through the winter of 1947 (the latter train commencing from Paignton), as did the 9.00 a.m. Taunton to Kingswear.

In the summer of 1947, the only daily through service was the 11.00 a.m. (12 noon on Saturdays) ten-coach Paddington to Kingswear dining car train; this timing was seemingly an isolated arrangement, as the traditional 12 noon departure was used both before and after this particular year's schedule. The Up train departed from Kingswear at 11.25 a.m., Torquay at midday (as pre-war), and was due to arrive at Paddington at 4.00 p.m. This was 25 minutes later than the 1932 schedule, accounted for by a stop at Exeter, and generally lower speeds en route. It again carried the title 'Torbay Express'.

In addition, through coaches were conveyed by the 1.30 p.m. (5 vehicles) and 5.00 p.m. (5 vehicles) departures from Paddington, returning by the 1.50 p.m. Kingswear (11.05 a.m. Penzance) and 8.45 a.m. Paignton (8.30 a.m. Plymouth) services respectively. On Saturdays, there were no less than six additional through trains between London and Torbay in each direction.

From the LMS, the 'Devonian' was running between Bradford and Kingswear on Fridays and Saturdays only, leaving the northern city at 10.15 a.m. The ten-coach train was balanced by the 9.05 a.m. departure from Kingswear, with each company supplying one train.

The 9.15 a.m. Liverpool train conveyed three LMS coaches for Kingswear, forwarded from Newton Abbot as the 6.25 p.m. departure. Five LMS vehicles formed the 9.00 a.m. Paignton to Newton, where they were attached to the 8.45 a.m. Ply-

An unidentified 'Hall' (possibly No. 4925 *Eynsham Hall*) approaching Kingswear with an early afternoon local passenger during the mid-'fifties. A 'Castle' waits behind the 'box, possibly to take the stock out as the next departure. The riverside footpath is seen again in the foreground, whilst the signalman waits at the side of the line near his box to accept the single line token from the Hall's fireman. Although much discussion over the doubling of the line took place, nothing was ever done about it, and the track to the south of Goodrington Sands Halt remained single for the six miles to the terminus at Kingswear. However, the double track through Churston station enabled trains to cross, and this assisted the flow of traffic.

M. E. J. Deane

'B' sets were not frequent visitors to the Kingswear line in Great Western days; only Kingsbridge saw that particular formation on a regular basis in the South Devon area. By the mid-'fifties, a 'near relative' of the 'B' set (Brake Second and Brake Compo) was running from Newton Abbot on the Moretonhampstead and Kingswear lines, and such a set is shown in the photograph behind an unidentified 'Castle'. The footpath connected to the long public footbridge over the station platform is seen in use in the foreground, the pedestrians having just passed over the Waterhead viaduct.
M. E. J. Deane

mouth to Crewe service, being destined for Manchester. Again, on Saturdays, there were extra direct trains running between the North, the Midlands and Torbay (4 Down, 5 Up).

Although post-war Sundays saw the 'Torbay Express' running in both directions during the summer months, the Down winter service had only TCs off the 'Cornish Riviera Express' (which travelled via Bristol); these were detached at Newton Abbot and reached Torquay at 4.48 p.m. There were also TCs off the 4.30 p.m. from Paddington, again via Bristol, arriving at Torquay at 11.11 p.m. The Up service consisted of TCs from Kingswear (dep. 9.55 a.m.) attached to the 9.30 a.m. Plymouth to Paddington, via Bristol, and the 2.40 p.m. Paignton to Paddington through train (via Westbury), arriving at Paddington at 7.20 p.m.

The through service to and from the North of England (via the Severn Tunnel) had continued throughout the war years. In the winter of 1947 there were TCs between Liverpool (dep. 9.15 a.m.) and Kingswear (arr. 7.08 p.m.), but the northbound service consisted of TCs from Paignton (dep. 9.00 a.m.) to Manchester (arr. 6.20 p.m.); this was similar to the daily summer service, though the loads were generally lighter. There was no service in either direction on Sundays.

In 1947 the freight service consisted of six trips in each direction along the branch; these were specified as two to Goodrington Yard (4.45 a.m. and 9.35 a.m. Hackney), two for Brixham (3.20 a.m. and 12.25 p.m. Hackney), and a pair to Kingswear (7.35 a.m. and 10.35 a.m. Hackney). These services called variously at Torre and Gas House Siding, plus Goodrington Yard, and Churston where relevant. Four of the return trips were mounted from Goodrington, with one each from Kingswear and Brixham. The only service on Sundays was a summer (run as required – RR) fish train from Brixham to Newton Abbot, worked by an engine sent up from Kingswear – though how such an engine would be available was not revealed by the working timetable! There were also the occasional special coal trains from Kingswear to Gas House Siding or Newton Abbot.

NEWTON ABBOT, TORQUAY, PAIGNTON AND DARTMOUTH.
Winter 1947.

	WEEKDAYS		SUNDAYS	
	No. of Trains	First/Last arrivals	No. of Trains	First/Last arrivals
DOWN				
Torre	23	4.52 a.m.	14	6.45 a.m.
		12.02 a.m.		11.08 p.m.
Torquay	23 + 1 FO, 1 SO	6.41 a.m.	14	6.48 a.m.
		12.05 a.m.		11.11 p.m.
Paignton	24 + 1 FO, 1 SO	5.20 a.m.	14	6.57 a.m.
		12.12 a.m.		11.20 p.m.
Churston	14 + 1 FO	5.35 a.m.	6	9.11 a.m.
		10.32 p.m.		9.22 p.m.
Kingswear	14 + 1 FO	5.50 a.m.	6	9.22 a.m.
		10.42 p.m.		9.32 p.m.
Dartmouth	14 + 1 FO	6.05 a.m.	6	9.35 a.m.
		10.52 p.m.		9.47 p.m.
UP				
Dartmouth	14	6.48 a.m.	6	9.45 a.m.
		9.50 p.m.		9.48 p.m.
Kingswear	14	7.00 a.m.	6	9.55 a.m.
		10.00 p.m.		10.00 p.m.
Churston	14	7.11 a.m.	5	10.05 a.m.
		10.10 p.m.		8.25 p.m.
Paignton	26 + 1 SO	7.02 a.m.	14	5.55 a.m.
		12.05 a.m.		12.05 a.m.
Torquay	25 + 1 SO	7.09 a.m.	13	8.02 a.m.
		12.12 a.m.		12.12 a.m.
Torre	25 + 1 SO	7.13 a.m.	13	6.05 a.m.
		12.19 a.m.		12.19 a.m.

There was the unusual feature of an early morning train from Paignton and Torre on Sundays only: this connected at Newton Abbot with the 11.50 p.m. overnight service from Paddington to Plymouth and Penzance, though no such connection was provided on weekdays! Kingskerswell's service was 20 Down (plus 1 SO) and 19 Up (plus 1 SO); and on Sundays 12 Down and 9 Up trains.

Bovey station, looking towards Moretonhampstead around the turn of the century.

L & GRP, cty. David & Charles

CHAPTER SEVEN

CITY BASIN TO SOUTH HAMS

MORETONHAMPSTEAD

'They seem to be guided by the stream, and (if it takes place) they will go right up the meadow under here ... and I cannot fancy it will take place, for people are a little cooled down; and not so made for speculation. Had it been projected some little time ago, no doubt it would have taken place.' (*Small Talk at Wreyland*, 1847. Cecil Torr). So reads a contemporary description of the surveys made from Newton towards the market town of Moretonhampstead, shortly after the SDR had been opened as far as the former. People must have cooled down even more, for in 1856 Thomas Brassey, the great railway contractor, appeared on the scene (which was still without any railway). 'He is staying at Torquay for the benefit of his health, and rides over some part of it every fine day.' (ibid).

Despite an incorporation in 1858 of the Newton & Moretonhampstead Railway, there was still no railway in the valleys of the Teign and the Bovey when, in 1862, the Earl of Devon reconstituted the company to form the Moretonhampstead & South Devon Railway (the SDR having a controlling interest). Originally estimated to require £88,500, the eventual cost of

the 12½ miles proved to be £155,000. Opened as a single line on 4th July 1866, it was worked by the SDR in return for 50 per cent of the gross receipts.

Between Teigngrace and Bovey, the line was laid on part of the route of the Haytor Tramway of 1820. The line climbed some 500 feet to Moretonhampstead, with gradients of between 1 in 49, and 1 in 70 between Heathfield and the terminus. The promoters entertained hopes of extending the line at some future date to Chagford, and possibly to Okehampton, though no such extension was ever authorised. Moretonhampstead station had one platform under an overall roof, and there were considerable goods facilities, not least for cattle traffic. An unusual feature was the signal box, built against one of the walls of the engine shed.

Originally there were two intermediate stations; Bovey had two platforms and a crossing loop, but Lustleigh had only one platform with a short siding to the rear. A third station, at Teigngrace, was opened in 1867, and Chudleigh Road (renamed Heathfield in October 1882) in 1874. Apart from the terminus, only Bovey was provided with a signal box. At the

Halfway between Newton and Moretonhampstead stood the crossing station of Bovey, provided with a passing loop (at which five pairs of trains crossed daily in 1934), a goods shed, and a 'back' siding. It also possessed a signal box, the only one between Heathfield and Moretonhampstead, giving a 2¼ mile section to the former, and 6¼ to the latter. Like Moretonhampstead, the station building was made of local stone, although the waiting shelter on the Down platform was built of brick, clearly a later addition.   *L & GRP, Cty. David & Charles*

A four-coach Down train at Bovey station, probably during the mid-'twenties, with a '45XX' 2—6—2 tank in charge. At around this time, during the summer months, Bovey had a number of terminating services from Newton in addition to the through Moretonhampstead trains; during the 'thirties, these were auto-trains, though one of the Exeter steam railmotors also worked through from Heathfield. The small signal box on the Up platform can be seen.
Lens of Sutton

insistence of the SDR, all bridges were constructed to allow for a subsequent doubling of the line, the company hoping to use the branch as a means of penetrating northwards into the 'enemy territory' of the LSWR. A signal box was provided at Chudleigh Road when it became the junction for the Teign Valley Railway. The SDR absorbed the Moretonhampstead Company in 1872.

In 1877 there were four trains each ways on weekdays and two on Sundays, the first and last departures from Moretonhampstead being at 7.05 a.m. and 7.15 p.m., with the first and last arrival times at 9.08 a.m. and 9.03 p.m. On Sundays the service consisted of a morning and evening train in each direction. By the end of the century, well-filled trains of six-wheeled carriages were running over the branch, and the provision for cattle traffic at Moretonhampstead had been enlarged. Thousands of cattle and sheep were transported over the branch each year, especially from Moretonhampstead itself, and the autumn potato traffic was so heavy that it was sent away in complete train loads. At Teignbridge there was a considerable traffic in clay, with sidings on either side of the line.

Apart from the opening of halts at Brimley and Hawkmoor (the site of a large sanatorium) in 1928 and 1931 respectively, the only other change of note took place in the very last months of the GWR's existence, when the engine shed at Moretonhampstead was closed. Rumour blamed the temper of one of the Moretonhampstead drivers, who was so morose that no fireman would work with him on a permanent basis! However, it was probably due to the need to make economies

in the working of the line; the sub-sheds at Kingswear and Brixham having both been closed during the 1920s, it was surprising that the Moretonhampstead shed survived for so long.

In 1902 there were five trains daily in each direction, with an extra train on Wednesdays and Saturdays and on 'the fourth Tuesday in each month', the latter in connection with a monthly cattle market. The last evening train left Moretonhampstead at 7.15 p.m., returning from Newton Abbot at 8.58 p.m. There were two trains each way on Sundays. The journey time from Newton Abbot was 44 minutes, but the return journey took only 35 minutes, reflecting the gradients encountered in that climb of 500 feet to the terminus. There was a daily goods train in each direction between Newton and Moretonhampstead, plus a conditional evening train as far as Heathfield.

One of the most interesting periods of railway history was the so-called 'golden age' of the years preceding the First World War. This was certainly so in terms of the summer services on the branch in 1911, which saw an increase to eight passenger services each way. These were mostly in the hands of 'A' sets – five-coach, six-wheel stock (Van Third, Compo, Compo, Third, Van Third), of which three could be seen daily on the branch, one being stationed at Moretonhampstead itself. In addition, a 'C' set (Van, Compo, Third, four- or six-wheel stock) and a three-coach, eight-wheel set were programmed for the branch.

Perhaps the most unusual aspect of workings on the branch at this time was the through coach to and from Paddington

Lustleigh station was situated 3½ miles to the south of Moretonhampstead, on the outskirts of the village it served. This 1921 view, looking southwards towards Bovey, typifies the delightful aspects of many branch line stations in South Devon; so very much part of the local scene, they did not appear to impose upon the environment. Great use was made of any 'spare' land within the company boundary, and allotments were commonplace. The staff were also encouraged to decorate the station with flowers and gardens, and the annual garden competition was fiercely fought.

L & GRP,

Lustleigh station building in later days, showing the expected similarities in architectural style with other stations on the line. The station was also provided with a small timber goods lock-up, served by a single siding. Gradients around Lustleigh were the most imposing on the line, with sections of 1 in 50 to the south of the station, and 1 in 49 to the north.   *I. D. Beale*

Moretonhampstead engine shed and goods yard, 1906, with one of the new (later '45XX') 2—6—2 tanks on view. This engine could possibly be No. 2161, which went to Newton Abbot on 12th November of that year. Earlier in 1906, one of the ('44XX' class) small-wheeled Prairies had also been running in the Newton area, and would most likely have visited the branch. The Moretonhampstead engines at this time were '1076' class 0—6—0 and 'Metro' class 2—4—0 tanks, although, within a year, the '2161' ('45XX') class had become the more or less permanent residents of the shed. The station signal box was unusual in being built onto the side of the engine shed, but at least the signalman would not have needed to walk very far for coal for his stove!   *L & GRP, courtesy David & Charles*

Small Prairie No. 2171 standing by the coal stage at Moretonhampstead, c.1908. This engine became No. 4510 in the new number series, and, like so many of her sisters, spent much of her Great Western career at West Country sheds, eventually moving up to Swindon and the MSWJ section in 1941.
E. Pouteau

Moretonhampstead c.1908, with the branch stock at the platform — mostly, if not entirely, six-wheel vehicles. The baulk road, with its longitudinal sleepers, was left over from the gauge conversion. It was becoming rare by this time, although remnants lingered in sidings for many years.
L & GRP, courtesy David & Charles

each day. This vehicle, a Corridor Brake Composite, worked down on the 11.50 a.m. Paddington to Kingswear express, and was detached at Newton. Together with two other eight-wheel vehicles, it then formed the 3.49 p.m. Newton to Moreton train. The return was made on the 10.45 a.m. Moreton to Newton (an 'A' set), at which venue it was attached to the 10.20 a.m. Kingswear to Paddington service. Both Down and Up expresses were dining car trains, giving the Moretonhampstead travellers an unaccustomed taste of luxury!

By October 1914, the service had reverted to the five daily trains, plus one Wednesday, and one Wednesday, Saturday and 'Fourth Tuesday' services.

Eight trains each way was again the order of the day in the summer of 1922 for Moretonhampstead. Half of these were through services from Kingswear, Paignton, and even Plymouth, though the returns, with one exception (to Kingswear), were all bound for Newton Abbot. The Paignton train utilised the corridor stock of the through Wolverhampton to Paignton service, which included one of the rare Buffet Van Thirds (though it is doubtful that this facility was opened for the benefit of the travellers on the Moretonhampstead branch!). Otherwise, 'M' sets were used (six-coach, six-wheeled stock). In addition, Bovey received two terminating services; one of these was nearly an express – the 10.15 a.m. Paignton called at Torquay, Torre, then ran non-stop to Bovey, passing even Newton Abbot 'at speed'! One goods train in each direction still sufficed for the branch traffic.

By 1934, auto-trains (based at Newton) had taken over the bulk of the branch services (nine in total during the winter),

whilst the resident 'E' sets (three-coach formations) worked only the first and last services of the day on the branch, spending the remainder of their schedules on a three-day cycle between Taunton, Kingswear and Plymouth. Bovey received a visit around midday from one of the Exeter's steam railmotors (Nos. 71, 80 and 96 were there during 1934, their penultimate year of service); this was a local working from and to Heathfield by one of the Teign Valley units.

During the war, the branch service became totally auto-train-operated (as were the Teign Valley, Ashburton and Brixham branches), with seven return journeys in summer, and six during the winter. Two of the Teign Valley autos were now extended from Heathfield to Newton and back, thus improving the service on the southerly section of the line. The service was no longer 'Newton Abbot and Moretonhampstead (for Chagford)' as in 1934, when road motor connections were still shown in the timetables.

The very last GWR timetable (6th October 1947, and until further notice!) gave seven return services between Newton and Moretonhampstead, with an extra return trip from Moreton on Saturday nights. These were operated by two auto-trains, which also served Totnes and the Torbay branch, and provided the characteristic 'through' services in two instances (7.25 a.m. from Totnes, and 10.05 a.m. from Paignton). The pre-war practice of two Sunday services was not reinstated. The Teign Valley auto-trains provided two extra trains in each direction between Heathfield and Newton on weekdays.

Moretonhampstead still received a single goods train each day (arriving at 12.55 p.m.) which spent 90 minutes at the

Moretonhampstead was amply provided with goods facilities, including a large goods shed and sidings (beyond the passenger station), and a cattle pen at the northern end of the site. This 1921 view shows the pens, together with a cattle van, all looking very hygienic. Those facilities concerned with the transport of cattle, sheep, etc., were traditionally washed with a solution of lime (hence the whiteness) to prevent the transfer of 'communicable diseases'; however, the practice was discontinued in the 'twenties when it was discovered that the lime was damaging the animals' feet. A less harmful disinfectant was subsequently used. The large, black wooden building beyond the cattle van was used to house the company's 'Road Motor Car' for the service to Chagford, some four miles distant. A rake of 6-wheel stock (probably a 6-coach 'M' set, scheduled to work the branch at this time) may be seen in the train shed, awaiting departures behind the almost inevitable '45XX' tank.

L & GRP, cty. David & Charles

'Metro' tank No. 470 replenishing her tanks at Moretonhampstead c.1933; this engine had been transferred to Newton from Truro during the previous year, and was to work out her remaining time there, being withdrawn from service in February 1934. Of the twelve passenger services in each direction at this time, six were operated by Newton auto-trains, whilst the remainder were formed of three-coach sets, one of which was stationed overnight at Moretonhampstead with the '45XX' engine. The vehicles of the auto are 'Clifton Down' stock, with Auto Third No. 3275 next to the engine, and most probably Auto Brake Third No. 3331 as the driving trailer, the two being almost inseparable!

M. D. England

terminus, before returning to Newton. Again, the southern end of the branch was busier in this respect, with three extra freights in each direction, two of which worked through onto the Teign Valley, whilst the third ran to and from Heathfield.

Although the engine shed at the terminus had been closed in November 1947, there was still an early morning train from Moretonhampstead (dep. 7.50 a.m.), and the last train in the evening was an outward working from Newton Abbot. There was thus the necessity for a twice-daily running of a light engine or empty auto-train.

In broad gauge days 4–4–0 and 2–4–0 saddle tanks were in charge of the service. The first standard gauge engines used were '517' class 0–4–2 Ts and 'Metro' class 2–4–0 Ts, with 0–6–0 STs on goods workings. The branch was one of the lines on which some of the first '4500' class 2–6–2 Ts (then numbered 2161–80) were used, but their advent did not see the total disappearance of the smaller engines. Prior to the Great War, successive engines shedded at Moretonhampstead were '517' class 0–4–2 T No.571; '1076' class double-framed 0–6–0 STs Nos.737 and 1658; 2–6–2 T No.2179 (later No.4518) and 'Metro' class 2–4–0 T No.3590. The 2–6–2 tanks had become established at Moretonhampstead by 1914, when No.4504 spent virtually the entire year there, being replaced by a brand new locomotive fresh from Swindon stock shed, No.4544, on 16th December of that year. Other 45XXs known to have been at Moretonhampstead shed included Nos.4538 (1921/2), 4522 (1923), 4540 (1924), 4565 (1924–7), 4535 (1925, 1930, 1934–

5, 4585 (1928, 1931/2), 4530 (1933), 4582 (1939), 4591 (1935–7) and 4557 (1938–9).

In the late months of 1939 the introduction of auto services on the branch to replace the ordinary trains brought 'new faces' to the shed. Collett 0–4–2 T No.4868 was probably the first to arrive, followed in 1940 by what was to become *the* Morehampstead engine, No.4827; this latter engine was the resident of the shed for nearly all of its remaining years, until closure, being relieved on the odd occasions by such as No.4866.

EXETER CITY BASIN

The short branch to the City Basin at Exeter was constructed by the SDR to provide access to quays and wharves, and was used exclusively for goods traffic. Its origins lay in the enthusiasm of the Corporation of Exeter to have rail communication with the City Basin of the Exeter Canal; after considerable pressure, the SDR finally agreed (in 1864) to build such a branch from their line near St Thomas station.

The Act required that the line should be of mixed gauge, and that standard gauge rails should be added to the main line from St David's station to the junction, this being for the benefit of traffic from the LSWR. Although the single-track branch, which was less than half a mile long, was opened for traffic on 17th June 1867, the third rail was not laid until March 1871, and then only on the Down line. The daily 'City Basin Goods', consisting of both broad gauge and standard gauge wagons (combined by means of a match truck), had to return *up* the

Totnes c.1937 with a Down express behind a 'Star' class 4—6—0 crossing onto the platform line. One of Newton Abbot's '31XX' class 2—6—2 tanks, with a target number on the buffer beam, is seen here shunting vans in the goods shed between banking duties.
Collection R. S. Carpenter

Brand new Collett '48XX' 0—4—2T No. 4865 standing in Totnes station with the Ashburton branch train in June 1936. She was delivered new to Ashburton in March 1936, remaining in the vicinity for about three years; in 1939 she moved to Central Wales, remaining there for the rest of her GW days. The auto-trailer, No. 132, was a 1922 rebuild of steam railmotor No. 35. The labelling of the non-smoking (red triangles) and smoking (white rectangles) saloons is clearly visible, reflecting a period when 60-75% of accommodation was given over to smokers on most trains.
W. Potter

Down line for the $1\frac{1}{2}$ miles to St David's station! This practice continued until the end of the broad gauge!

Restrictions on the types of locomotives allowed to work over the branch, and the weight of the daily train, meant that for many years one of the '4400' class 2–6–2 Ts was shedded at Exeter specially for this working; No.4405 was a familiar sight from 1935 until 1946 on such duties.

ASHBURTON

The Ashburton branch, opened in 1872, was the last branch to come into existence during the lifetime of the SDR, and one of the last broad gauge branches to be built. Like several other local lines, its birth took place after a protracted gestation and more than one abortion! As early as 1848 the Ashburton, Newton & South Devon Junction Railway had been authorised, and was to have extended some $10\frac{1}{2}$ miles from Newton through Buckfastleigh to Ashburton. However, difficulty in raising the required capital resulted in the company being dissolved in 1851, before any work had been commenced.

The next serious proposal was not made until 1863, this being for a line from Totnes to Buckfastleigh – the Buckfast-

leigh, Totnes & South Devon Railway, which was authorised on 25th June 1864. A second Act of Parliament, on 26th May 1865, authorised the extension of the line to Ashburton. However, construction was at a standstill by the end of 1867, pending negotiations with the contractor. Work was eventually recommenced after a further Act granted an extension of time in which to complete the line, another contractor having been appointed in 1868. The line was opened on 1st May 1872, and was worked by the SDR.

The single-track line was $9\frac{1}{2}$ miles long, with intermediate stations at Staverton and Buckfastleigh, the latter by far the most important station on the branch. The Act had also authorised the construction of a railway or tramway, three-quarters of a mile long, from the SDR at Totnes to a quay on the River Dart, on which the use of 'locomotives, stationary engines and ropes, or "Atmospheric Agency"' was prohibited. It was highly unlikely, to say the least, that the SDR of all lines would be tempted into using the latter means of propulsion! The tramway was eventually opened on 10th November 1874, when locomotives began to work over it as far as the level crossing, powers for this having been obtained that year. Horses con-

The Symonds Cyder premises dominate the riverside at Totnes quay. This branch was not closed until 1969, although this end section would appear to be little used. The operation of the quay line would seem to have changed little over the years, with an early morning freight onto the branch (at around 8.0 a.m.) as far as Tram Gate, with the engine returning light to the station. An engine would return light during the late afternoon to pick up outbound traffic, departing from Tram Gate between 4.30 and 5.0 p.m. (although in 1902, this departure was 6.55 p.m., no doubt reflecting the longer hours of work then prevailing). The maximum speed over the branch was 10 mph (15 mph post-war), and the maximum load 35 wagons. Horse power was used to distribute the wagons along the branch, and onto the Quay. *R. W. Kidner*

Three miles from Totnes along the Ashburton branch was the modest station of Staverton, opened in 1872, and serving the small village nearby; this picture shows Collett '14XX' tank No. 1470 at the platform with an evening Totnes-bound train during the early 'fifties. This little station had a curious arrangement of two level crossings, one after the other. The first, normally left open to road traffic, crossed the goods siding whilst the second, seen here, traversed the running line. The signal box was an intermediate block post, dividing the 7-mile length between Totnes and Buckfastleigh into two sections, for operating purposes.

M. E. J. Deane

tinued to work the quay lines as late as 1948! The company was not absorbed by the GWR until 28th August 1897.

Ashburton station had one platform under an overall roof, in Brunel style. There was no signal box; indeed, the station only possessed one signal! All points were worked from levers in a ground frame situated near the small engine shed. At Buckfastleigh there were two platforms and a crossing loop, though one platform does not appear ever to have been used for passenger traffic; there were several goods sidings and a signal box. When the wool trade was still prosperous in the Dart Valley and the mills were working at full capacity, Buckfastleigh's goods revenue exceeded that of any main line station on the SDR!

Staverton also had a signal box, made necessary by the level crossing at the Totnes end of the single platform. The siding which served the small goods shed to the rear of the platform

was unusual, as the points were on the far side of the level crossing, which thus traversed two lines. In later years a siding for Staverton Builders was provided on the Totnes side of the crossing.

A regular source of revenue was provided by cattle traffic, especially by the four cattle fairs held annually at Ashburton. These required up to 90 wagons and lasted until 9 p.m. or 10 p.m. Wagons were brought to Buckfastleigh two or three days beforehand and worked to Ashburton as required, with wagons full of cattle worked back in batches until there were enough to justify a trip from Buckfastleigh to Totnes. The loop at Ashburton could only take 17 wagons, and trains of empties were often too long for that facility. On such occasions, the engine used the release cross-over into the station and then pulled the wagons 'alongside' by means of a 'wire rope' or steel towing cable. The cattle pens at Ashburton appear to have

Staverton, 1st June 1921, looking towards Ashburton; the brick-built structure on the right was a goods lock-up, with the shed and the station building beyond. The corrugated iron shed served as a lamp hut. The barrels on the platform were no doubt awaiting the arrival of the daily goods train from (and to) Newton Abbot, scheduled to spend 15 minutes at Staverton in each direction. Across the meadow behind the signal box is the River Dart, whose valley had attracted the Kingswear, and Totnes Quay lines in addition to the Ashburton branch. Passenger services at this time were operated by '517' class 0–4–2 tanks (No. 1440 in particular).

L & GRP

An unidentified '14XX' class engine (possibly No. 1470 again) at Staverton during the mid-'fifties. The destination board showing 'Totnes' on the side of the coach was reversible, and had 'Ashburton' on its other face; in view of the Down home signal being 'off', it should perhaps have been showing the latter. The auto-coach is an ex-GWR vehicle, one of the 60ft units built in the 1930s. Having enountered easy gradients on the run from Totnes, the train is about to be confronted with a 1 in 50 section on the way to Buckfastleigh.

J. H. Moss

Buckfastleigh in Edwardian times, with a '517' class 0—4—2 tank leaving the station with a southbound train for Totnes around midday. The stock allocated to the branch at this time was a 3-coach set (Brake Third, Composite, Brake Third) of 4-wheel stock (seen in this view) with an extra 'Market Third' added as required on Wednesdays, Fridays and Saturdays. The station master's imposing residence is seen to the rear of the train; clearly a man of some standing in the community. The train is about to cross the bridge over the River Mardle, a tributary of the Dart; it would then follow the River Dart itself for the seven miles to Totnes.

Chapman & Son

'517' class 0—4—2T No. 1466 arriving at Buckfastleigh with the three-coach branch set on an Ashburton to Totnes service in the years before the Great War. *Lens of Sutton*

The station building at Buckfastleigh, the join in the differing stonework making a later extension apparent, the middle chimney also marking the limit of the original. The station master's office was at the left-hand end of the building in this view, with the parcels office next. The booking office occupied the end of the original structure, with the general waiting rooom next to it, behind the slightly extended facade of the passenger entrance. The ladies waiting room and gentlemen's lavatory completed the facilities within the main building, though a large, corrugated, 'pagoda' style building to the right provided storage room. Although built of local stone, the building differed in style to that at Ashburton (the latter bearing a striking resemblance to the terminus at Moretonhampstead). *J. H. Moss*

This 'fifties view, looking southwards from the overbridge carrying the Totnes to Buckfastleigh road, shows the delightful situation of Buckfastleigh station, a scene now so completely transformed by the construction of the A38 dual carriageway. The signal box, goods shed and station building can just be seen, together with the loop siding (to the left of the running line) and the goods yard headshunt (to the right) in the near distance. The bracket signal to the right provided for running over either route through the station, with the longer arm controlling the running (platform) line, and the smaller arm the loop; a ground signal (to the left of the first point) controlled the entrance to the goods yard. The River Dart crossed beneath the railway at the girder bridge beyond the bracket signal, leaving the railway to follow the course of the River Ashburn for the last two miles of its route.   *J. H. Moss*

been constructed after 1905, which suggests that there must have been a considerable increase in traffic at the beginning of this century. In 1929 the side screen from the train shed was removed, and an extra platform constructed to allow the loading of cattle from pens made of hurdles.

On cattle fair days, the normal daily goods train from Newton Abbot ran only as far as Buckfastleigh, where traffic for Ashburton was left to be worked forward on the following day. As the normal amount of traffic was often quite considerable, this meant that two trips were often worked from Buckfastleigh to the terminus on 'the morning after the night before'. Passenger services on such days continued according to the timetable, though they can hardly have been 'as normal'. Congestion at Ashburton often prevented the auto-train

(which had superseded the '517' class 0–4–2 T and its train of 'four-wheelers') from running into the station any further than the foot of the platform. As the cattle traffic was more important and much more lucrative, in later years the company gave up the attempt to combine passenger and cattle traffic; on fair days, passenger trains were therefore terminated at Buckfastleigh, and passengers were taken to and from Ashburton by 'bus.

In common with most of the other branches, there were four trains in each direction on weekdays in 1877, the first departure from Ashburton being at 7.20 a.m. and the last at 7.10 p.m. The first arrival was at 9.09 a.m., and the last train reached Ashburton from Totnes at 9.19 p.m. There was a morning and evening train in each direction on Sundays. By 1902 this had

Ashburton in the mid-1920s, with an unidentified '517' class 0—4—2T on the branch train of 4-wheel stock. The 80ft long train shed could just accommodate the passenger compartments of the three coaches comprising the normal branch train at that time. During the latter 'twenties, the eastern side of the train shed was modified to allow the loading of livestock (via the pens) along the whole length of the siding, thus speeding-up the process on busy market days. The central section of the roof was left open along its length to allow the dispersal of smoke, and to permit some daylight into the gloomy interior.   *Lens of Sutton*

The southern approaches to Ashburton c.1947. The line at this point dropped sharply at 1 in 60, and special instructions as to the braking of vehicles not connected to an engine were in force. The large building in the centre of the picture belonged to Edwin Tucker & Sons, Maltsters and Seed Merchants, and was served by a private siding.   *P. J. Garland*

increased to six trains daily, plus an additional one on Saturdays. The last departure from Ashburton was now at 7.30 p.m. and that from Totnes was at 9.10 p.m. There were still two trains in each direction on Sundays.

The daily goods train operated from and to Newton Abbot, conveying a maximum of 40 wagons over the branch, and was scheduled for a 'six coupled tank'. Engines of the '1854' class became associated with this working.

In the summer of 1911, the branch train was scheduled for a Brake Third, Composite, Brake Third (4-wheel stock) formation, with an 'extra Market Third' being attached on Wednesdays, Fridays and Saturdays as required.

The 1922 (summer) service saw six trains in each direction, the first leaving Ashburton at 7.45 a.m. and the last arriving back at 8.05 p.m. The Newton Abbot goods arrived at Ashburton at 1.45 p.m., departing fifty minutes later.

Auto services on the branch appear to have commenced during 1927. By 1934 there were seven daily return trips to Totnes, with additional services (return) at around midday, and late evening, on Saturdays.

During the war, the service seems to have altered little, although the Saturday late evening return trip had been suspended. With the return of peace (and austerity), the branch services were reduced to six daily return trips, with the midday and late evening trips operating on Saturdays in addition. The Newton freight now spent ninety minutes in the yard at Ashburton, departing again at 1.15 p.m. (1.00 p.m. Saturdays).

In 1947 the 'signal box' at Ashburton opened at 7.00 a.m. each morning for the 7.50 a.m. departure to Totnes, closing at 7.30 p.m. (thirteen minutes after the last scheduled arrival from

At the station throat, the track passed between the engine shed (on the left) and Tucker's premises. Ashburton's Home signal can be seen in the distance, whilst a ¼-mile beyond that, down the incline, was a very short 'tunnel', Gulwell, formed by the post-war construction of the Ashburton bypass. After closure, a subsequent road-building programme isolated Ashburton from the rest of the branch, with part of the new carriageway being constructed over the old trackbed.   *P. Rickard*

The station yard, Ashburton, showing the goods shed and passenger station c.1947. Apart from livestock traffic (which at times was considerable), goods handled at Ashburton was relatively modest, and the limited facilities reflected this; Buckfastleigh was busier, its traffic including the despatch of cloth and agricultural products. The pressure of the war years on the railway shows in the 'neglected' condition of the yard, with little manpower available to carry out other than essential work.

Totnes) on weekdays. It remained open until 9.55 p.m. on Saturdays to receive the 9.42 p.m. arrival from Totnes.

The competing bus service run by the Western National from Totnes to Buckfastleigh had obviously contributed to the decline.

In broad gauge days the little 0–6–0 ST *Taurus* worked on the branch, while c.1890 the 2–4–0 STs *Cerberus* and *Bury* were the regular engines. After 1892 the usual engines employed were 0–4–2 Ts of the '517' class, No.1466 being a regular engine in the early years of this century. During 1914, No.571 was

allocated to the shed, with No.205 putting in an appearance towards the end of the year. Other locomotives shedded at Ashburton during the 'twenties included Nos.1440 (1923), 571 again (1924–5), 1439 (1926), and 559 and 838 during 1927. In the latter part of 1927, No.530 appeared from Exeter, the locomotive being auto-fitted; this probably heralded the introduction of auto services, as subsequent locomotives were similarly equipped. Nos.205 (1932), 1165 (1929), 1443 (1933/4) and 831 (1935) were also residents on the branch; 'Metro' No.1415 too (1936).

Ashburton in better days, possibly the mid-'fifties. There was no signal box at Ashburton, the various levers for points and signals being scattered around the site. The starting signal lever, for instance, was situated on the platform (just outside the southern end of the train shed), whilst a three-lever frame outside the entrance to the engine shed controlled the home signal, and the adjacent points at the southern end of the loop and the entry to the goods shed siding. Basic locomotive facilities were provided, and the branch's only water column can be seen to the left of the engine shed.
P. J. Garland and Lens of Sutton

Churston station, c.1936, with the Brixham train (comprising autotrailers Nos. 167 and 160 – Diagram A27, built 1928) waiting at the branch platform. As the two platforms used by the service were on different sides of the train, the coach destination boards probably remained *in situ*, with the nearside showing 'Churston' and the far side 'Brixham'. With the gradual demise of the '517' class engines in the first half of the 1930s, 'Metro' tanks were allocated to Newton Abbot to assist in the working of local services, and the Ashburton and Brixham branches; they were only ousted completely by the new '48XX' class engines during the early 'forties. One of Newton's three examples of the Large Metro class is seen at the head of the train.
G. Platt, courtesy W. G. Rear

In 1932, Collett's 0–4–2 auto-tanks appeared from Swindon, though it was not until March 1936 that a brand new example arrived at Moretonhampstead from Swindon Works in the form of No.4870 during 1938, after which the latter became 'Ashburton's own' for many years. No.4866 made many re-appearances on the branch with Nos.1429 and 1427 (after the closure of Moretonhampstead shed). No.4870 (later No.1470), however, managed to be absent on the very last day of the GWR's existence, when No. 1429 was in charge of 'Bulliver', as the branch train was known to its regular patrons.

BRIXHAM

That Brixham had a railway at all was due almost entirely to the efforts of one man, Mr R. W. Woolston, of that town, who obtained an Act for the line, held most of the shares, undertook the construction after a contractor had defaulted, and purchased a small locomotive to work it! The Act was obtained in 1864, for a line just over two miles long from Brixham Road station (later Churston) on the Dartmouth & Torbay Railway. The capital consisted of 1,880 £10 shares, of which Woolston held 1,770, the remainder being taken by two relatives and a friend. The line was opened for passenger traffic on 28th February 1868, and for goods on 1st May. The small engine *Queen* had been purchased second-hand, and other rolling stock was hired from the SDR who staffed and managed the railway as agents for the owning company.

What should have been quite a normal operation proved to be the makings of a great dispute involving both companies

with the Railway & Canal Commissioners. Brixham was the foremost fishing port in the country, and considerable quantities of fish were sent away daily, despite the inconvenience of the station being situated at the top of a steep hill on the outskirts of the town. However, the periodical accounts rendered by the SDR showed consistent losses on the working, and Woolston was forced to mortgage his engine to them as security for their claims. Eventually, when he was nearly ruined, friends engaged an experienced railway accountant to examine the accounts. The SDR was found to have been failing to credit the Torbay & Brixham with the terminal charges to which it was entitled, and had been invoicing all the traffic as from Churston, thus only accounting for the mileage rate on the two miles from Brixham!

The SDR refused to negotiate, so the small company took the matter to the Railway & Canal Commissioners. At a hearing in July 1876 the SDR's lawyers raised every possible objection to the Commissioners' jurisdiction, but these were speedily over-ruled and a decision was given in favour of the Torbay & Brixham. The SDR were obliged to provide revised accounts which allowed the terminal charges previously appropriated by themselves, but in retaliation imposed new and exorbitant charges for the use of the station at Churston. Encouraged by their previous experience, the small company made another appeal to the Commissioners, which was heard in March 1877. The result was that far from receiving any extra money, the SDR was forced to disgorge some £2,000 which they had illegally appropriated!

Brixham, c.1906, with what appears to be an '850' class 0—6—0ST engaged on shunting duties. The Brixham branch engine around this time was normally (though not exclusively) a '517' class 0—4—2T, and the engine pictured may well have been based at Newton, working through on a goods turn.   *Lens of Sutton*

The branch set, standing at Brixham station c.1920. The use of four or six-wheel passenger vehicles on the branch persisted until the late 'twenties, when auto services were inaugurated.   *L & GRP, courtesy David & Charles*

Brixham Harbour, photographed on 5th May 1936, with a wonderful selection of fishing vessels on view.

M. F. Yarwood

The passenger station buildings were a curious mixture of stone, timber and brick structures, which served the needs of the town until closure in 1963. After the First World War, the station had approximately an hourly service to Churston, utilising a three-coach set of 4-wheel stock, with a fourth vehicle added on Wednesdays (an arrangement which dated back at least to the early years of the century). By the mid-'thirties, with an autotrain in operation, the service was nearer half-hourly; however, in the last years of the company's existence, it was back to one train per hour in each direction.

Lens of Sutton

The humiliated SDR had to enter into another agreement with the Brixham Company, even though they were no longer working any lines, since the GWR had taken over in February of the previous year. However, the SDR remained legally separate until 1878, so the directors had to make the agreement which would be carried out by the GWR. The T & BR now worked its line with its own engine and stock hired from the GWR – no doubt the same stock as had previously been hired from the SDR.

Relationships with the GWR were far friendlier than they had been with the SDR; indeed, when *Queen* was in need of repair, the GWR loaned the company an engine. Further, in January 1877 (two months before the still legally existing SDR was taken before the Commissioners for the second time), the GWR sold the ex-SDR engine *Raven* to the T & BR! Finally, the company agreed to sell its undertaking to the GWR for £12,000, and on 1st January 1883 the Torbay & Brixham Railway ceased to exist, and the little line became just another GWR branch.

Connection with the Kingswear line meant that Brixham enjoyed a better service than was provided on many other branches. In 1877 there were seven trains in each direction, when other branches had only four or five. There were also the usual two trains each way on Sundays, one morning and one evening, as on the other local branches. The first train left Brixham at 7.10 a.m. and the last at 9.00 p.m., the first and last arrival times being at 9.10 a.m. and 9.16 p.m. By 1902 there were ten trains each way, with an extra late-evening service on Saturdays. The 10.45 a.m. from Churston was 'mixed'. The last trains left Brixham at 8.20 p.m. and Churston at 9.00 p.m. (SO 11.00 p.m. and 11.15 p.m.). The branch had five trains each way on Sundays, connecting with two of the three trains from Newton Abbot and with all three trains from Kingswear.

The never-ending cycle of maintenance on the fishing fleet is highlighted in this view of Brixham Harbour, 5th May 1936.

M. F. Yarwood

The station throat, Brixham, c.1936, with a '57XX' class 0—6—0PT shunting the yard. The engine shed seen in the centre of the picture originated from the Goonbarrow mineral branch in Cornwall, being moved to Brixham just before the turn of the century to replace the original shed, which had stood since the opening of the line in 1868. The station was arranged on a continuous curve, to fit the contours of the land. One curious operating requirement (at both Churston and Brixham) shown in the working timetables was that branch trains should 'stop dead' at the home signal of each, and thereafter 'be steadily drawn to the platform'; this, no doubt, had its origins in the forward gradients into each station.

G. H. Platt, cty. W. G. Rear

A Newton Abbot '57XX' class tank, No. 8709, shunting the goods shed line, c.1936. This engine, built in 1931, spent the GWR era within the Newton Abbot Division, though only at Newton itself during the period 1934-7. By this time, the branch engine originated from Newton each morning with the 3.25 a.m. goods, arriving at Brixham at 5.32 a.m., and disposing of the train before its first passenger departure at 6.30 a.m. (Brixham engine shed had been closed in July 1929). During the late afternoon, with the branch auto at Churston, an engine and van from Goodrington made its way to Brixham to shunt the yard. It remained at Brixham for about 1½ hours (during which time the auto made three return trips down the branch from Churston) before departing at 6.48 p.m. with the Up goods to Newton Abbot, the maximum load to Churston being 33 wagons of 'general merchandise'. The two Goods Brake Vans behind the engine are Nos. 35627 and 35650, both of which were allocated to Newton Abbot. Note the 'Renwick, Wilton & Dobson' wagon behind the front of the engine; originally a local concern, the company had grown into a countrywide coal distributor by this time.

G. H. Platt, cty. W. G. Rear

The branch train in 1911 was formed with three 4-wheel vehicles: Brake Third, Compo, Brake Third, with an extra Third added on Wednesdays. The service had by this time expanded to thirteen daily return journeys, with an extra late trip on Saturdays. One of these daily journeys involved a visit to Brixham of the Kingswear branch steam railmotor, running through as the 10.55 a.m. from Paignton; the unit returned working the 11.25 a.m. to Torre.

The number of return trips had risen to seventeen by the summer of 1922, plus a late night Friday extra. There was also a late evening goods trip from Churston to Brixham and return, before the engine brought back the last passenger train of the day at 10.15 p.m. The branch train formation was identical to that of 1911. There were no Sunday trains.

It is probable that auto-train services on the branch began around 1929, when the working of the line was transferred to Newton Abbot. The number of return workings had exploded to twenty-three by 1934, with an additional late-night Wednesday and Saturday trip. There were now four trips each way on Sundays, with three-coach 'E' sets and four-coach 'M' sets (bogie stock) working through to the branch from both Exeter and Newton Abbot (as detailed in Chapter 6).

This intensive service remained intact until the outbreak of war, when it was reduced to twenty trains each way, and no Sunday service. By 1944, it had further reduced to fifteen

return trips, at which level it remained (apart from a short period of 16 trips in late 1946) until the end of the company's existence.

Freight services post-war comprised through trains from and to Hackney (around mid-afternoon), with the branch engine also operating a goods trip to Brixham from Churston as it positioned for the day's passenger services at 5.30 a.m.

The engine shed at Brixham was closed in 1929, and henceforth the engine returned to Newton Abbot each night, though the last working was from Churston. Few passengers travelled by rail from Brixham to Kingswear, which had a direct bus service, and increasing numbers forsook the railway in favour of the Devon General's service to Paignton and Torquay. The only trains normally well-filled were the 8.03 a.m. from Brixham and the 4.50 p.m. from Churston during term time, when they carried local children on their way to and from the Torquay grammar schools.

Queen and *Raven* were replaced by the 2–4–0 ST *Prince* and the 0–6–0 ST *Taurus*, and the latter engine returned to work on the branch after being converted to work on the standard gauge. By 1901 '517' class 0–4–2 T No.1472 was the branch engine shedded at Brixham, and in 1921 it was No. 571. Other 'non-auto' engines allocated to Brixham included Nos. 1158 (1923), 1466 (1924), 838 (1925), 845 (1927) and 559 (1928). Auto engines used by Newton Abbot included members of both

An unidentified steam railmotor departing from Newton Abbot with the 3.0 p.m. (Wednesdays and Saturdays only) Newton to Heathfield service during the spring of 1935, with a 4-wheel Van Third as strengthening. It had become customary by this time to run one of the Exeter units working on the Teign Valley service through to Newton Abbot (via Heathfield), a tradition that was to be perpetuated by Exeter autotrains (after the demise of the SRMs) until the very end of the company's existence. During 1935, Exeter had Steam Railmotors Nos. 37 and 71 in residence, both of which would be withdrawn from service in October of that year along with the eight other surviving units.

G. N. Southerden

the '517' and 'Metro' classes, and, from 1936, locomotives of the 48XX class.

THE TEIGN VALLEY AND EXETER RAILWAYS

The Teign Valley was a line with a very chequered career, needing no less than *nine* Acts of Parliament to bring it into being and a further three Acts subsequently, which must be a record for a line less than 8 miles long! Originally, it had been authorised as early as 1863, as a broad gauge line from the embryo Moretonhampstead & South Devon Railway to Chudleigh and Doddiscombleigh. However, the company was not content with this modest aim, and proposed an extension to Exeter – an ambition which did not endear it to the SDR, who considered that passengers travelling from Chudleigh to Exeter should rightly go via Newton Abbot, thus filling the company's coffers! It was soon in Chancery, and had to make a scheme

of arrangement with its creditors, after which its powers were allowed to expire. Despite this, the ambitions of the promoters had not abated, and powers were revived in 1872, but little or nothing was done.

The next step was calculated to endear the company even less to the SDR, as help was sought from the LSWR, and an Act obtained for an extension to Crediton, the whole line to be *standard gauge*! By this time the SDR must have been getting more than a little alarmed, for the scheme suggested an ultimate penetration to Newton Abbot – or even to Torquay – by the arch-enemy. Again, nothing resulted from this Act, so the plan for extension was abandoned in 1880, and power obtained to enter into a working agreement with the GWR on whom the SDR's mantle had fallen. This resulted in such an agreement being reached shortly before the line was, at long last, completed and opened on 9th October 1882.

A busy time at Heathfield station in the early evening of 9th September 1933 with, on the Up Main, the 4.58 p.m. auto from Bovey to Newton (with a '517' class 0–4–2T in charge of what appears to be 'Clifton Down' auto stock) crossing the 3.45 p.m. Kingswear to Moretonhampstead train, hauled by a '45XX' class 2–6–2 tank. Steam railmotor No. 80 is waiting in the bay with the 5.10 p.m. departure to Exeter via the Teign Valley line, with a 6-wheel saloon (possibly a Dia. G20) in tow. During the early months of 1933, No. 80 was in store at Cirencester, being transferred down to Exeter for the summer services; she left Exeter in 1934 for the Swindon Factory 'Pool', being in the last group of SRMs to be withdrawn on 19th October 1935. *G. N. Southerden*

Heathfield station, c.1925, showing the original layout, with a single through platform on the left, and the Teign Valley bay to the right. The '45XX' tank is waiting with a mid-afternoon train for the Moretonhampstead line, whilst an Exeter '517' class 0—4—2T is about to depart with a Teign Valley train, running through to Tiverton, according to the coach destination board. Exeter autotrains (and steam railmotors before them) regularly operated through between the Teign Valley, Exe Valley and Dulverton lines.

Lens of Sutton

Heathfield, again c.1925, showing the timber-built station building, with the goods lock-up beyond. At this time, there was a short loop situated beyond the signal box seen in the distance, from which a connection was made onto the Teign Valley line for through running. The only crossing place on the line between Newton and Moreton-hampstead was Bovey, although dispensation was given to enable a goods train to use this loop at Heathfield to enable a passenger or another goods train to pass it.

Lens of Sutton

Steam railmotor No. 76 alongside the Up platform at Heathfield on 11th April 1928; the recent remodelling of the station is apparent, with the clean flagstones and neatly raked gravel. The railmotor may have worked to Newton, and is awaiting departure for Exeter via the Teign Valley line. No. 76 was not a West Country unit; it had been at Neath during January 1928, and, after a prolonged visit to Swindon later in the year, was allocated to Pontypool Road in April 1929, and St. Philip's Marsh in the following year, where it worked for most of its remaining life. The overbridge behind the SRM carried the A38 trunk road between Exeter and Plymouth!

G. N. Southerden

Heathfield station on 9th September 1933, showing the modified station layout as constructed in 1927. A new Down platform was built (left) with a loop line to serve it, making Heathfield a crossing station, whilst the Up Main line platform was considerably extended northwards. The goods lock-up on the Up platform (next to the station building) was truncated at about the same time. The steam railmotor No. 80 was waiting in the Teign Valley bay with the 5.10 p.m. to Exeter. The large factory on the left of the picture was the 'Great Western' pottery and brickworks of Candy & Co. Ltd., manufacturing glazed brickwork, stoneware pipes, tiles, etc. The company owned its own fleet of wagons, some of which can be seen on the factory siding, loaded with fuel for the furnaces.

G. N. Southerden

Just 2½ miles out of Heath-field on the Teign Valley line, was the attractive little station of Chudleigh. The buildings were very similar to Heathfield, and, like that station, the A38 trunk road passed nearby on an overbridge. This picture shows steam railmotor No. 81 at the station c.1923; the unit arrived at Exeter shed on 12th November 1922, and stayed for about 2½ years. It was one of the two motors at the shed during the early 'twenties, and one was sched-uled for an afternoon Exeter—Heathfield—Christow—Heath-field—Exeter turn, with an evening trip to Dulverton and back on Saturdays. The other unit worked a main line stop-ping service between Exeter and Teignmouth.

Lens of Sutton

The Teign Valley Railway consisted of a standard gauge, single-track branch from Heathfield to Ashton, with a short extension to a goods siding at Teign House, near Christow. The stations, at Chudleigh, Trusham and Ashton, had a single platform, and no crossing loops were provided, the loop at Trusham being for goods traffic only. In later years, Trusham was provided with a signal box, but the points and signals at the other stations were worked from ground frames. There were sidings to quarries at Trusham (Crockham Sidings) and at Whetcombe Quarry (between Trusham and Ashton), there being a considerable traffic in crushed stone in later years.

As the Moretonhampstead branch remained broad gauge until 1892, the Teign Valley railway was isolated for nearly ten years. It possessed a small tank engine, a handful of carriages, some goods stock, and an 'esprit de corps' all its own! Both the engine, a '517' class 0–4–2 T, and the rolling stock

The rather neat timber-built station building and goods shed are shown in this view, looking towards Exeter, c.1930. The steam railmotor at the station platform is believed to be No. 97, and was photographed on a Heathfield-bound service, with a trailer attached; No. 97 resided at Exeter between 1928 and 1931. The station was sandwiched between the River Teign (to the left), and a minor road which meandered from Kingsteignton in the general direction of Exeter (behind the station buildings), whilst the A38 crossed the bridge. A loop with a siding was provided at the Heathfield end of the station site to cater for the modest goods traffic.   *Lens of Sutton*

Trusham station was four miles from Heathfield on a gently rising gradient towards Exeter. The original station, seen in this c.1905 view, consisted of a single running line, with a short loop and siding on the west side. Before the First World War, a number of alterations were made at Trusham; the original loop was converted into a siding, and the station platform was extended towards Heathfield, this being made possible by the removal of the original signal box from the location shown in the photograph. A new 'box was built further along the line on the same side. On the opposite side of the running line, a new, longer loop was built, with a second (short) loop serving a loading bank running from it.   *Lens of Sutton*

An unidentified '517' class 0—4—2T arriving at Trusham with an Exeter-bound train during 1906. The normal formation of the branch set was Van Third, Composite, Van Third (4-wheel stock), although an extra Third was added on Wednesdays, Fridays and Saturdays, which would seem to be the case in this instance. The brick-built station building, which bore a greater family resemblance to the stations towards Exeter than to those towards Heathfield, provided adequate facilities for the local communities. The smoke in the distance (above the engine) marks the site of Crockham Quarry, at which granite was excavated. There were a number of sidings at the quarry, which also served other concerns (including a cement works) in the same area. The course of the River Teign lay behind the trees, and had been crossed by the train a quarter-mile before reaching the station by means of an iron girder bridge.   *Chapman & Son*

Trusham c.1933, with steam railmotor No. 96 and a trailer (probably the 6-wheel ex-saloon) on a Heathfield to Exeter service. The SRM had spent some time in Swindon stock before moving down to Exeter in 1933; she was withdrawn from service in January 1934, and the body rebuilt as autotrailer No. 213. The station is seen in its 'intermediate' form, with a long loop beside the running line, and a second, short loop off this for the loading bank in the distance. In 1943, this short loop was removed, and a passenger platform was constructed alongside the loop line, making the station a crossing place; previously, the long loop could only be used by a goods train being passed by a passenger (or another goods) train.   *G. N. Southerden*

were provided by the GWR, the former being stabled in a small shed at Ashton. Even after 1892 it continued in isolation, the only access from the Moretonhampstead line being by means of a connection facing towards Moretonhampstead, and leading into the short bay at Heathfield station into which the Teign Valley trains ran. In 1901 No.540 was the branch engine, while No.1466 also worked on the line during the early 1900s.

In 1902 the Teign Valley's service between Ashton and Heathfield provided five trains each way on weekdays, of which the 9.20 a.m. from Ashton and the 6.00 p.m. from Heathfield were 'mixed'. The last evening departure from Ashton was at 7.08 p.m., that from Heathfield being at 9.20 p.m., providing a connection from the late evening train from Newton Abbot to Moretonhampstead. There were no trains on Sundays. The normal journey time was 25 minutes, but the 'mixed' trains were allowed an additional 10 minutes.

The following year, a 'conditional' goods train (run when required) was shown, leaving Heathfield at 11.05 a.m., and returning from Ashton at 11.40 a.m. The 'mixed' train now left Ashton at 10.25 a.m.

The Exeter Railway provided the Teign Valley with its eventual link with the county town, though this did not take place for over 20 years. It was the only GWR branch in Devon to be opened in this century. Although officially known as the Exeter Railway, it soon lost that name and became known by that of its older companion, the whole line between Exeter and Heathfield being described as the Teign Valley line. The two lines made an end-on connection at Christow, where the mile-posts changed from 8.07 miles to 7.57 miles, the former being from the Exeter Railway's junction with the main line, and the latter from the Teign Valley's junction at Heathfield.

The Exeter, Teign Valley & Chagford Railway, for such was its original title, had been authorised in 1883, the year after the long-awaited opening of the Teign Valley, but, like the latter, it was fraught with setbacks and disappointments, though it never produced the plethora of Acts of Parliament which so distinguished its neighbour. The opening of the only section built, as far as Christow, did not take place until 1st July 1903, twenty years after it had been authorised! It was worked by the GWR on behalf of the owning company, and was still in existence at the grouping, when it achieved fame in its own style by being one of two small companies whose absorption created such difficulties that it had to be dealt with by the Amalgamation Tribunal!

Ashton station on 26th September 1928. The first part of the Teign Valley line was opened for passengers in October 1882 between Heathfield and Ashton, a distance of 6¼ miles (to the 'narrow' gauge), although the line continued beyond Ashton for another 1½ miles to a siding at Teign House (near Christow). In January 1903, Ashton was credited with a signal box, the only one on the branch at that time (apart from Heathfield); however, by 1914 it had 'gone', and the layout was controlled by ground frames. The station building was very similar to that of its neighbour, Trusham.

G. N. Southerden

An unidentified '517' class 0—4—2T arriving at Ashton with what appears to be a five-coach train for Heathfield during the years before the Great War. Before 1914, five passenger trains in each direction called at Ashton, as did three of the four goods trains using the branch (though work in the yard would seem to have been minimal, with just 12 minutes maximum allowed). The goods work was handled by Exeter 0—6—0 tanks, with a maximum load of 30 wagons scheduled for the section through Ashton; the same shed supplied the tanks (normally '517' class) for the passenger services. *Lens of Sutton*

Ashton yard and engine shed, looking south towards Heathfield, on 26th September 1928. The engine shed, which opened in October 1882, housed the branch locomotive (possibly a '517' class from the outset); in 1902, '517' class No. 1468 was resident in the shed until April, when No. 1472 took over for the remainder of the year. The pattern of work at this time was five passenger or mixed trips to Heathfield and back, with goods trains to Teign House and to Heathfield in between when required. The shed's days were numbered from 1903, when through working from Exeter began, and it was finally closed in 1908 (though it was still standing in the late 'fifties). *G. N. Southerden*

The most substantial station on the line during the earlier days was Christow, laying approximately half-way between Exeter and Heathfield, and until the Second World War, the only station between the two extremities where passenger trains could cross. It was situated at the foot of the climb to Longdown, involving gradients of 1 in 64; the single line beyond the station can be seen to rise towards the cutting. The inevitable '517' class 0—4—2T is standing at the station platform with the branch train of four 4-wheelers in the early years of the century, on a Heathfield-bound service. Note the absence of quarrying, a feature which was to dominate the Christow of later years. The station building was similar to those at Trusham and Ashton, though a hipped roof was used in preference to gable; a matching waiting shelter, also with a hipped roof, was provided on the Down platform, whilst the goods facilities were to be found on the Up side.

Collection J. E. Kite

The single track ran from a junction on the main line, just to the north of that for the City Basin branch. Stations were provided at Ide (later Ide Halt), Longdown and Christow, the latter having two platforms as well as extensive sidings in connection with traffic from local quarries. The gradients were fairly severe, averaging between 1 in 56 and 1 in 58 on the section from Alphington to Longdown. Initially, only Christow was provided with a signal box, though there was also one at Longdown in later years.

From the time of opening, the passenger service was integrated with that of the Teign Valley branch, but goods traffic was initially worked to Christow from Newton Abbot and Exeter in two distinct sections. Although there was a daily working from Newton Abbot on weekdays, that from Exeter was Saturdays excepted.

By 1914, a daily goods ran in each direction between Exeter and Heathfield, whilst a Newton to Trusham (and return) and an Exeter to Trusham (and return) were also scheduled for weekdays.

The traditional three-coach four-wheel set was provided for passenger services, with an extra Third being attached on Wednesdays, Fridays and Saturdays.

The southern approaches to Christow, with Collett 0—4—2 tank No. 4808 on the 3.0 p.m. Heathfield to Exeter service on 9th September 1933. The engine arrived at Exeter shed as new in October 1932, and remained in the area until 1935 when it began a remarkable series of moves, which saw it at Southall, Weymouth, Lydney, Kidderminster and Gloucester sheds before the outbreak of World War II! This particular combination may have been substituting for a steam railmotor, which still operated most services on the line (including, it is believed, this one). '45XX' class 2—6—2T No. 4549, also from Exeter shed, is standing in the siding with the late afternoon Christow to Exeter goods; the engine arrived from Exeter with a goods train around lunchtime, and spent about four hours shunting the station and nearby quarry lines.

G. N. Southerden

The road bridge to the south of Christow station (looking towards Heathfield), the effective boundary between the old Teign Valley and Exeter railways, where the 8 mile 7 chain mark from Exeter met the 7 mile 57 chain from Heathfield, almost at the end of the run to the old Teign House siding. The railway was still in close contact with the River Teign (on the far side of the field on the right). *J. H. Moss*

Steam railmotor No. 53, in company with the six-wheel (ex-saloon) trailer, departing from Christow with an afternoon service to Heathfield on August Bank Holiday Monday, 3rd August 1931. The unit had arrived from Bristol (St. Philip's Marsh) earlier that year, and left again during 1932, ending up in storage at Cirencester; No. 53 was withdrawn on 1st July 1933, the body being converted into autotrailer No. 199. The end of 6-wheel Brake Third No. 1685 (Diagram T51) can also be seen; this vehicle survived until December 1937, by which time very few 6-wheel passenger-carrying vehicles remained in revenue-earning service. *G. N. Southerden*

Christow station, probably in post-war days, with an autotrain at the Down platform, awaiting departure with a lunchtime service to Heathfield. The Scatter Rock Quarry buildings and sidings can be seen beyond the signal box; these were fed by an aerial ropeway system, which originated at Scatter Rock itself, some 1½ miles to the west of the station. In addition, a standard gauge tramway ran adjacent to the ropeway, serving the barytes mine near Bridford. This again provided a source of mineral traffic for transportation by rail from Christow.

W. A. Camwell

At the Exeter end of the line, a large new goods shed was opened at Alphington Road in July 1903, and a new low-level line, passing under the main line and giving access to the City Basin, was opened in May 1904. The former Teign Valley engine shed at Ashton was closed about 1908.

A halt was opened at Chudleigh Knighton in the early 1900s, others being opened at Dunsford and Alphington in 1928. Prior to the Great War, Chudleigh Knighton was the starting place for twice-weekly trips to Newton Abbot by steam rail motors, which visited the line soon after the Exeter Railway was opened. They re-appeared on the line after the Great War, sharing the passenger services with trains of four-wheel stock.

The 'through' route from Exeter to Heathfield assumed greater importance after October 1916, following extensive alterations to the junction which allowed through running between Exeter and Newton Abbot. In 1927 a passing loop and second platform were installed on the Moretonhampstead line at Heathfield, and these alterations (together with the provision of a signal box at Heathfield) allowed the Teign Valley line to be used as an alternative route for main line trains should the coastal section of the main line become blocked. However, weight restrictions did not allow for the use of main line engines, the largest type permitted being the '4500' class 2–6–2 Ts.

During the Second World War, further improvements were made; the crossing loop at Christow was extended in 1943, a second platform and crossing loop provided at Trusham at the same time, and a loop was installed at Longdown. These new works achieved considerable significance when special ambulance trains worked over the line to Heathfield and thence

During the latter months of 1932 and the early part of 1933, Exeter shed received no less than six of the new Collett 0–4–2 tanks of the '48XX' class to replace a similar number of ageing '517' class engines. No. 4819 was allocated to Exeter as new in April 1933, and is seen at Christow with a Down auto in the early evening of 19th August of that year. This engine remained in the West Country until 1941, moving on then to Fishguard and Swansea for the remainder of the GWR's existence. A good view is afforded of the Quarry sidings, with the gantry carrying the aerial ropeway from Scatter Rock. The Devon Basalt Quarries tramway line fed off to the left from the goods yard siding in the distance, which also served the cattle pens.

G. N. Southerden

Dunsford Halt was situated two miles to the north of Christow, and nearly two miles to the east of Dunsford village. It was positoned on the climb between Christow and the summit at Longdown, which involved gradients as steep as 1 in 64; as may be seen. This view, taken on 4th April 1928 (just three months after it had been opened), looks towards Exeter, and shows the short platform provided; this was long enough for a steam railmotor and trailer, which operated almost all of the services on the line at that time.   *G. N. Southerden*

'48XX' class 0–4–2T No. 1440 entering Longdown station with a late morning autotrain to Exeter, c.1947. This engine was allocated to Exeter when new, in May 1935, remaining there until the 'fifties; during that time, she alternated between Exeter and the sub-shed at Tiverton Junction, and was no stranger to the Teign Valley line. Originally No. 4840, the engine was renumbered to 1440 during October 1946. Longdown was situated at the summit of the line, with significant falling gradients on either side. It possessed a fairly substantial station building, similar to Christow, and a small signal box (being a staff station). In 1943, a long passing loop was constructed at the station; this could be used to hold a goods train whilst a passenger service used the platform. It was, however, utilised to cross two passenger trains during emergency working of express services, diverted from the Teignmouth section; in that instance, engines of the '51XX', '43XX', '78XX' and '2251' classes could be seen on the line.   *W. A. Camwell*

Steam railmotor No. 77 on a Heathfield to Exeter train approaching Longdown on 11th April 1927; this motor was allocated to Exeter in January of that year, and remained there until mid-1928. The unit has just reached 'level ground' after the climb from Christow, and the stop board for Down goods trains can be seen immediately behind the car. There was another stop board at the opposite end of the station where Up trains had to pin down their brakes before descending the incline; just beyond that board was the 836-yard Perridge Tunnel.
G. N. Southerden

to Moretonhampstead, where the GWR's Manor House Hotel had become an army hospital. These brought about the first appearance of 4–6–0s on the line, and the first appearance of LNER engines(!), in the form of ex-GER B12s. Furthermore, GWR '41XX' class 2–6–2Ts, '43XX' Class 2–6–0s and 'Manor' Class 4–6–0s were permitted on the line in connection with emergency wartime diversion workings, as were '2251' Class 0–6–0s.

Perhaps the most varied passenger workings could be found in the early/mid thirties. In 1934, the Teign Valley line had seven trains running through between Exeter and Heathfield; five of these return journeys were operated by two of Exeter's steam railmotors, one by a two-coach (bogie stock) train, and one by an Exeter auto-trailer. In addition, the ordinary train worked an early morning Exeter to Christow (and return) train, whilst the auto operated a late evening Exeter to Trusham (and return) service on Thursdays and Saturdays only. One of the steam railmotors carried out some complicated manoeuvring on the branch, working the 2.45 p.m. Exeter to Trusham, the 3.53 p.m. (empty) to Christow, and the 4.12 p.m. Christow to Heathfield, before returning to Exeter as the 5.10 p.m. departure. It had earlier worked down the More-

tonhampstead branch to Bovey (12.01 p.m. Heathfield), returning to Heathfield as the 12.40 p.m. Bovey. The second steam railmotor worked up to Newton Abbot (2.40 p.m. Heathfield) and return (Wednesdays and Saturdays only) in addition to its Teign Valley duties.

Goods services were worked from Newton and Exeter, both terminating at Trusham, and returning to their respective origins. In addition, a further goods trip ran from Exeter to Christow, and return.

After the withdrawal of steam railmotors from the branch in 1935, their workings were taken up by auto-trains, with three separate units operating on the line. The ordinary train service remained unchanged.

The wartime service saw a reduction in trains to Heathfield, with just four return trips being run; two of these worked through to and returned from Newton Abbot. The early morning train between Exeter and Christow survived, as did the afternoon Heathfield and Christow service previously operated by the steam railmotor. All of these trains were now worked by auto-trailers.

The post-war service consisted of five through autos to Heathfield, with an extra lunchtime service on Saturdays; two of

An unidentified steam railmotor standing at the timber-built Alphington Halt, c.1930. Opened for traffic in April 1928, this station was situated about two miles from Exeter St. David's, in open countryside, with the platform positioned on the south side of the line. It survived until the withdrawal of passenger services on the line in June 1958.   *G. N. Southerden*

Alphington Halt, on 18th April 1928, with steam railmotor No. 76, and trailer, approaching the station with a late-morning Up service (possibly the 10.35 a.m. Heathfield). The car was a South Wales unit, and spent only a short period at Exeter. Facilities provided at Alphington Halt were similar to those at Dunsford, which was opened at around the same time (1928). The Distant signal is that of City Basin Junction 'box (Exeter), about three-quarters of a mile away at the junction of the branch to the main line. *G. N. Southerden*

Steam railmotor No. 97, with a third class coach, departing from Exeter St. David's station with a Heathfield train on 2nd May 1931. No. 97 had a three-year allocation to Exeter from 1928, moving on to Neath in early 1932 after a spell at Swindon Factory. The motor ran on the Down main, calling at St. Thomas' station (about a mile distant) before turning off to the right onto the branch at City Basin Junction, 1¼ miles from St. David's. Steam railmotors were a common sight on the Teign Valley line from the years of the First World War until their demise in 1935.

G. N. Southerden

A Down express passing through Brent station behind 'Star' class 4–6–0 No. 4023 *King George*, c.1912; No. 4023 was an Old Oak engine at this time. The branch set (designated as four-wheel stock) is standing at the platform, whilst the engine (2–6–2T, almost certainly a '44XX') is busy in the yard. From Brent, west bound trains had a fairly easy two-mile climb to the summit at Wrangaton, after which came a continuous falling gradient to the outskirts of Plymouth, including the steep descent of Hemerdon bank. The rolling hills of Brent and Ugborough moors provided a delightful backdrop to this compact main line station.

Collection Graham Beare

The Kingsbridge branch train arriving at Brent (c.1955) behind '45XX' class 2–6–2T No. 5533, comprising a Fruit Van (possibly in use as a parcels van), a non-corridor Brake Composite, and an ex-LNER Brake Third. *Lens of Sutton*

.these ran through to Newton. The early morning trip from Exeter was extended to Trusham, which also received a late night Saturdays only service from Exeter. Again, these were auto services, as was the late afternoon Heathfield and Christow.

Freight services were again changed, with a through service from Newton to Exeter and return, and another morning trip from Newton to Christow and back. The independent trip from Exeter did not survive the war.

Chudleigh and Chudleigh Knighton now had no late evening train on Saturdays; both places were served by the Devon General service between Exeter and Newton Abbot, which had taken away much of the line's former traffic.

KINGSBRIDGE FOR SALCOMBE

The Kingsbridge branch, opened from Brent in December 1893, was yet another line whose realisation had taken many years; it had been no less than 30 years since a local company had first obtained an Act of Parliament, then constructed some four miles of line, after which both money and enthusiasm seem to have run out. Although other proposals had followed, none had resulted in the completion of the line. Kingsbridge had considerable sea-borne traffic, and was not so isolated as some other towns, hence there was perhaps not the same urgency as shown elsewhere. The town continued to be linked with the GWR by means of a stage coach which ran to and from Kingsbridge Road station (Wrangaton). The GWR, having taken over the powers of the Kingsbridge & Salcombe Railway in 1888, at last completed the construction of the line.

It was a typical GWR branch line, initially worked by engines of the '517' or 'Metro' classes, with the usual assortment of carriages, with a '1901' class 0–6–0 ST handling the goods traffic. The line had some severe curves, which considerably restricted the number of classes permitted to run over it, the terminus itself being situated on a curve. Although Kingsbridge station had only one platform (which was considerably lengthened in later years), the layout was quite spacious, and there was a large goods yard. A stone-built engine shed was provided, but there was no turntable; rather unusually, there was also a carriage shed built of corrugated iron, which could hold two carriages. The intermediate stations were at Avonwick, Gara Bridge and Loddiswell. Gara Bridge had two platforms, a passing loop and a signal box – the only one on the branch apart from that at Kingsbridge. The other two stations had only one platform, and ground frames, though both had a

The timeless charm of Avonwick station c.1950, looking southwards towards Kingsbridge, some ten miles distant. As may be expected, the buildings of the intermediate stations on the branch bore a striking family resemblance, although they were not identical. The goods shed was a common feature, being situated on the platform alongside the station building in each case. The main passenger building provided the basic facilities of station master's office, a general waiting room, a ladies waiting room, and gentlemen's toilets. *J. H. Moss*

Gara Bridge station, looking north, in May 1920. Gara Bridge was the only passing station on the branch between Brent and Kingsbridge, and was accordingly provided with a signal box. It was also the only intermediate staff station on the line, being about 5½ miles from Brent, and 7 from Kingsbridge. During the mid-'thirties, three of the eight daily trains in each direction were scheduled to pass at this location.   *L & GRP, cty. David & Charles*

Gara Bridge signal box also controlled the level crossing, which carried the Modbury to Dartmouth minor road across the railway. Signalling at the station was conventional, with the provision of a fixed distant, home, starter, and advanced starter in each direction, although the Down line was additionally provided with an intermediate starter.   *A. Attewell*

goods loop siding and cattle pens; Loddiswell also had a small goods shed.

Following the use of 'Metro' class 2–4–0 Ts, (of which Nos. 470, 1448 and 1487 worked on the line in 1902), two of the small-wheeled 2–6–2 Ts, Nos.3101 and 3104, worked on the branch in the early years of this century. During 1914 no less than seven of the class of eleven engines worked on the Kingsbridge line. After the First World War, two '4400/4500' class engines were shedded at Kingsbridge, working on passenger and goods turns on alternate weeks. The restriction on the branch being partly due to the curves, engines of the '2021' class were not allowed because of their longer wheelbase. From around 1940, allocation of 4500 class engines was reduced to one.

There was considerable agricultural traffic over the branch in earlier years, though this gradually decreased as road transport became available. However, during the war years, 1939–45, the branch was called upon to handle an almost incredible amount of freight traffic in connection with the use of the coast at Slapton as a battle training ground prior to 'D-Day'. At the height of this operation, several special trains had to be run each day, providing the line with its heaviest traffic since it had been opened.

Unlike most of the other branches under consideration, the Kingsbridge line did not convert to auto-train operations; the

four-wheel stock operating during the 'twenties was replaced by 'B' sets, pairs of non-corridor Brake Composites. Kingsbridge had two such sets allocated, together with a spare all-Third for strengthening purposes.

The initial service on the branch was for five trains in each direction; the first departed from Kingsbridge at 8.00 a.m.,

The northern end of the Down platform at Gara Bridge, showing the ornate rustic woodwork of the garden. The photograph was taken in 1937 and the Union Jacks are flying to celebrate the Coronation of King George VI. *E. A. Bovey*

Gara Bridge, looking south, probably during the 'fifties showing the three Down starting signals, the first (with the Down main to siding starter) is situated at the end of the platform, the intermediate starter is on the right-hand side of the running lines, and the advanced starter is in the distance (with a calling-on arm below it). The rear face of the Up home signal can also be seen above the hill. The railway crossed and re-crossed the River Avon ten times between Avonwick and Loddiswell, before parting company with it at the latter. The bridge of one of those crossings can be seen on the near side of the intermediate starting signal, and to the far side of the cattle pens on the left. Behind the bracket signal is the lamp room, with a small permanent way hut beyond that. Another PW hut can be seen in the distance near the advanced starting signal; there were twelve of these huts spread between the stations on the branch. *J. H. Moss*

The sylvan setting of Gara Bridge can be seen in this 1934 photograph of the station, looking westwards. The River Avon ran just beyond the station, along the edge of the wood; there were no villages nearby, the station taking its name from the adjacent road/river crossing. A new camping coach can be seen at the old loading dock, which had been modified to accommodate it.

National Railway Museum, York

The Camp Coach at Gara Bridge in August 1934, the year of their introduction. Other vehicles were also based at Avonwick and Loddiswell. No. 9953 (a 48ft ex-composite, built in 1891), in pristine condition, is resting amongst the rustic woodwork. In the second and carefully posed photograph, a gentleman (were ties and cuff-links obligatory dress for holidaymakers?) is about to receive what appears to be an empty cup!
National Railway Museum, York

whilst the last arrived back at the terminus at 8.59 p.m. Ten years later, the timespan of passenger operations was much the same, except that there were not six return trips within the working day. Of those trains, two Down and one Up were mixed. The branch was also visited by a goods train, the 5.45 a.m. from Laira Junction; on arrival at Kingsbridge (8.52 a.m.), the locomotive was scheduled to run the 9.15 a.m. passenger train to Brent, the 10.30 a.m. 'Mixed' back to Kingsbridge, then depart for Laira Junction with the 12 noon Kingsbridge freight. The branch locomotive worked the other five return passenger trips.

The branch train itself consisted of a Brake Third, Compo, Third, Brake Third (four-wheel) combination, with extra Thirds available for duplication and strengthening (1911). Seemingly, a three or four-coach formatioin was the norm up to the time of the arrival of 'B' sets.

The previous year, 1910, had seen a Sunday service in operation, worked by one of Plymouth's steam railmotors. The unit left Plymouth at 3.30 p.m., Brent at 4.25 p.m., arriving at Kingsbridge 5.00 p.,m.; the return journey commenced at 6.20 p.m., with an arrival at Plymouth of 7.48 p.m.

During 1922, there were still six return journeys made, with a branch freight running to and from Brent in connection with main line services. This was worked by the second branch locomotive.

By 1934 the service had expanded to seven trains each way, with an extra train on Saturdays during the summer.

Loddiswell station, 3½ miles from Kingsbridge, was very similar in layout to Avonwick, with a goods loop at the north end (controlled by ground frames), and a goods shed and station building side by side on the platform. Like Avonwick, it was a 'brisk stroll' from the hillside village to station which was down in the river valley below. The line from Brent had been in continuous descent to a point just north of Loddiswell, and then began a climb through the station towards the high ground separating it from Kingsbridge, reaching a gradient of 1 in 50. At the summit of this final section of the line was the 638 yard Sorley tunnel, which was followed by an equally steep descent towards the terminus.   *J. H. Moss*

'45XX' class 2—6—2T No. 4583 at rest outside the engine shed at Kingsbridge, probably in the 'thirties; a second engine of the same class can be seen inside the shed. A truly West Country engine, No. 4583 spent the years between her first allocation (March 1927) and the mid-'fifties at sheds between Taunton and Truro, with the great majority of her work being on the numerous branch lines in the three counties. The coal stage and the ash pit and water tower were situated outside the shed entrance but the water column was positioned on the end of the platform, a short distance along the bay line towards the signal box to enable it to be used by engines standing on either the running line (main platform) or the bay line.   *W. A. Camwell*

'45XX' class 2–6–2T No. 5558 is pictured on the run-round loop at Kingsbridge station c.1955. During GWR days this engine was allocated to the Swindon/Bristol area, moving to Taunton soon after nationalisation. It was transferred west in the mid-fifties. *R. C. Riley*

One interesting aspect of the line was the working of the through Paddington coach, which started c.1905. During 1907, a 70ft Brake Tri-Compo (corridor stock) was attached to the 11.50 a.m. Paddington to Kingswear train, and detached at Newton Abbot. The vehicle was taken by the 3.35 a.m. Newton to Plymouth train as far as Brent, from where it completed its journey on the 4.22 p.m. to Kingsbridge. The return was made on the 11.25 a.m. Kingsbridge to Brent, thence to Exeter by the 11.15 a.m. Plymouth service, and on to London attached to the Up 'Limited', 10.00 a.m. Penzance. This arrangement was in force until at least October 1914.

During the summer of 1922, the through portion (now a 70ft composite and 70ft Van Third) left Paddington on the 11.00 a.m. Penzance train, and was detached at Exeter. There, it was attached to the 9.05 a.m. Wolverhampton to Plymouth train as far as Brent, and the 4.05 p.m. thence to Kingsbridge (arr. 4.40 p.m.). The departure from Kingsbridge was still 11.25 a.m., but now the 9.50 a.m. Truro express called at Brent to attach the coaches. Arrival at Paddington was 4.34 p.m.

By the mid 'twenties, the coaches were worked on the 11.10 a.m. Paddington to Penzance train during the summer, and briefly found themselves on the Down 'Limited', 10.30 Paddington, for the late summer schedule, and from April until July. In the latter case, a Brake Compo was used, and the return was effected on the 11.25 a.m. Kingswear 'Torbay Express'.

By 1931, the pair of coaches (four on Saturdays) were working during the summer (July to September) timetable only, on the 11.00 (SO) or 11.05 a.m. (SX) Paddington, returning on the 9.15 a.m. Falmouth. During September and October, 1932, and May to July 1933, a Brake Compo for Kingsbridge was again attached to the Down 'Limited', returning on the Up 'Torbay', and this 'winter' arrangement continued until at least 1937. The summer workings (11.10 a.m. Paddington, 9.00 a.m. Penzance) remained in force until the outbreak of war.

The 'National Emergency' timetables of February 1940 show five return trips operating on the branch, but this had increased to six by 1946, with one extra Saturdays only trip. There were now two return branch freight trips each day.

Although the GWR had given up trying to persuade passengers that Moretonhampstead was 'For Chagford', they persisted in stating in 1947 that Kingsbridge was 'For Salcombe'. The passenger train arrangements during the last months of the GWR were the same as in 1946, except that an extra 'Wednesdays and Saturdays' trips ran from Kingsbridge to Brent only. As in 1932, the timings were such that two engines were required to work the service; some trains left Brent and Kingsbridge at almost the same time, crossing at Gara Bridge. However, in post-war days, only one '4500' class 2–6–2T was shedded at Kingsbridge, so the operation of such a service presented some difficulty! The solution lay in a return passenger working over the branch being in the charge of the engine which worked the daily 'pick up' goods from Laira. Last departures were at 7.45 p.m. from Kingsbridge and at 9.40 p.m. from Brent; the reason for the later times, compared with earlier years, was the connections made at Brent with the 8.05 p.m. Plymouth to Manchester and the 12.15 p.m. Manchester to Plymouth trains: few, if any, people were likely to go from Kingsbridge to Brent for an 'evening out'.

THE 45s OF KINGSBRIDGE

A representative allocation of the 2–6–2Ts during the Grouping:

First Series	Second Series
4503 (1928)	4576 (1930)
4510 (1928/29)	4582 (1936/37; 1946)
4520 (1925)	4587 (1942)
4521 (1923/24)	4589 (1930/31)
4522 (1924/25)	5501 (1932)
4523 (1927)	5505 (1936)
4525 (1926)	5516 (1939)
4538 (1934)	5525 (1930/31)
4540 (1932/33; 1937)	5530 (1940–42)
4542 (1926/27; 1934; 1938)	5551 (1947)
4547 (1935; 1943)	5552 (1944)
4549 (1923; 1943)	5557 (1945; 1947)
4553 (1925)	5567 (1939)
4571 (1935; 1937)	
4574 (1933; 1936)	

Barbican Quay, Plymouth. W 1674.

A late Victorian view of Barbican Quay (later Sutton Wharf), Plymouth, looking northwards.

CHAPTER EIGHT

PLYMOUTH SOUND

Plymouth, being the birthplace of the SDR (and with the company's offices situated at Millbay station), might have been expected that it would become an impregnable citadel of the broad gauge. However, the SDR had only just settled into their new station at Millbay when the first rumblings of invasion by the narrow gauge were heard. At that time the LSWR had not reached beyond Salisbury, but had already assisted with the

ocean liner traffic, and it was to be the first stretch of track over which *City of Truro* ran at the beginning of the 'Record of Records' journey!

In 1852 the company's own branch to Sutton Harbour was completed. Running from Laira, it was a single line ($1\frac{3}{4}$ miles long) made in part from the Plymouth & Dartmoor Railway, which was adapted and improved for that purpose, though the

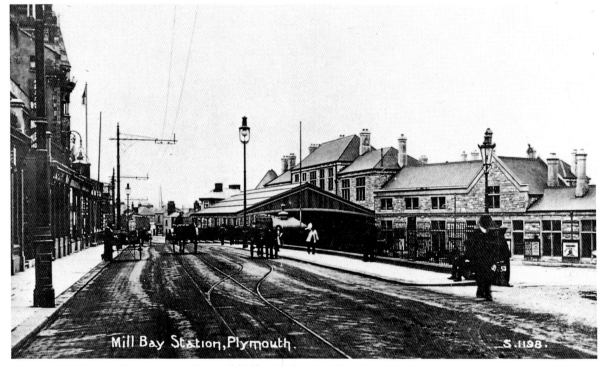

Plymouth Millbay station was opened in April 1849, with the extension of the SDR line from its temporary terminus at Laira. Ten years later, in May 1859, trains of the Cornwall Railway were running westwards from Millbay to Truro, and the following month the SDR's service to Tavistock began; thus was Millbay's future traffic pattern established. This view of the station approaches was taken from Millbay Road (looking towards Millbay docks), probably in the years around the turn of the century.
Lens of Sutton

promotion of the Cornwall & Devon Central & Plymouth Railway; they had also formed an alliance with the promoters of a company for the improvement of Sutton Harbour, even lending them the capital! It was obvious that sooner or later a major offensive would be launched to bring the narrow gauge – either the LSWR or one of its satellites – into Plymouth.

The broad gauge immediately looked for an ally in respect of the Plymouth Docks, and found it in the Plymouth Great Western Dock Company, incorporated in 1846 to construct the Millbay Docks. The SDR, together with the GWR and the B & ER, had contributed financially towards the venture, and had provided a rail connection from Millbay in 1850; the Dock Company laid a railway to their Millbay Pier and to other wharves. Over fifty years later this line was to acquire considerable importance when the rivalry of the GWR and the LSWR resulted in the race from Plymouth to London with

Act of 1846 had made provision for a completely independent line. The use of the trackbed of the Plymouth & Dartmoor was not the only example of thrift in connection with the branch, as the old arrival station at Laira Green was re-erected as a goods shed at Coxside! The branch was worked by horses until April 1869, though the SDR had obtained powers to use locomotives as early as 1854; they had almost entirely reconstructed the branch between May 1856 and October 1857, during which time it was closed to all traffic. It was never used for anything other than goods traffic. In November 1879 a short branch off the line was opened to give the GWR access to the North Quay, the LSWR having opened a branch to the quay a few days previously; the latter branch later became the LSWR's means of access to a new terminus at Friary.

The Millbay Docks were the sphere of operation for a number of small tank engines. In broad gauge days these were

Through trains and coaches from and to Plymouth itself often originated (or terminated) at Millbay; some of these ran through to their destination independently, whilst others were attached to (or detached from) Penzance services at North Road station. In this September 1928 view, a rake of London-bound coaches, almost certainly the 8.35 a.m. Plymouth service, stand at No. 3 platform awaiting the locomotive from Laira shed (probably a 'Castle', though possibly a 'King'). A '45XX' class 2–6–2T is waiting at No. 1 platform (on the right), possibly with a Tavistock train. Millbay shed can just be seen in the distance, to the left of the running lines. Although this shed closed in 1924, it was temporarily re-opened in 1925 with a small stud of 2–6–2 and 0–6–0 tanks, plus some engines for the docks ('1361' class). It was closed again in 1931, when Laira was able to absorb all the stock. The goods shed was positioned alongside the passenger station.

G. N. Southerden

mostly SDR 0–4–0 Ts, including *Tiny*, though *Taurus* was also used at one period. After being converted to standard gauge, some of the ex-SDR 0–4–0 Ts continued to work in the docks for many years, Nos.1330–3 being so employed in 1901. Other engines which saw service there included two exiles from the former North Pembroke & Fishguard Railway in West Wales, both being 0–6–0 STs. No.1380 *Ringing Rock* had been built by Manning, Wardle in 1874 and rebuilt at Swindon in 1902; it was in the Plymouth area from about 1898 until sold in 1912 to the Kent & East Sussex Railway (becoming No.8 *Hesperus*). No.1378 *Margate* was of Fox, Walker origin and built in 1878; it was sold out of service in 1910 (and survives as a preserved locomotive).

One or two of the ex-Cornish Minerals Railway 0–6–0 STs (Nos.1392–1400) may also have been used at some time; cer-

tainly engines of the '1901' class were used, among them No.1973, and these had the trailing coupling rods removed when on these duties. In later years it was mandatory for them to be converted to 2–4–0 Ts! From 1911, a couple of the '1361' class 0–6–0 STs were allocated to the small sub-shed in the docks. The class was developed from the ex-Cornish Minerals engines built by Sharp, Stewart & Co., and was built at Swindon specially for this type of work.

Considerable improvements to the Docks station were completed in 1936, including the provision of a fine new reception hall with seating for 170 passengers, and facilities for the exchange of money, the despatch of cables and telegrams, and a buffet. During the early 1930s a significant amount of first class transatlantic traffic was passing through Plymouth, and the GWR did its utmost to develop this, with the slogan 'Land

'Castle' class 4–6–0 No. 5003 *Lulworth Castle* at the end of Millbay's Platform 3 with a main line departure on 24th May 1936. This engine had just been transferred to Newton Abbot shed from Cardiff (Canton), and could be working through to Newton or Exeter with this Sunday train. No. 5003 was allocated to Old Oak when new, in June 1927, moving to Cardiff in 1934; after her brief stay at Newton, she was transferred to Exeter in 1937, and on to Taunton in 1942, where she saw out the GWR.   *G. N. Southerden*

The north end of Plymouth Millbay, showing the carriage and engine shed complex. The main engine accommodation is seen to the left of the approaching goods train, whilst the carriage shed is situated to its right. At the extreme left-hand edge of this view is a third building, which housed both engines and carriages. The signals at Cornwall Junction can be seen behind the goods train where the routes to Penzance (left) and North Road and Paddington (right) diverged. *Collection Paul Karau*

A Millbay to Saltash autotrain heading along the triangle behind a '64XX' class 0—6—0PT and about to cross the Stonehouse Pool viaduct on 24th May 1936. The viaduct to the right was Cornwall Loop, which carried the North Road to Penzance direct route. Off the bottom of the photograph was the third side of the triangle, the North Road and Millbay Loop, with the adjacent turntable and engine sidings visible in the foreground. These facilities were used by engines visiting the nearby North Road station, avoiding the inconvenient run up to Laira shed. The front end of Penzance shed's 'Hall' class 4—6—0 No. 4940 *Ludford Hall* can be seen at the bottom right edge of this view.

G. N. Southerden

Millbay level crossing, seen from the adjacent footbridge, looking towards the docks in September 1928. These lines were used by the Ocean Liner Specials to Paddington, latterly the preserve of 'Castles'.

G. N. Southerden

The eastern suburbs of Plymouth were well served with halts and stations, with no less than three intermediately on the four-mile stretch of main line between Plympton and North Road. Lipson Vale Halt was the central one of that trio, with Laira about a mile to the east, and Mutley half a mile to the west, North Road being a further quarter-mile beyond that. It was opened during the 'explosion' of halts, in 1904, coinciding with the introduction of steam railmotor and autotrain services. This view was taken on 6th July 1922, looking west towards Mutley, whose tunnel was about 300 yards beyond the bend of the line. Lipson Vale Halt was closed on 23rd March 1942.

L & GRP, cty. David & Charles

at Plymouth and save a day'. This traffic encouraged the construction of the famous 'Super Saloons' of 1931, the GWR's luxurious answer to the Pullman cars; they were named after members of the royal family. The greatest event, apart from the 'Record of Records' in 1904, was the first call of the RMS *Queen Mary* on 15th March 1937, when a civic reception by the Mayor of Plymouth took place on board the liner in Cawsand Bay, the civic party being taken out to her by one of the GWR's tenders.

Local passenger traffic in the Plymouth area had received little attention from the GWR until the LSWR made strenuous efforts to develop this during the 1890s. At the turn of the century there were a few stopping trains running to Newton Abbot or into Cornwall, two trains each way between Millbay and Plympton, three in each direction between Millbay and Saltash (one of which was extended to and from St Germans), and about sixteen trains each way between Millbay and Mutley on the Tavistock, Launceston and Yealmpton services. In 1903 about 100 trains passed through North Road on weekdays; four years later there were no less than 250!

The first move was the opening of a new station at Keyham on 1st July 1900, in response to the LSWR's successful efforts in developing traffic between Devonport and St Budeaux. Little more was done until 1904, when steam rail motors were introduced on a greatly expanded local service, and several halts were opened. Laira, Lipson Vale, Wingfield Villas and

Ford all came into use on 1st July 1904, as did St Budeaux Platform, followed exactly a year later by Dockyard Halt. Later in 1905 a similar halt was opened at Mount Gould and Tothill, served by trains to and from Yealmpton. At the same time, fares were drastically reduced, there being a 6d. return from Saltash to Millbay.

The success of the steam railmotor in generating new traffic soon resulted in trailers being required, the railmotor often hauling two of these; even with the eventual replacement of the railmotors by auto-trains, the GWR still insisted on calling the latter 'Rail Motor Cars' in the timetables. Such was the volume of traffic during the morning and evening 'rush hours', that a conductor was required for each of the four trailers used, when the service was being worked by the auto-trains; thus, there were seven men on each train – something which was unique to Plymouth. The conductors issued bell-punch tramcar style tickets.

The engines usually converted for auto-working were 0–4–0 Ts of the '517' class, though a few of the 'Metro' class 2–4–0 Ts were also auto-fitted. However, Plymouth required six-coupled engines for such work, and in 1906 two 0–6–0 STs of the small '2021' class were converted for these duties. No.2120 was rebuilt with a short, square saddle tank, and the whole engine was covered with dummy coachwork; the intention was to sandwich the engine in the middle of the four trailers which became a regular formation for the Plymouth suburban

Against a backdrop of the River Plym, this Millbay to Yealmpton autotrain was taking the Plymstock line at Mount Gould South Junction (c.1925). The engine, an unidentified member of the '1076' class ('Buffalo') 0—6—0PT, might be No. 1168, whilst the auto-coach appears to be a converted 'matchboarded' steam railmotor, possibly of the SRM 3 to 8 series (auto 99-104). The train is approaching the site of Mount Gould and Tothill Halt, opened in 1905, though closed around the time of the Great War. The two lines in the foreground served the Southern Railway's Friary terminus, and the Great Western's Sutton Harbour branch, whilst the route taken by the auto also connected with the Southern's Cattewater and Turnchapel lines. Between the two sets of tracks runs the Lee Moor (Plymouth & Dartmoor) tramway line, suitably arranged for non-mechanised traction! *F. H. C. Casbourn*

Ford, one of six stations on the normal westerly limit of suburban services around Plymouth, pictured here on 21st May 1922. Ford 'Platform' (being of *train* length, rather than the *railmotor plus* length of a halt) was three miles to the west of North Road on the main line, and this view was taken facing the city. The parapet of Keyham viaduct can just be seen in the distance, beyond the platforms. Like most of the halts in the district, Ford Platform was opened in 1904 to combat competition from trams, and a certain degree of success was obtained. Ford was closed on 6th October 1941. *L & GRP, cty. David & Charles*

Plymouth North Road station, probably in the early 'thirties, looking west. At the right-hand end of the line of coaches in the carriage sidings on the far side of the station is one of the 70ft twelve-wheel 'Dreadnought' sleeping cars which ran to North Road on the midnight train from Paddington, returning the following night attached to the 9.0 p.m. Penzance to Paddington sleeping car service. The vehicle on its left may well be one of three-compartment Sleeper/Thirds, with which the 'Dreadnought' was paired on those trains.
Lens of Sutton

services. This work was done at Swindon, but No.2140 was similarly dealt with at Newton Abbot. Nos.2117 and 2135 were also auto-fitted but did not receive the dummy coachwork.

The result of these conversions was what may be called the 'Plymouth Sound', as the continuing of the regulator through the front of the smokebox produced what was described as a 'shrill yelping exhaust note', which was recognisable from afar. For these engines, which were the nearest thing the GWR

possessed to the famous Brighton 'Terriers', this was especially appropriate! During the Great War, the double-framed 0–6–0 STs of the '1076' class, Nos.1168, 1235, 1252, '1271', 1284 and 1600, were also auto-fitted, and replaced the '2021' class engines on these services. In the 1930s, the Plymouth suburban services were taken over by the new auto-fitted engines of the '6400' class, eight of which were shedded at Laira (reduced to six engines by 1938). An unusual addition during the war years

'Buffalo' 0–6–0PT No. 1252 at North Road station, Plymouth, pictured with a goods train at 1.30 p.m. on Thursday, 16th September 1920. This engine was at Newton Abbot at the turn of the century, moving to Plymouth during the Great War; she remained at Laira until withdrawal in October 1932. Originally built with saddletanks, No. 1252 was fitted with panniers during 1911.
Collection R. C. Riley

Another auto-fitted '1076' class tank, No. 1271, entering North Road station with the 3.55 p.m. Yealmpton to Millbay service on Saturday, 11th July 1925. The leading trailer is No. 4, one of the first purpose-built vehicles for use in auto services (constructed in April 1905), the second vehicle is probably trailer No. 3. This engine tended to wander around during its career, being at Laira in early 1902, and moving to Oxford in December of that year. No. 1271 was at Llanelly in 1906 and 1910, Bristol in 1914, and back at Laira by 1918. Apart from a spell at Swansea (Landore) in 1928-30, she remained at Plymouth until 1936, when a final move was made back to Landore, from which place she was withdrawn in April 1937.   *F. H. C. Casbourn*

No. 1235, one of Laira shed's stud of '1076' class 0—6—0 tanks, heading a Down autotrain between Laira and Mutley on Thursday, 14th May 1925. The autocoaches invariably operated as 'twin sets', coupled together on one side of the engine, as most had a connecting gangway. In any event, West Country auto units in general adopted this formation, unlike some London Division sheds who seemed to favour a trailer on each side of the locomotive. The majority of Plymouth area services operated with just two cars, with three and four-car operation reserved for peak traffic hours.

F. J. Agar

Mutley station c.1920, looking towards London, with the 183-yard tunnel in the background. The station was only ¼ mile from North Road, and one minute was allowed for the journey between the two. Like North Road (and Lipson Vale Halt), it was served by trains of both companies, and shared with those stations (and Exeter) the rather unusual 'reverse direction' running of Southern services. Having served the locality for 68 years, Mutley was closed on 3rd July 1939, the beginning of the summer timetable for that year. *Lens of Sutton*

was No.5412, of the larger-wheeled '5400' class, which worked the newly restored passenger service on the Yealmpton branch.

Prior to the introduction of the steam railmotors in 1904, the local service was worked by 'Metro' class 2–4–0 Ts or by the '517' class 0–4–2 Ts. In 1901, Millbay's allocation was only two of the former class Nos.1450 and 1464 (the former engine spent each night at Liskeard), and No.218 of the latter class – which worked the Yealmpton branch. Laira had two 'Metros', Nos.1448 and 1457, and both sheds had a selection of 0–6–0 tanks of the 850, 1016, 1076 and 1854 classes. No doubt the six-coupled tanks found themselves on passenger as well as goods duties.

In December 1902 2–4–0 T No.1 arrived at Millbay. This was a fairly large engine with double frames, which had originated in 1880 in the shape of a very unsteady 4–4–0 T, and which had been rebuilt as a 2–4–0 T two years later. It was considerably larger than the 'Metro' engines, and in later years carried a boiler similar to that fitted to the 'Dukes'. Being both powerful and free-running, it was very popular with the enginemen, and there was considerable lamentation when it was transferred to Chester after several years at Plymouth. The large 2–4–2 T No.3601 was also given trials on the local services during 1902/3.

Mutley was by far the busiest local station in early days, apart from North Road and Millbay, and was served by some long-distance trains as well as by stopping services on the main line, and the Yealmpton, Tavistock and Launceston trains. In 1902 over 30 trains in each direction called on weekdays and about a dozen on Sundays. Plympton and Saltash, the effective limits of the suburban service, had 11 Down and 12 Up trains, with about half-a-dozen on Sundays. Only a handful of these trains actually terminated at Plympton or Saltash, the majority being stopping trains to or from Newton Abbot and Truro.

In 1914 the three towns of Plymouth, Devonport and Stonehouse were united – and with them their tramways. The closure of some halts soon afterwards was evidence that the railways

could not compete with the newly integrated tramway system. By this time, the steam railmotors had left the district, leaving the services in the hands of autotrains. Between 1881 and 1914 the population had grown from 138,000 to 214,000, but increasing numbers were travelling by tram rather than by train. The introduction of 'bus services in 1920 caused a further loss of traffic for the railways, and Wingfield Villas Halt was closed in June 1921. Most 'rail motor' services were withdrawn between Millbay and Plympton in 1930, when some of the Saltash trains were diverted from Millbay to North Road.

By 1932 the main line and suburban services appeared in separate timetables, the latter under the heading 'Plymouth, Plympton and Saltash Suburban Service'. There were now only 24 Down and 25 Up trains stopping at Mutley on weekdays, the reduced number being largely due to the withdrawal of the passenger service on the Yealmpton branch (which also resulted in the closure of Laira Halt). However, although Plympton's service was now no better than in 1902, Saltash enjoyed a greatly increased service, with no less than 43 Down trains and 47 Up trains on weekdays, and 19 Down and 20 Up trains on Sundays. Apart from the ferry across the Tamar, Brunel's Royal Albert Bridge, with its railway, provided the only connection between Saltash and Plymouth! The majority of the Saltash trains were railmotors – auto-trains with a double-framed 0–6–0 PT operating between two to four trailers (depending upon the time of day). Millbay had 45 Down trains and 46 Up trains on weekdays, but only 15 in each direction on Sundays.

In 1947 the service had been considerably reduced, while Millbay and Mutley stations had been closed. The closure of Mutley took place in 1939, and Millbay was closed to passenger traffic on 23rd April 1941. The shortness of the platforms at Millbay had long caused difficulties and, when the adjacent goods station suffered severe bomb damage, all the limited room in the passenger station was needed for goods traffic. Another war-time closure was that of Lipson Vale Halt (used

A four-coach auto-train passing the Royal Albert Bridge signal box with an Up service to Millbay in the late 1920s. This would have been an evening rush-hour train, comprising four vehicles; at non-peak periods, these trains were reduced to two or three coaches. The signal box controlled the entry and exit to the single line section across the bridge. *B. Y. Williams*

A July 1946 view of Plymouth North Road, with '64XX' class 0—6—0PT auto No. 6417 at the head of a 'motor' from Saltash. The coaches are still in their wartime brown livery which much of the lesser stock carried into nationalisation. The station and its approaches were scheduled for major rebuilding in the 'thirties, and a start had been made on the new platforms when the war brought a halt to such activities. No. 6417 is standing at one of the new platforms on the Up side of the station, which had its train shed removed in the process. The engine had arrived at Laira shed as new in December 1934 for a continuous allocation through into the 1950s.
S. C. Nash

'64XX' class 0—6—0 Autotank No. 6409 passing the Royal Albert Bridge 'box with an afternoon Up service during July 1934. The token setting-down equipment was situated on the front of the signal box, and the fireman is placing the token on the catcher in this photograph.

B. Y. Williams

One or two autotrains ran further west than the normal outer limit of Saltash, and in this view a '64XX' class 0—6—0PT is working a four-coach set near the site of Defiance Platform with a Liskeard-bound service in April 1949.

R. E. Vincent

A panoramic view of the approaches to Millbay station, Plymouth, taken in 1947. Millbay was closed to passengers in April 1941, and was thereafter used for parcels and goods traffic only. Extensive use was still made of the carriage sidings (to the north of the signal box), and stock for both main line and branch services was kept there; the autotrailers were stabled at Laira by this time. The main business of the station was carried out by a series of transfer trips to and from Tavistock Junction, with a lesser number of similar trips to and from Devonport. A small number of parcels trains used the station, too. Millbay had one passenger shunting engine operating throughout the day, forming and disposing of the passenger sets, whilst a goods shunting engine (possibly the '57XX' class engine in the photograph) worked around the clock. In addition, two engines (normally the '1361' class saddle tanks) worked the docks at Millbay, one of which resided in the small shed within the dock area.
P. J. Garland

The old No. 4 platform at Millbay station in 1947, with its goods and parcels role now clearly evident. Beyond the two sidings next to the platform line, the tracks to the docks (via Millbay crossing) can be seen dropping to a lower level; these tracks also served the fish dock, situated beside the station, near to the level crossing. The lines from the station and the docks continued northwards independently for just over ¼ mile, although there were connections between the two pairs at the station throat. The station was largely demolished in 1959, and the area converted into carriage sidings; these survived for a further ten years, and the closure of the dock lines in 1971 finally concluded the Millbay chapter.
P. J. Garland

Just 400 yards along the Launceston branch from the main line at Tavistock Junction, sat the small crossing station of Marsh Mills; it was, in fact, a double-track station, the line only becoming single at its northern end, and possessed the first of the eight signal boxes to be found on the 32 mile branch to Launceston. In this view, an Up local passenger pauses behind a '45XX' 2–6–2T at the station, whilst a northbound special departs from the Down platform. 29th March 1937.   *G. N. Southerden*

only by Southern trains following the closure of the Yealmpton branch), which was closed on 4th May 1942 and then dismantled, as the wooden platforms constituted a major fire risk; Ford Halt had been closed as from 6th November 1941.

Plymouth had two branch lines which ran far out into the surrounding countryside. The branch to Launceston, which was the second major branch line built by the SDR (originating as a nominally independent line to Tavistock) had the distinction of being the only branch line which crossed the border into Cornwall. The Yealmpton branch in the South Hams was the next-to-last branch line opened by the GWR in South Devon, and had the rather gloomy distinction of being the only one whose passenger service was withdrawn during the lifetime of the GWR – and one of few branches anywhere that had it withdrawn twice!

Throughout 1852 and 1853 two groups of local worthies in Plymouth were engaged in a fierce combat, each intent on securing the honour – and, doubtless, the profit – from linking Tavistock with Plymouth. The 'Plymouth & Tavistock' group were led by the ex-Chairman of the SDR, Thomas Gill, but it was the second group (the South Devon & Tavistock), led by Lord Morley, who secured the support of the SDR's directors. Not to be outdone, the 'Plymouth & Tavistock' looked northwards and sought other allies; by the end of 1852 they had expanded both their title and their ambitions, having become the 'Plymouth, Tavistock, Okehampton, North Devon and Exeter'. They were, nevertheless, defeated in the House of Commons who passed their rivals' proposal. However, as the Lords declined to follow the Commons in accepting the 'South Devon & Tavistock', Thomas Gill and his friends made a third

attempt. This time, as the 'Plymouth, Tavistock & Devon Central Railway', a rather feeble attack was made, but, once again, the South Devon & Tavistock won the day.

The engineer appointed, A. H. Hampton, died in the spring of 1857, but little work had been done by that time, and Brunel was appointed to bring the work to a successful conclusion. The line was single and just under 13 miles long from its junction with the SDR, later to become familiar as Tavistock Junction. There were many cuttings and embankments, three tunnels – Shaugh (307 yards), Yelverton (641 yards) and Grenofen (378 yards) – and no less than six large viaducts of Brunel's typical design, timber on stone piers. Walkham was the most impressive of these, being 376 yards long and standing at a height of 132 feet; it has been described as 'the most mature of Brunel's timber viaducts'.

The line was opened for passenger traffic on 22nd June 1859 (goods traffic did not commence until 1st February 1860), with intermediate stations at Bickleigh and Horrabridge. The terminus at Tavistock had an impressive overall roof and two platforms, with three lines between them. The large goods shed was situated behind the Down (Launceston-bound) platform, and a small engine shed with a typical SDR turntable (23 ft 7 in diameter) at the Plymouth end of the station site. From the layout, it was obvious that Tavistock was not intended to be a permanent terminus, and that there were intentions of extending northwards. The company leased the line to the SDR until July 1865, after which it became South Devon property.

The extension to Launceston was the result of aggression by the standard gauge, led by the old enemy, the LSWR. There had been two schemes before Parliament in 1861; one to connect the North Devon Railway with Tavistock, the other for a new line from Exeter to Lydford, by way of Moretonhampstead, Chagford and Okehampton. Neither was passed, and the SDR took the next step, with the intention of securing their frontiers against incursions inspired by the LSWR, who were obviously casting acquisitive glances in the direction of Plymouth. Broad gauge lines to Launceston and Moretonhampstead were incorporated in 1862.

The Launceston & North Devon Railway Act authorised a broad gauge line from the existing terminus at Tavistock to the small East Cornwall town of Launceston, the only place outside Devon to be served by the SDR. As with the South Devon & Tavistock's Act in 1854, the Board of Trade were given powers to order standard gauge rails to be laid over it, and for running powers to be given to any connecting company. The Okehampton Railway had obtained powers for an extension to join the Launceston line at Lydford, while in 1865, as part of an Act obtained for the construction of the City Basin branch in Exeter, the SDR was required to lay standard gauge

An Edwsrdian view of Yelverton, a delightfully situated station just over eleven miles from Millbay. Opened in 1885, Yelverton assumed the role of the junction station for the Princetown branch which, since the opening of that branch in 1883, had been undertaken by Horrabridge (1½ miles to the north of Yelverton). The station was positioned on the southern edge of the village it served, and was in effect provided with passenger facilities only (although one or two goods trains did call briefly).

Lens of Sutton

The Up platform at Yelverton, during the early years of the century. The main station building was situated on the right, between the fork of the Up and Princetown lines, and was connected to the Down platform and station forecourt by the footbridge. The Down platform itself possessed a waiting shelter and a 'pagoda' hut, seen at the left of the picture. Yelverton was located at the summit of the seven mile climb from Marsh Mills, involving gradients as steep as 1 in 58. At the far end of the Down platform, the line started a continuous descent to Tavistock (with similar gradients), some five miles distant.   *Lens of Sutton*

The four-mile section of the Launceston branch between Horrabridge and Tavistock contained fairly heavy works, with a tunnel and two major viaducts in addition to a significant number of cuttings and embankments. The challenge brought out the best of Brunel, who responded with some truly magnificent viaducts; the Magpie viaduct, 216 yards in length, carried the line at a maximum height of 62ft above the valley of the River Walkham, some ¾ mile to the north of Horrabridge station, near Bedford Bridge. An Up train is shown on the viaduct behind a 4–4–0, probably a large-boilered member of the '3521' class (some of which were shedded at Launceston at this time). The viaduct was replaced in 1902 by a brick-built structure.

Lens of Sutton

rails from Lydford into Millbay (and also to Sutton Harbour) if requested to do so by the Okehampton Railway. The latter changed its name to the Devon & Cornwall Railway in the same year, but did not manage to reach Lydford until 1874.

The line to Launceston was opened for passenger traffic on 1st July 1865, a day with such rain that similar weather is still known locally as 'railway weather'(!), and was opened for goods traffic in August. The Tavistock Company had already been absorbed by the SDR by the time of the opening of the extension to Launceston, but the Launceston & South Devon Railway retained its independence until 1873 (though always worked by the SDR). In contrast to the line between Plymouth and Tavistock, there were no heavy engineering works on the 19 miles to Launceston. Stations were provided at Marytavy, Brentor, Lydford and Coryton, in addition to the new terminus at Launceston. The latter had two platforms (with cattle pens situated at the rear of one of them), and there was a small engine shed.

With the opening of the extension to Launceston, the small engine shed at Tavistock fell into disuse, and deteriorated to such an extent that the GWR refused to take it over (or be responsible for it) in 1876! It was still standing, half blown down, in 1885; two years later the station, which was built of wood, was burnt down, and was replaced by a stone structure of almost identical design.

South of Tavistock, a station was opened at Marsh Mills in 1861, whilst Yelverton, and the platforms at Plym Bridge, Shaugh Bridge, and Whitchurch Down were opened under the aegis of the GWR. The most important of these was that at

Yelverton, which was the junction for the Princetown branch; however, this was not opened until 1885, two years after services commenced on that branch, and trains initially ran to and from Horrabridge. The original Brunel viaducts were all replaced between 1893 and 1910, the impressive Walkham Viaduct being the last to go.

In 1877 Tavistock and Launceston had five trains in each direction, the latter station then enjoying the most generous service ever provided; during this century the maximum number of daily trains was four, although an extended Tavistock train (on Wednesdays and Saturdays only) did increase the total. The first departure from Launceston was at 7.55 a.m. (Tavistock dep. 8.45 a.m.) and the last at 5.40 p.m. (Tavistock dep. 6.31 p.m.); the first train from Plymouth arrived at Tavistock at 9.11 a.m. and at Launceston at 10.02 a.m., with the last arrival times being 8.56 p.m. and 9.47 p.m. respectively. There was also a morning and evening train in each direction on Sundays.

By 1902 there were four trains each way between Plymouth and Launceston, the 11.50 a.m. from Plymouth being 'mixed', and the last train left Millbay at 6.50 p.m. On Saturdays the 5.10 p.m. Plymouth train worked through to Launceston, returning to Plymouth as the 8.15 p.m. departure; on other days, the last train from Launceston was at 6.25 p.m. There were two trains each way on Sundays, a curious feature being that the evening train did not leave Millbay until 9.50 p.m.

Tavistock had an additional five trains, making nine daily, with a tenth train on Wednesdays and Saturdays, the latter being a late evening train. The 10.45 a.m. from Plymouth was

Yelverton, on Monday, 25th May 1931, with a '44XX' class 2–6–2T at the head of a recently arrived branch train from Princetown. The engine is most probably No. 4402, which had been at Plymouth since 1928. It had moved to Princetown in 1931 for a more or less continuous allocation into nationalisation. It is fitted with the experimental flange oiling device to minimise the excessive wear being experienced on this sharply curved line. The Westinghouse pump apparatus (from an ex-ROD 2–8–0 engine) forced a fine spray of oil onto the driving wheel flanges, and also unfortunately onto the tyres (which caused slipping!); the experiment was therefore deemed a failure.

'Buffalo' class 0–6–0PT No. 1570 waiting to depart from Yelverton's Down platform with a Millbay to Tavistock autotrain, propelling the trailers (probably a 'twin set') northwards as was the custom with the Millbay set. No. 1570 had probably waited at Yelverton for an Up service to arrive (given the smoke still issuing from the tunnel in the background from the latter's passage), and has now been signalled for the next leg to Horrabridge. This engine arrived at Laira shed from Worcester in 1928, and was at Millbay shed in January 1930, around which time this photograph was probably taken. She moved on from Laira to Neath in 1932, being withdrawn from South Wales in October 1935.   *Photos: G. N. Southerden and Dr. I. C. Allen*

Horrabridge station in the pre-Great War period, with the wide track spacing divulging its broad gauge origins. Between August 1883 and May 1885, this station served as the junction for the Princetown branch, until relieved of that function by Yelverton. The track at that time was of mixed gauge, the 'standard' element of which was provided to accommodate LSWR trains between Exeter and Plymouth (via Lydford), and the 'narrow' gauge Princetown branch service would also have made use of that facility. Horrabridge was provided with passenger and goods amenities, and continued to handle the majority of freight traffic for the Princetown branch into the 'fifties. In this view a 4–4–0 engine, probably a '3521' class rebuild, is approaching the station with a Plymouth-bound train consisting of Composites and Thirds sandwiched between six-wheel Brake Vans, a typical formation of the period.   *Lens of Sutton*

another 'mixed' service, a peculiarity of the branch being that there were no such trains in the other direction. Except on Wednesdays and Saturdays, the last evening train from Millbay was at 9.25 p.m., returning from Tavistock at 10.30 p.m. However, on those two days the departure was not until 10.55 p.m. from Millbay, with the return working leaving Tavistock at 11.55 p.m. and arriving back at Millbay at the somewhat unearthly hour of 12.40 a.m.! The normal weekday last train from Tavistock at 10.30 p.m. was a considerable improvement on 1877 when there were no trains after 6.31 p.m.; the service of nine trains daily compared very favourably with the five of 1877.

In the years leading up to the First World War, the service had again expanded. Launceston still had its four regular trains in each direction (with a fifth on Wednesdays and Saturdays), formed of 6-wheel stock with a Van, two Thirds, two Composites and a Brake Third specified. One branch set resided at Launceston, the other at Plymouth.

In addition, Tavistock received and despatched seven services (eight Wednesdays and Saturdays only), five of which (six WSO) were of 6-wheel stock (Van, Third, Compo, Compo, Third [8-wheel], Van), the other two being steam railmotors. Furthermore, Yelverton had two trips, both railmotors (one of which ran WSO). During 1911, auto-trains worked two of the four 'motor' services.

There were three branch goods services, from Laira Junction to Tavistock, Lydford, and Launceston respectively, with the balancing return trips.

Sunday services saw some variations, ranging from two return trips to Yelverton, one to Lydford and one to Launceston (6/8-wheel stock), to three trips for Yelverton (auto-trains) and three to Tavistock (2 auto-trains, 1 passenger). There were two goods trains in each direction in 1914.

Early post-Great War services settled down to four Launceston and six Tavistock trips each way, with two additional Wednesday and Saturday trips (one of which was auto-train-worked). Branch freights ran to Tavistock and to Launceston, again mounted from Laira Junction. On Sundays there were three return trips to Tavistock, and one to Yelverton.

In 1934 there were still only four trains daily between Plymouth and Launceston, but Tavistock now had no less than thirteen trains daily and an additional train on Saturdays; six of the Tavistock trains were railmotor workings. Plymbridge Platform, Shaugh Bridge Platform, and Whitchurch Down Platform had all been opened between 1906 and 1908, whilst Clearbrook and Liddaton were opened during the inter-war period. The difference between a 'platform' and a 'halt' does not appear to have been very clear (Burrator Platform, on the neighbouring Princetown branch, having begun life as Burrator Halt!). The last weekday train from Millbay to Launceston was now at 6.10 p.m. (6.50 p.m. in 1902 and 8.00 p.m. in 1877), but the last train still left Launceston at 6.25 p.m. (On Saturdays these times were 9.05 p.m. and 9.16 p.m. respectively.) Tavistock passengers, for many years more favoured than those for Launceston, could now leave Plymouth as late as 11.00 p.m. on each weeknight, the last train back

Probably deputizing for the usual '64XX', 2–6–2T No. 4409 is shown here at the spacious Tavistock station with an Up (non-auto) train. Tavistock was the usual destination for auto-trains on this line, the Launceston services normally being provided with compartment stock.

Lens of Sutton

Coryton station was situated eight miles to the east of Launceston, adjacent to the River Lyd, and a mile to the west of the village it served. The station was provided with a goods loop siding at its west end, controlled by a ground frame; a loading bank was provided on this siding. This view shows '45XX' class 2-6-2T No. 4555 entering the station with a Launceston to Plymouth (North Road) train on 23rd June 1962, just six months before passenger services were withdrawn on the line.   *R. C. Riley*

leaving Tavistock at 11.58 p.m. Launceston had lost its Sunday trains, but Tavistock still had three auto-trains in each direction; another two (one auto, one passenger) ran between Plymouth and Yelverton, whilst a further two ran to the same destination when required; the Princetown branch now had no service on Sundays.

Branch goods services in 1934/5 had again expanded to three in each direction, leaving Laira Junction at 5.45 a.m. (for Tavistock), 8.00 a.m. (for Horrabridge) and 9.32 a.m. (for Launceston).

Passenger stock on the branch during the mid/late 'thirties consisted of a mixture of 'E' sets (Brake Compo, Lavatory Third, Van Third) and 'B' sets (Brake Compo, Brake Compo), whilst the auto-trains conveyed two trailers.

With the outbreak of World War II, Tavistock lost three of its nine return services, leaving three auto and three passenger trips; Launceston retained its four trains in each direction. On Sundays, the branch service was reduced to three auto-trains in each direction as far as Tavistock.

During the winter of 1946/7, Launceston again retained its four immutable trains, with the fifth running on Saturday nights. Tavistock maintained its wartime quota of six, with an extra Saturday service. The 'Saturdays only' late night trains to and from Launceston were also operated on 'Wednesdays only' to and from Tavistock, and as such could be operated by one set of coaches. The three pre-war goods services remained.

The usual 4-4-0 and 2-4-0 saddle tanks worked on the branch in broad gauge days, *Melling* and *Ostrich* being shedded

Launceston station building, photographed shortly after closure to passengers, c.1963; the line had served the local community for 97 years, and the site survived into its century as a freight-only complex operated by the adjacent Southern Region line. The station was provided with a substantial goods shed, whilst the locomotive facilities comprised a 100ft single track shed (which could comfortably hold a pair of '45XX' class engines), water tank, coal stage, sand-drying bin, and a 45ft turntable.   *R. S. Carpenter*

at Launceston in 1890. Following the gauge conversion in 1892, 0-4-4 Ts of the '3521' class were responsible for the services, with 0-6-0 STs on the goods turns. The turntable at Launceston was replaced by one of larger diameter in 1899, apparently to allow tender engines to be used, as the '3501' class 2-4-0s and the '3521' class rebuilt as 4-4-0s were used during the first decade of this century.

A view of Yelverton station, looking south towards Plymouth, taken a few years before the Great War, with a '44XX' class 2—6—2T in the branch platform. The station signal box was situated at the south end of the Down platform, and can just be seen at the right-hand end of the footbridge. Beyond the 'box was a refuge siding, having the capacity of an engine, 25 wagons and a brake van. The main platform loops were 720ft in length, capable of holding around 12 coaches (or a 36-wagon goods train), whilst the platforms themselves could accommodate six or seven vehicles.

L & GRP, cty. David & Charles

There was no run-round loop on the branch line at Yelverton station, engines reaching the opposite end of their train with the assistance of gravity. After the passengers had left the coaches, the empty vehicles were propelled towards Princetown until they were well clear of the point leading to the turntable siding (seen in the foreground). The brake was then screwed down on the coaches, the engine uncoupled and moved into the turntable siding (as seen in the photograph). The points were then reset for the branch and, under the control of the branch guard, the coaches were allowed to run down the gradient into the branch platform, clear of the turntable siding point. The point at the far end of the branch platform was set for the dead-end siding, to protect the main line in the event of a misjudgement! The engine would then back out of the turntable siding onto its train in readiness for departure.   *Lens of Sutton*

During 1902, '3201' ('Stella') Class engine No.3512 was at Plymouth, together with '3521' Class Nos.3535, 3537, 3555 and 3559, whilst 3528, 3543, 3554 and 3555 (again) of the same class spent periods at Launceston shed in the same year.

By 1914, the locomotive power on the line had changed considerably; during that year, small 2–6–2 tanks of the 44XX Class were at Launceston (Nos.4402, 4405 and 4410), alternating with duties at Kingsbridge, and were 'rubbing shoulders' with 'Duke' 4–4–os Nos.3261 *St. Germans*, 3262 *St. Ives*, 3282 *Chepstow Castle* and 3287 *Mercury* variously.

In the same year, the Lydford goods was rostered for an 0–6–0 tank, and the Launceston for a 2–6–2 tank (a 44XX, or perhaps Laira's single 45XX, No.4530). The Launceston could convey 37 wagons to Yelverton (with assistance), 40 on to Horrabridge, 30 to Lydford, and 40 beyond.

After the First World War, 45XX class engines gradually took over the services, with the auto-trains securely in the hands of eight of the '1076' ('Buffalo') Class 0–6–0 tanks. From 1932, the latter were displaced by the new 64XX Class auto-tanks, with Nos.6406–09 arriving at Laira during that year.

Closely associated with the Launceston branch was the steeply graded and sharply curved line climbing from Yelverton to Princetown, which was opened as a *standard gauge* branch in 1883. The GWR had been considering building such a railway when the Plymouth & Dartmoor Company offered their line in return for shares in what became the Princetown Railway Company. Authorised in 1819, the Plymouth & Dartmoor ran from Laira to Princetown via Dousland; passengers were carried, and large quantities of granite were brought

The station approach road ran southwards from the south-western outskirts of the village.   *Collection P. Karau*

down from the Dartmoor quarries, all handled by horses. The lower course of the line had already been utilised by the SDR in constructing the Sutton Harbour branch many years previously.

The new line was just over 10 miles long and ran from a point just south of Roborough Tunnel to a new terminus at Princetown, with an intermediate station at Dousland, signal boxes being provided at both stations. The single line was built almost entirely on the course of the old P & DR. Worked by the GWR, it was opened to traffic on 11th August 1883, and all trains ran to and from Horrabridge; the line had previously been 'mixed' for the benefit of the LSWR. This arrangement

A Princetown train waiting at the branch platform in Yelverton station during 1948 behind '44XX' class 2—6—2T No. 4402. This engine had, in effect, been the 'branch engine' since 1931, and remained so more or less until its withdrawal in December 1949, the first of its class to go. The small 23ft 6in diameter turntable can be seen beyond the inspection pit, a unit designed for use with the 0—6—0 and 0—4—2 tanks which had operated the line in the early days. With a wheelbase of 26ft 6in, the '44XX' engines could not be turned on either this table or the similar unit at Princetown. The turntables were useful, however, to turn the 0—6—0T and snowplough from Laira shed during really bad weather.

R. J. Doran

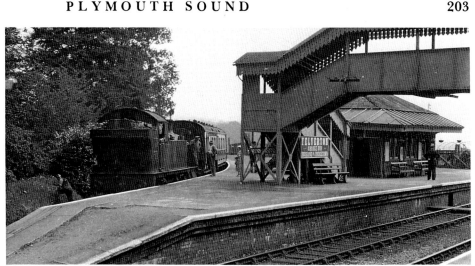

A 45XX alongside the branch platform prior to propelling the stock back along the branch to effect the run-round procedure.
Lens of Sutton

continued until a new station was opened at Yelverton on 1st May 1885.

An engine shed was provided at Princetown for the branch locomotives, and initially these were two small 0–6–0 side tanks inherited by the GWR from the Llynvi & Ogmore Railway. Nos.919 and 923 were the surviving members of a class of five engines built in 1865 by Sharp, Stewart & Co. No.923 was withdrawn in June 1888 and No.919 exactly four years later. They were replaced by '517' class 0–4–2 Ts and '850' class 0–6–0 STs, though how the little 0–4–2 Ts were expected to be able to cope with such gradients is a mystery! Nos.561 and 563 were employed during the 1890s, together with Nos.990 and 992 of the '850' class, one of the latter engines being derailed during the great blizzard of 1891. Turntables were provided

No. 4410 alongside the branch platform with a Princetown-bound train in the early 'fifties. This engine had a long association with the branch, first being allocated to Princetown in December 1906. The station building was a rather curious five-sided design, situated in the fork between the Up main and branch lines. On occasions, through coaches would be worked between Plymouth and Princetown, and this would involve much manoeuvring by the branch train. The through vehicle would be left at the Down platform by a Tavistock or Launceston-bound train; having 'run round', the branch train would reverse out onto the Up main, then run forward towards Plymouth until clear of the loop. It would then reverse onto the through vehicle sitting at the platform on the Down main, couple up, and reverse again towards the tunnel until clear of the northern end of the loop. The train would then run forward on the Up main, and subsequently onto the branch, having used nearly every function of the lever frame.
R. J. Doran

Yelverton station on 20th August 1954, with '45XX' Class 2—6—2T No. 4542 on a Launceston train at the Down platform. This engine was allocated when new (27th November 1914) to Newton Abbot, spending many years working on (and allocated to) the Kingswear branch. During the grouping period, No. 4542 was allocated to various sheds between Minehead and St. Blazey, remaining mostly in the Plymouth area during nationalisation.

H. C. Casserley

Yelverton, looking south towards Plymouth on 23rd September 1948. The rear end of a Launceston-bound service is seen at the Down platform, the coach being a non-corridor Van Third. The siding beyond the 'box was occasionally used to house the odd goods vehicle, although its designated use was that of a refuge siding. *L. E. Copeland*

Collett 0—4—2T No. 1434 accelerating down the gradient towards Plymouth with an auto service during the late 'fifties. These engines were latecomers to the branch, not arriving in the area until around 1954. *Roye England*

at both Princetown and Yelverton, being of 23 ft 6 in diameter. Their purpose was not to permit the branch engines to be turned at the end of each journey (which might have been highly desirable when it is remembered that they all had open cabs!), but in connection with the turning of the engine employed for snow clearing during the winter months, when one of the '850' or '1901' classes was so employed.

In later years the branch became famous for the regular use of two of the small-wheeled 2–6–2 Ts of the '4400' class, which were sub-shedded at Princetown. They were fitted with a special device to provide a supply of water on the flanges of the front coupled wheels, in an attempt to reduce the wear encountered on the sharp curves which abounded on the line.

The branch service was always shown in the public time-tables as being part of the Tavistock and Launceston service, the whole being headed 'Plymouth, Princetown, Tavistock and Launceston'. In 1902 there were four trains in each direction, with a fifth at midday on Saturdays. The last departure from Princetown was at 6.50 p.m., that from Yelverton being at 7.42 p.m. The maximum speed limit of 20 mph in each direction resulted in the Up and Down times being almost identical – between 33 and 36 minutes – despite the differences in effort required. There was also a late afternoon goods trip from Princetown (4.00 p.m.) to Horrabridge, arriving back at the

Churchward 2–6–2T No. 4410 entering Dousland with a Yelverton to Princetown train c.1953. By this time, the single coach sufficed for most trains, being strengthened by a second vehicle when necessary.
R. C. Riley

A mixed train leaving Dousland station for Yelverton behind the inevitable '44XX' class 2—6—2T No. 4410 on 5th July 1955.

R. J. Doran

A view of Dousland station, showing the only intermediate signal box on the branch. This structure replaced the function of the older cabin, situated near to the level crossing.

Lens of Sutton

Dousland, looking east towards Princetown. The line turned sharply southwards after this crossing, beginning its tortuous climb onto the moor towards Princetown, taking a nine mile route to cover the remaining five (direct) miles to the terminus, climbing some 800ft in the process.

Derek Clayton

'44XX' class 2—6—2T No. 4410 with a mixed train approaching Burrator and Sheepstor Halt, against a backdrop of typical Dartmoor scenery, in the mid-'fifties. Having skirted the southern edge of Yennadon Down, the line turned northwards towards Burrator Reservoir and the halt, just 1¼ miles from Dousland.

R. C. Riley

Burrator and Sheepstor, opened in 1924, with No. 4410 pausing at the platform with its mixed train. Burrator Reservoir, behind the train, supplied most of Plymouth's water, and provided the passenger with yet another breathtaking view on this line of contrasts. The rocky crags of Leather Tor can be seen on the skyline above the engine.

R. J. Doran

No. 4410 climbing away from Burrator with her train in July 1955, having about thirty minutes journey time ahead of her to Princetown, 7½ miles distant. The line continued northwards to pass to the left of Peck Hill (1312ft AMSL), seen in the centre of the photograph with the aerial of Sharpitor Wireless Station visible immediately beyond it.

R. J. Doran

THE PRINCETOWN RAILWAY & INGRA TOR 1586

Just over three miles beyond Burrator, the railway skirted the outcrop at Ingra Tor, at about 1000ft AMSL. Here a '44XX' class engine is pictured rounding the Tor during the early 'twenties (well before the adjacent halt was constructed) on a Yelverton-bound service, showing the bleak aspect of this portion of the line. Eight-wheel stock was used from the earliest days of the branch, although there are indications that 4-wheel coaches were also utilised; due to the sharp curvature encountered on the line, six-wheel stock was prohibited.

Chapman & Son

'44XX' class tank No. 4410 leaving Ingra Tor Halt with a train for Princetown on 5th July 1955. The headcode carried signified a light engine, or in certain circumstances a branch passenger train, but this may have been laziness (!) as other photographs taken of this service on the same day clearly show the conventional 'B' class code (lamp at chimney) being carried. No. 4410 was a much-travelled engine within the Newton Division, being allocated variously to Penzance, Helston, St. Ives, Newquay, St. Blazey, Moorswater, Millbay, Launceston, Kingsbridge, Newton and Exeter sheds in addition to Laira and Princetown. She was withdrawn from service in September 1955, just two months after this photograph was taken. To the right, the wooded valley of the River Walkham provides relief to the sparse moorland, whilst the town of Tavistock lay some four miles beyond.

R. C. Riley

A misty day on the moor, this photograph was taken from a mixed train as it negotiated the curves near Swell Tor, about three miles out from Princetown. At this point, the railway made a major detour around King Tor, running for over two miles in order to get ¼ mile closer to Princetown.

H. C. Casserley

King Tor Halt, with an Up train coasting down the gradient in 1955; the engine is No. 4410 again. This station was opened in April 1928 to accommodate walkers on the moor, as essentially were the other two halts between Dousland and Princetown. This view looks south, with the mast of Sharpitor WT station visible on the skyline, just two miles away.

R. J. Doran

No. 4410 at King Tor Halt during 1955, with Princetown just 1½ miles ahead of her. The engine was fitted with a flange lubricating system, using a 'coolant' fluid force-fed by steam pressure onto the outer rail of a sharp curve, being actuated by the 'misalignment' of the leading pony truck. The reservoir for the fluid can be seen on the footplate of No. 4410, to the right of the smokebox. It was the practice on the Princetown branch to run the engine's chimney towards Princetown, so that the crown of the firebox would be covered by water on the successive steep gradients. Apart from one section between Lowry Road (a mile to the north of Burrator) and Ingra Tor, the line was in continuous ascent from Yelverton to Princetown, with gradients between 1 in 40 and 1 in 55 being commonplace; operating on this line required great skill on the part of the engine crew.   *R. J. Doran*

terminus at 6.25 p.m., in time for the final return passenger trip of the day. There was no intermediate crossing place on the branch.

Although there was a service on Sundays, this consisted of just one train in each direction, and was a through working from Millbay (dep. 2.00 p.m.) which arrived in Princetown at 3.10 p.m., after reversal at Yelverton. The return working left Princetown at 5.00 p.m. and arrived back in Millbay at 6.15 p.m. This was the only such through working, and the only regular working over the branch by an engine and crew from Millbay. This Sunday service continued until the 1920s, at least during the summer months (though in 1901 it was 'all the year round'). In 1927–28 it commenced from Millbay at 10.17 a.m., arriving in Princetown at 11.47 a.m. and then returned to Millbay (arr. 1.43 p.m.); leaving again at 2.27 p.m., Princetown was reached at 3.57 p.m. The train then made a return trip to Yelverton, where it connected with an auto-train which ran from Millbay to Yelverton and back, finally leaving Princetown at 7.25 p.m. and arriving back at Millbay at 8.49 p.m.

The only goods working in 1927 was on alternate days (Mondays, Wednesdays and Fridays), leaving Princetown at

12.55 p.m. and running to Horrabridge (arr. 2.12 p.m.). Returning as a Goods to Elverton, it then became the daily 2.50 p.m. mixed train to Princetown. On other days, a mixed train left Princetown at 12.20 p.m. but ran only as far as Yelverton. The first train from Yelverton (dep. 8.36 a.m.) was also 'mixed'.

In 1934/5, there were five trains in each direction. In the Up direction, the 12.14 p.m. departure from Princetown was mixed (Tuesdays, Thursdays and Saturdays) whilst on the other three days of the week, it became a 12.55 p.m. (goods) departure. Two of the five Down trains were also mixed. On Saturdays, an 8.00 p.m. departure from Princetown connected with the 8.30 p.m. Tavistock to Plymouth auto, whilst the branch departure from Yelverton at 9.47 p.m. catered for passengers off the 9.05 p.m. Plymouth service. Two additional stops on the journey, at Burrator Halt and King Tor Halt, increased the overall time to between 33 and 40 minutes, although the first down 'mixed' train took 53!

The timetables advised passengers that 'Trains call at Burrator Halt during the hours of daylight only'; whether this was because would-be passengers would be unlikely to find that halt after dark or the engine driver unable to see it in time to

A '44XX' and its one-coach train climbing away from King Tor Halt on the last leg of the journey to Princetown (c.1955), with the gradient (about 1 in 50) clearly discernible. The line at this point was at about 1250ft AMSL, with just over 100ft more to climb in the last 1½ miles of the branch. The PW hut to the left was the last before Princetown; they were spaced at intervals of about a mile along the length of the line.   *R. J. Doran*

An **Edwardian view of Princetown**, looking south-eastwards, affording a rare glimpse of the station's carriage shed (extreme right-hand edge of photograph).   *Collection R. S. Carpenter*

The station throat, Princetown, with No. 4410 arriving with a mixed service during July 1955; the train has just entered the only significant level section of the line. The desolate nature of the moor may be gathered from this picture, and it doesn't take much to imagine the difficulties facing a would-be escaper from the nearby prison! During the winter period, only the first Up train of the day, and the two evening departures from Yelverton carried any real number of passengers, and the services were the subject of regular assessments; the findings invariably called for a reduction in the number of trains. However, the 'lifeline' aspect of the services was clearly more important than the financial considerations, and the timetable altered little up to closure.
R. C. Riley

Princetown, viewed probably in the mid-'thirties, showing all the usual facilities provided at terminal stations. The engine shed is situated on the extreme right, with the siding serving the 23ft 6in turntable leading from it; the table was mainly used by Laira shed's '850' class 0—6—0Ts sent to the line on snow clearance duties. Originally, Princetown possessed a carriage shed at the far end of the platform line; this is just visible in the picture on the facing page but it was removed around 1930.
S. R. Loxton

Plymouth (Millbay) station on 24th May 1936, with a Saltash autotrain about to depart from Platform 2. At this time, the daily suburban services in the Plymouth area were operated by four autotrains, one of which was stationed at Millbay. Local trains to Truro and Penzance, and to Newton and Exeter, were formed of 'conventional' stock, as were the Launceston-bound services. The Yealmpton trains, latterly auto-operated, were withdrawn in 1931 and replaced by a 'bus service; however, a late afternoon train (seemingly unadvertised) did run during the summer months in the late 'thirties. The autotrain service to Yealmpton was reinstated in November 1941, running from the Southern Railway's Friary station.
G. N. Southerden

stop, was not explained! King Tor Halt was opened to serve a group of quarrymen's cottages, and there was a siding into a quarry. A third halt, at Ingra Tor, was opened on 2nd March 1936, becoming famous for its warning about the danger of snakes!

In 1947 there were five trains each way, the first and last departures from Princetown being at 7.35 a.m. and 6.00 p.m., and those from Yelverton at 8.36 a.m. and 7.00 p.m. respectively. The working arrangements were virtually identical to those in force during 1934/5, although the 'Saturdays Only' trains no longer ran.

The South Hams remained without railways for much longer than other areas of South Devon. The Kingsbridge branch was not opened until December 1894, to be followed within five years by the opening of a branch, a few miles to the west, to Yealmpton. This was a single-track line from Plymstock, on the LSWR Turnchapel branch, over which the GWR had running powers from Cattewater Junction. A line from Mount Gould Junction near Laira to Cattewater Junction had been opened on 17th January 1898, and enabled GWR trains for Yealmpton to run direct to Plymstock.

The opening, on 17th January 1898, was of the usual 'brass bands and bun fight' description, though a unique feature was the presence of a 'Duke' class 4–4–0 specially renamed *Lady Morley* for the occasion. This was not typical of the motive power provided; '517' class 0–4–2 T No.218 was the usual engine for the first few years, until steam rail motors took over

Plymstock station was situated on the north-western outskirts of the village, four miles from Millbay, on the Yealmpton branch. This view shows the station, looking east, at around the end of the Great War; a Yealmpton to Millbay train is drawing into the platform, with perhaps one of Laira's auto-fitted '2021' class 0–6–0 tanks in charge of the two trailers. The line to the right is the LSWR branch to Turnchapel, the latter just a mile away to the south.
Lens of Sutton

the workings in 1905. Proposals for extension to Modbury or beyond, and rumours of such proposals, were in circulation for some years after the branch was opened, but traffic was never very heavy, hence the substitution of the rail motor for the branch train. Following the introduction of the rail motors, Mount Gould and Tothill Halt was opened in October 1905, only to be closed on 1st February 1918.

Billacombe, one mile to the east of Plymstock station, stood immediately to the north of Plymstock village, and was perhaps a more convenient station for the latter. However, it did not enjoy so intensive a train service as the junction did, with its frequent LSW trains to Friary in addition to the Yealmpton services. This photograph was taken on 7th June 1930 from the road bridge, looking east towards Yealmpton; the lines to the right served the small goods yard.

G. N. Southerden

The intermediate stations were at Billacombe, Brixton Road and Steer Point, the latter station having a siding serving the South Hams Brickworks. Crossing loops were provided at Billacombe and Brixton Road, the latter station and Yealmpton having signal boxes. The Brixton Road box was closed around 1918, never really having been justified. All four stations were provided with a goods shed and cattle pens, and each had only a single platform. Trains also stopped at Lucas Terrace Halt (opened in October 1905) on the LSWR's branch, and at Plymstock, where the GWR used a separate platform.

In 1902 there were six trains in each direction, with the last evening train leaving Plymouth at 7.05 p.m. and returning from Yealmpton at 7.55 p.m. A goods train also ran, leaving Laira Yard at 8.10 a.m., crossing the first Plymouth-bound passenger service at Plymstock. It remained at Yealmpton

A mile down the Yealmpton branch from Billacombe was the small station of Elburton Cross, the summit of the 2½ mile climb from Cattewater Junction. This station served the village of Elburton, immediately to the east of Plymstock; with the LSWR providing facilities at Oreston, on the Turnchapel branch, Plymstock and its environs were served by no less than four stations. This picture shows the morning Laira to Yealmpton pick-up goods passing Elburton Cross at around 10.50 a.m. on the morning of Saturday, 7th June 1930, behind one of Laira's pannier tanks, possibly a member of the '850' or '1854' classes, several of which were resident at this time.

G. N. Southerden

Having skirted around Plymstock, the branch turned south, passing midway between Elburton and the village of Brixton; the bridge carrying the road between those two villages can be seen immediately beyond the station which, in true Great Western fashion, was called Brixton Road! It was situated a mere three-quarters of a mile from Elburton Cross station, although it was considerably more substantial than the latter, with passenger and goods facilities constructed of stone. The photograph, looking towards Billacombe and Plymouth, was taken on 7th June 1930.   *G. N. Southerden*

Brixton Road, looking north towards Billacombe, on Saturday, 7th June 1930. Branch trains were normally arranged so as to cross at Plymstock (or to the west), although it was permissible in later years to cross a passenger and a goods train at Brixham Road 'when absolutely necessary'; in that event, the passenger train would, of course, take the running (platform) line, whilst the goods would occupy the loop. It was also permitted to cross two goods trains at the same location. The two-road goods yard can be seen to the right, with its attractive stone-built goods shed. There was a signal box here for a short period before and during the Great War; it was situated at the southern end of the station platform but was replaced by the two ground frames controlling the loop and access to the goods yard, one of which was accommodated in the small timber structure shown here in the foreground.   *G. N. Southerden*

Continuing southwards from Brixton Road, the line followed the east bank of Cofflete Creek towards Steer Point, where it turned eastwards for Yealmpton. The station at Steer Point was situated about a quarter of a mile to the north of the point itself and, as seen in the photograph, consisted of a single running line, with a goods shed loop to the east. The two wagons on the right of the picture are on a siding which ran behind the station to the South Hams Brickworks. In this view a steam railmotor and trailer are leaving the station for Yealmpton, c.1908. At the peak of passenger services in the years before the Great War, Laira had six SRMs plus a number of auto-train sets, with the daily suburban services requiring four of the former and three of the latter. Examples of both forms were to be seen on the Yealmpton branch during that period.

Lens of Sutton

'1076' class 0–6–0PT No. 1252 propelling a pair of autocoaches on a Millbay to Yealmpton service on Tuesday, 8th July 1924. The train is about three-quarters of a mile away from the terminus, and is running along the northern bank of the River Yealm, which it will shortly cross. No. 1252 arrived at Laira shed during the Great War (possibly 1917, having been fitted for auto-working in that year), and remained there until her withdrawal in 1932.

H. C. Casserley

during the arrival and departure of the passenger train, and left for Laira at 10.30 a.m. Yealmpton was the only branch terminus not provided with an engine shed. The early evening final departure cannot have contributed to the prospect of any great success for the branch, which was the only line in Devon to lose its passenger service during the lifetime of the GWR. There was no service on Sundays at this time, and the absence of such a service on both of the South Hams branches was probably due to their late dates of opening, by which time it had become evident that Sunday services on such branches were not generally economic.

By 1911, the service had expanded to nine trains in each direction, worked by a two-trailer auto-train on Mondays to Fridays, and shared by a steam railmotor and trailer (three return trips) and an auto-train (four trailers) on Saturdays. The latter also ran an additional late-night trip on Saturdays. On Sundays, the auto-train ran four return services; by 1914 this service had been reduced to three.

In the summer of 1922, there were seven return trips, with an additional late-night service on Saturdays; the goods train now ran on Mondays, Wednesdays and Fridays only. The Sunday service consisted of three return trips. All passenger services were again 'motor' operated.

The passenger service was withdrawn in 1931, and the 1932 timetables contained the statement 'A Road Motor Service is operated by the Western National Omnibus Company'. The

Yealmpton station throat on 7th June 1930, looking towards Plymouth. Although a terminus, Yealmpton had the design of a through station, no doubt with the possible extension to Modbury in mind. It was situated on the south bank of the Yealm, opposite the main part of the town, and crossed the river on the way to Plymouth about half a mile to the west of the station. *G. N. Southerden*

'Buffalo' ('1076') class 0–6–0PT No. 738 at Yealmpton station with an auto for Millbay on Saturday, 7th June 1930. This engine, built as a saddle tank in 1873, spent part of its earlier life in South Wales, before moving to Paddington in the early years of the century; she remained in London until 1923, having been fitted with panniers in 1917. In 1923, No. 738 was fitted for auto working and transferred to Laira shed. Her duties in the area involved the working of main line suburban auto services, with trips to Tavistock and to Yealmpton included. The class were also occasionally used for shunting and light goods turns. No. 738 was rebuilt with an extended smokebox, and rectangular cab windows in place of the usual round spectacles. She was transferred back to South Wales in 1932, ending her days at Swansea in 1936.

G. N. Southerden

times of the buses to and from Plymouth were also given, showing that the service provided eighteen buses in each direction on weekdays, compared with the eight trains in 1927, and on Sundays twelve buses each way, compared with four trains, during the summer months only. Yealmpton could not be said to have been unduly deprived by the transfer from rail to road, especially as the road journey took eight minutes less! However, most unusually for such branches, the service was later restored. This took place on 3rd November 1941, when the combination of a severe petrol shortage and ever-increasing numbers of people moving out from bomb-damaged Plymouth meant that the bus service could no longer cope with the situation. The restored service ran to and from the Southern's Friary station and was worked by an auto-train. From 1942, this auto was in the charge of one of the large-wheeled auto-tanks of the 54XX class; No. 5412 was moved down to Laira from Taunton during that year, and remained in the Plymouth area until nationalisation. There were eight trains in each direction.

The 1946/7 service consisted of seven weekday trips each way, with a late-night Saturday trip in addition. The goods train left Laira Yard at 11.30 a.m., and returned from Yealmpton at 2.18 p.m. (3.55 p.m. on market days).

The final closure to passengers came on 5th October 1947. The timetables which came into use on the following day warned passengers 'SERVICE SUSPENDED. A frequent bus service is operated by the Western National Omnibus Company'. However, unlike the 1932 timetables, no bus times were shown, and passengers were advised 'For particulars, see local announcements'. The 'Plymouth Sound' was no longer that of the steam rail motor, or the auto-train with its tank engine indulging in the indecent gurgling noises peculiar to the GWR's 0–4–2 Ts, but the grinding of gears on a Western National Bristol 'K'.

No. 738's branch train on 7th June 1930 consisted of autotrailer No. 151, seen at the platform in Yealmpton station. This coach was a 1927 rebuild of steam railmotor No. 63, which itself was no stranger to the West Country, having spent periods both before and after the Great War at Penzance. Yealmpton signal box, the only one on the 6¾ mile branch from Plymstock, was closed at the cessation of passenger services in July 1930. Thereafter, a single goods train ran between Laira and Yealmpton, and the branch was worked by the 'one engine in steam' principle. After the re-introduction of passenger services in 1941, the branch was worked by Electric Train Token; the line finally closed in October 1947.

G. N. Southerden

The east end of Yealmpton, again photographed on 7th June 1930, looking for all the world like a through station. The loop was of a considerable length, and the arrangement of the track gives the impression that through trains to Modbury could be crossed here — yet the buffer stops were a hundred yards or so beyond the bridge. The goods yard, served by the line off to the right, was provided with five roads, one of which ran through a sizeable goods shed. The water column was positioned to serve engines on both the running and goods yard lines.
G. N. Southerden

An unidentified Milnes Daimler single deck car (Reg. AF139) pictured here in Station Road, Moretonhampstead c.1908. The 'bus is probably on the Chagford service, a run of four miles in each direction.

L & GRP, cty. David & Charles

CHAPTER NINE

BY ROAD AND
BY WATER

The advent of the motor bus may have signalled the 'end of the line' for rail services on some country branches, such as that to Yealmpton; but the GWR were among the first users of buses, their first service being between Helston and the Lizard, which began on Monday, 17th August 1903. Only a few months later, on 2nd May 1904, the first GWR bus service in Devon was introduced between Modbury and Yealmpton, no doubt helping to dispel the lingering rumours of the company's intentions to extend the Yealmpton branch to the former village. However, it was not the only bus service on that route, another being operated by Sir Tristram Eve and a local company, the South Hams Motor Carriers Ltd. The rival service did not last for very long, as the company was bought out by the GWR in 1905, this being one of the first 'take-overs' in the motor bus industry. The service was subsequently extended from Yealmpton into Plymouth, thus creating a most unusual situation in which a railway was in competition with itself!

The second route in Devon also created a similar situation when, in July 1904, the GWR commenced running buses between Torquay and Paignton on a route more or less parallel with the railway, but serving the developing district of Preston which had no station; it was significant that when this service was withdrawn in 1911, a halt was immediately opened at Preston!

The first vehicles on the Torquay and Paignton route were petrol-driven, consisting of a double-decker, which carried 18 inside and 20 on top, and a single-decker in the form of a wagonnette, with room on top for luggage, open sides with waterproof curtains, and longitudinal seats for 20 people. The service was half-hourly 'when both ran', the journey taking 22 minutes, with a fare of 4d. for the full journey. The two original buses were replaced later in the year with double-deckers, each with a 22 hp engine, and which were lit at night by acetylene gas. The GWR continued to run this service until trams began operating as far as Paignton in 1911.

Among the buses known to have been in service during this period were Milnes-Daimlers Nos.16, 20 and 21, 32 and 33, 52, 57 and 59, 68, 90 and 93, 114 and 115, the last two being ex-Paignton & District. Nos.20 and 21 were wagonnettes. Also in use was a solitary Straker Squire, No.80. Although all were granted licences by Torquay, they were garaged at Paignton.

ON THE WAY TO BIGBURY-ON-SEA. YEALMPTON STATION.

Yealmpton station saw two GWR road motor services running in connection with its trains. The first was a through service between Dartmouth, Kingsbridge and Plymouth (Millbay) via Modbury, whilst the second was a single car running from Bigbury-on-Sea and Modbury to Millbay. This view, probably taken in the years before the Great War, shows a road motor waiting in the station forecourt.
Lens of Sutton

Two months after the start of the Torquay and Paignton service, another was instigated from Plymouth to Crownhill and Roborough, in September 1904. The following year further developments took place in the Paignton and Totnes areas, with the opening of a service between these towns (which did not stifle all talk of the possible opening of a railway between them). On 9th April 1906 a service between Moretonhampstead and Chagford was inaugurated, again fulfilling earlier notions of an extension of the rail service. A much more adventurous affair was the service across Dartmoor to

more modern vehicles which were mostly of AEC manufacture. These vehicles were in a new livery of green, this colour being generally adopted for GWR passenger vehicles for several years, after which the original chocolate and cream was again introduced.

No further double-deckers were purchased, and some of the rural services had one-man operated buses, Burford 18-seaters, which also had pneumatic tyres, being the first GWR vehicles so fitted (no further solid tyres buses were introduced). They were followed by a series of Thornycroft 18-20 seaters, mostly

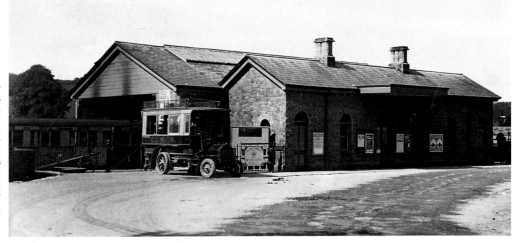

Moretonhampstead station, c.1910, with a motor bus (Reg. T399, possibly a Milnes Daimler) standing in the forecourt, again probably on the Chagford run. In addition, a charabanc tour between Bovey, Princetown and Tavistock also called at the station.

L & GRP
cty. David & Charles

Princetown, commenced in 1909; in this case, no one appears to have contemplated building a railway along that route!

Two vehicles for the services from Moretonhampstead were kept in a wooden garage close to the branch terminus. The Chagford service continued for many years, eventually being taken over by Devon General, and becoming part of the Newton Abbot to Okehampton route. Single-deckers were used, the larger rear wheels having solid tyres, while the smaller front wheels *may* have had pneumatic tyres. One bus used on the Chagford service was a Milnes Daimler, registered AF 139.

However, this was not the only bus service to Chagford; the LSWR had beaten their rivals by opening a service between Exeter, Queen Street station, and Chagford (via Whiddon Down) in 1905. For the next four years this service was maintained by two Clarkson steam buses (whose hill-climbing abilities and smoothness of running were superior to those of petrol-engined vehicles, though repairs were expensive). They were replaced in 1909 by Thornycroft petrol-engined vehicles.

In those days petrol was 4d. per gallon, but the most expensive single items on the early buses appear to have been the solid tyres, which cost £200 per set and worked out at 4d. per mile! This expense at one time threatened to cause abandonment of such services by the GWR. The railway colours of chocolate and cream were mainly used for livery, but there were some variations – some buses had red bonnets!

By 1912 the GWR bus fleet in the Plymouth area comprised six Milnes-Daimlers, three being garaged at Plymouth and three at Yealmpton. However, the Plymouth depot closed in 1916 owing to war-time petrol shortage and the consequent reduction of services (that to Roborough being abandoned). During the 1919-24 period the entire pre-war fleet, with the exception of some Maudslays acquired in 1913, was replaced by

one-man operated. Thus the GWR were among the pioneers of the now familiar OMO bus service.

The 1920s saw a rapid expansion of bus services in general, as the GWR and the newly-formed Southern found to their cost in Plymouth. GWR expansion in South Devon was concentrated in three areas: Bovey Tracey, Paignton and the South Hams. The acquisition of the Manor House Hotel at North Bovey was followed by the provision of a bus service from the station at Moretonhampstead. Among the first buses so employed was No.1613 (UV 4087, a Thornycroft FY BC), which was used for about a month in August/September 1929, to be followed by No.1661 (UV 916, a Guy OND with Duple bodywork) which took over the service on 6th September.

The Manor House was originally the country residence of the family founders of W. H. Smith & Co. and was of considerable splendour, including a lounge complete with minstrels' gallery, and a handsome carved stone fireplace resplendent with the carved coats of arms of Eton, Winchester and Harrow schools (really more suitable for the Southern Railway!). While these facts were not advertised, the GWR took good care to mention that there were 200 acres of grounds, an 18-hole golf course and a private trout stream (also that there were 10 miles of trout and salmon fishing in the River Teign), as well as hard and grass tennis courts, central heating and electric light, and also lock-up garages (and all in 1932!).

Other services which started from Bovey were to Haytor Rocks; Bovey–Becky Falls–Manaton; Bovey–Moretonhampstead–Princetown–Tavistock (this being a tour, with one trip daily each way on Charabanc Car No.14); Bovey–Haytor–Widdecombe–Grimspound–Becky Falls–Bovey (another tour on which a charabanc car was used). These local tours had been started before the war(!) and were resumed in 1920, at

A number of charabanc trips were mounted by the GWR from Bovey station, and four such vehicles are portrayed here in the forecourt, c.1925. On the left, bus No. 238 (Reg. T7692), an AEC 3½ ton car, is on the Haytor Rocks service; this beauty spot was situated four miles to the west of Bovey, and the trip involved a degree of hill-climbing! To the right of No. 238 is bus No. 857, a Burford 30 cwt (Reg. XY2110) on the Becky Falls and Manaton run, these were about five miles to the north-west of Bovey, and encountered the same sort of terrain as the adjacent Haytor route.

Collection Paul Karau

a time when there was a great increase in their popularity and availability in the West of England. They were followed in 1927 by 'Land Cruises', these lasting from 6 to 13 days, which were extended tours of areas such as Exmoor, Dartmoor, the Wye Valley, etc. Three 15-seat Thornycroft parlour coaches, the last word in luxury for that period, were used.

Paignton was another centre for GWR bus services, these including Paignton to Totnes (employing two buses), Paignton–Berry Pomeroy–Totnes, and Totnes–Berry Pomeroy–Brixham (this serving Churston station). There were about 35 buses allocated to Paignton in the late 1920s (including some at Kingswear). In 1929 the Paignton local services were purchased from Messrs Ashcroft and Kent.

The Plymouth to Roborough service was not resumed after the war, but the Modbury route was developed, and became a through Plymouth–Kingsbridge–Dartmouth service. Services in the South Hams were quite extensive: Dartmouth–Torcross–Stokenham–Frogmore–Kingsbridge (employing two buses), with an extension of the service through Modbury and Yealmpton to Plymouth (which was covered by only one bus). Another service worked by a single bus and terminating at Millbay station was Bigbury-on-Sea–Modbury–Yealmpton–Plymouth. There was competition on the Plymouth–Yealmpton–Newton Ferrers section from the Devon Motor Transport Co. until 1925, when an agreement was concluded with that company (and with Cornwall Motor Transport) which allocated routes and eliminated wasteful competition. Although certain GWR activities were discontinued in favour of Cornwall Motor Transport, it was the GWR services which continued in the South Hams.

Special market cars ran between Dartmouth, Halwell and Kingsbridge or Totnes. From Torcross there was another single bus service to Stokenham and East Portlemouth, while from Kingsbridge there radiated a number of similar services, to

The GWR provided garages for its road vehicles wherever possible, and such a structure is pictured here on the Yealmpton branch. *E. T. Day*

Hope Cove, to Thurlstone, to Loddiswell (Mondays, Wednesdays and Saturdays), to Frogmore and South Pool (Saturdays), to Salcombe and to Totnes. The latter service was extended on Sundays to run between Salcombe and Newton Abbot, there being no train service on the Kingsbridge branch, and as late as the 1940s a Western National bus ran from Totnes station to Salcombe on Sunday evenings. Although Kingsbridge had about 18 buses allocated to its garage (which included a small out-station at Salcombe), there appears to have been only one GWR bus allocated to Plymouth!

Railway type tickets were issued at first, but bell punch machines were later used. There were also books of tickets at 12½ per cent discount. Staff uniform consisted of leather cap, jerkin, waistcoat, breeches, gaiters and greatcoat. Although each garage was in the charge of a leading driver, the con-

Tendering on ocean liner traffic at Plymouth dated back to 1873, and by the 'thirties the Great Western had a quartet of vessels to carry out such work. *Sir Richard Grenville* was built by Earles of Hull and launched on 18th June 1931, being 170 ft long, 42 ft 6 in wide, with a draft of 11 ft 9 in. The promenade deck was usually kept clear for the carriage of mails, bullion, and other bulky items such as motor cars, whilst the passengers transferring were accommodated on the main deck, which had a large, fully-fitted saloon.   *R. C. Riley*

ductors were under the control of the station masters, and cash was paid into the booking office.

In 1928, after at last obtaining comprehensive road powers (there had always been some question of the legality of the railways' bus operations), the 'Big Four' decided to give up direct operation in favour of large-scale investment in major provincial bus companies. A large proportion of the GWR's services were concentrated in Devon and Cornwall, and in 1929

the Western National Omnibus Company Ltd was formed to amalgamate the GWR services with those of the National Omnibus & Transport Company Ltd. Although eminently suitable in the West of England, and not altogether inappropriate in the Trowbridge area, it was always somewhat strange to find Western National as the local bus company at Stroud in the Cotswolds! The railway employees engaged in bus operation were given the option of transfer to the new

Sir John Hawkins was the 'elder sister' of *Sir Richard Grenville*, being built earlier by the same engineering company, Earles of Hull. Whilst her primary duty, along with her sister ships, was the transfer of passengers and mail, etc., to and from visiting ocean liners, she was also in great demand for excursion traffic during the summer months. Regular sailings were made from Plymouth to neighbouring beauty spots such as Looe, Fowey, Salcombe, and Torquay. Whilst the other three tenders were acquired for Admiralty service in August 1939, *Sir John Hawkins* remained with the company at Plymouth. She was severely damaged in a bombing raid on Plymouth, and when repaired, she too 'joined up', in January 1941. All four had rejoined the Great Western by 1946.   *R. C. Riley*

Perhaps the most famous 'railway station without trains' was Dartmouth. Opened in 1889, the building was similar in general style to its counterpart across the river at Kingswear, to which it was connected by a ferry service. The station building survives to this day, although now used as a restaurant.
Lens of Sutton

company, retaining their railway rates and privileges, being termed 'loaned staff'; those who did so could always be recognised by the fact of their continuing membership of the National Union of Railwaymen!

Although seldom realised, after the grouping, the GWR were the nation's largest dock owners. Long before then, GWR interest in the Millbay Docks at Plymouth had resulted in considerable investment and development there. In their final state, Millbay Docks included an inner basin and an outer basin, as well as a graving dock. Nineteen grain sheds and fifteen transit sheds were situated on the quays, unloading being done by nine hydraulic cranes (the largest of which could lift 25 tons), three electric cranes and five smaller steam cranes.

The inner basin covered 13 acres, while the much larger outer harbour covered over 31 acres, the respective depths of water being 17 feet and 28 feet. The entrance to the inner basin was by means of an 80 ft wide entrance lock.

Several railway-owned vessels were employed in Millbay Docks, the most important, and the best known, being the tenders which ferried passengers and mails from the ocean liners anchored off Plymouth Sound. These were named after famous Devonshire 'Sea Dogs' of the Elizabethan era: *Sir Francis Drake* and *Sir Walter Raleigh*, the original vessels, were joined in 1936 by the new vessels built that year, *Sir John Hawkins* and *Sir Richard Grenville*. However, they were not the only vessels used for such work, and at the time of the 'racing' in 1904, passengers from across the Atlantic might have thought they had been landed at the wrong port when they saw that the

vessel on which they were ferried to the shore bore the name *Cheshire* and was registered in Liverpool!

An equally important, though perhaps less glamorous role was that performed by the vessel which maintained the ferry service between the stations at Kingswear and Dartmouth. For many years this service was operated by the SS *Dolphin*, obtained second-hand from the River Dart Steamboat Company for whom it had been built. The vessel was rather singular in appearance, as it had a bow at each end! Another unusual feature, not so apparent, was the provision of a drop rudder, enabling the vessel to steam ahead in either direction! A paddle steamer, she was fitted with a tall and slender funnel. Despite the 'reversible' design, there was only one bridge, and passenger comfort was ensured by a rather cramped deck cabin 'aft' of the main superstructure. It is thought that she was fitted with inclined compound engines. Captains Thorn and Gurney were successively in command, while the First Engineer was Frederick Roper, Edwin Roper being Second Engineer.

The highlight of her career was undoubtedly in 1902, when she carried His Majesty, King Edward VII and Queen Alexandra across the river to lay the foundation stone of the Royal Naval College at Dartmouth. Six years later, in 1908, the *Dolphin* made her last voyage across the Dart, having been replaced by a new vessel.

Her successor became known to many thousands of local people and to hundreds of thousands of holiday-makers, being the famous *Mew* (though her real name, which she carried, was *The Mew*). She was named after a well-known rock just off the estuary of the Dart. Built at Falmouth by Cox's, she had a boiler of GWR design, coal fired by two furnaces, which proved to be the least successful feature of the vessel. It appeared to have been designed by those who were better acquainted with locomotives than with ships, and was the exception to the rule that 'Swindon knew best'! The boiler supplied steam to two compound engines driving twin screws. She entered service on 20th May 1908. Successive captains were Boxhall, Brown, Palmer, Harris and Legge; in 1908 the First Engineer was Edwin Roper (promoted from Second Engineer on the *Dolphin*) and the Fireman was Fred Roper. The Roper family appear to have had a vested interest in the running of the ferry!

A much larger vessel, *The Mew* was licensed to carry 543 passengers, though it is doubtful if this figure was ever reached, except perhaps on one occasion in 1914, when a photograph was taken showing *The Mew* crowded from stem to stern with soldiers (believed to be the 7th Battalion of the London Regiment). Originally, there was an open bridge just forward of the tall and raked funnel, while the upper deck extended almost to the stern. However, in 1924 she was completely modernised in the local yards of Philip & Co., during which a funnel of much larger diameter was fitted, a raised and closed bridge replaced the original, and the rear portion of the top deck was removed. The reason for the latter alteration was to provide space on deck for the conveyance of vehicles, there being room for two lorries or four cars. GWR goods lorries were regularly ferried across from Kingswear to deliver consignments in Dartmouth.

The greatest adventure and moment of glory for *The Mew* came in 1940, when she steamed alone up the English Channel to Dover in a noble attempt to offer assistance at Dunkirk. In the event, she was not used as her draught was too great to allow her to get close to the beach, and she was reckoned too small to carry large numbers from off-shore. Another reason for her non-use was possibly the fact that the unaccustomed high speed and non-stop steaming up the Channel had resulted in her fire bars fusing together! A record of this 'run' with an analysis of horse-power exerted would surely have furnished an unusual, not to say unique, contribution to the annals of Great Western Steam!

The Mew returned to her accustomed duties, the less glamorous but nonetheless essential service, on the Dart, no doubt, after a much-needed operation on her grate! She remained on that service for many years afterwards – and for some years after the GWR itself had been sunk by enemy action. She sustained another extensive refit, again by Philip & Son, in 1948, and made her last voyage on 8th October 1954, when there was many a wet eye. It would be good to think that there may have been one of the Roper family there to 'see out' the end of steam on the ferry across the Dart – though, happily, not the end of steam on the Dartmouth & Torbay.

The Mew at the landing stage, Kingswear. Clearly the most famous of the Dart ferries, this vessel replaced the paddle steamer *Dolphin* in 1908. Built by Cox & Company of Falmouth, she was 90ft long, 22ft wide, with a draft of about 6ft when loaded. In the course of an average year, *The Mew* made 23,000 trips across the River Dart, carrying some half a million passengers and 8,000 vehicles. Her trips connected with the trains at Kingswear, and she sailed from Dartmouth fifteen minutes before a train was due to leave; passengers from the trains at Kingswear were usually in Dartmouth ten minutes after their arrival at the former.   *National Railway Museum, York*

APPENDIX A

WORKING TIMETABLES — MAIN LINE   1st October 1934 to 7th July 1935

These tables show the regular weekday services running on the South Devon section during the winter schedule of 1934/5. Additional passenger services ran on Saturdays (not shown), especially during the periods around the summer timetable (late June/early July; early October); however, *daily* trains which ran in those periods are included in these tables.

The times given are for arrival and departure; a single time placed centrally in the column indicates the *passing* of that train. They refer to the appropriate locality, i.e. Exeter station, or goods yard; Newton Abbot station, or Hackney yard; Plymouth North Road or Millbay stations, Tavistock Junction or Laira Junction yards. The traditional GWR manner of indicating a.m. (3.0) or p.m. (3/0) is used.

DOWN TRAINS

Class		Train			EXETER arr	dep	NEWTON ABBOT arr	dep	PLYMOUTH arr	dep	To	
C	10/55	Bristol	Goods		1.6	1.18	1.50		..	..		
C	9/10	Cardiff	Parcels		1.37	2.0	2.28	3.5	4.0	4.20	Penzance	8.20
A	10/10	Paddington	Postal		2.19	2.25	2.51	2.58	3.44	3.53	Penzance	6.21
A	9/50	Paddington	Passenger		2.46	2.58	3.26	3.37	4.30	4.40	Penzance	7.30
J	8/15	Swindon	Goods		5.2	5.35	6.25		..	..		
C	9/32	Old Oak Common	Goods		3.8		3.38	4.8	5.29		Penzance	10.15
C	10/10	Paddington	Goods		4.1		4.32	4.53	6.38	..		
A	12.50	Paddington	News		3.38		4.3		4.50	4.58	Penzance	8.0
A	1.40	Paddington	Passenger		4.42	4.49	5.15	5.19	6.8	6.14	Penzance	8.48
C	10/35	Paddington	Parcels		4.20	4.54	5.25	5.55	7.10	..		
E			Goods		..	..	..	5.25	7.50	..		
E	10/0	Avonmouth	Goods		5.42	6.0	6.42	7.50	10.19	..		
A	12.0 mn	Paddington	Passenger		5.19	5.30	6.8	6.20	7.22	7.40	Penzance	10.57
C	11/35	Paddington	Goods		6.0	6.15	6.55	..	..	..		
C	9/20	Oxley Sdgs	Goods		6.18	6.38	7.10	..	..	..		
J	2.25	Bristol	Goods		7.25		8.15	8.35	11.15	..		
K			Goods		..	..	..	6.30	..	..	Brent	
B			Auto		..	..	..	7.2	..	..	Totnes	
E	10/30	Reading	Goods		7.28	7.50	8.30	9.35	11.50	..		
B			Passenger		..	6.50	7.36	7.45	..	..	Kingswear	8.35
B			Passenger		..	..	..	7.49	8.57	..		
B			Passenger		..	..	..	8.25	9.37	..		
J	8/45	Cardiff	Goods		7.55	8.20	9.25	..	..	..		
B			Passenger		..	8.7	8.49	8.55	..	..	Paignton	9.17
A	2.35	Shrewsbury	Passenger		8.30	8.42	9.8	9.16	10.3	10.25	Penzance	1/19
B	9.0	Paignton	Passenger		..	..	9.22	9.30	10.40	..		
B			Passenger		..	9.10	9.48	9.53	..	..	Kingswear	10.40
K			Goods		..	9.0	2/5	..	..	..		
B			Passenger		..	9.20	10.2	10.7	..	..	Kingswear	10.52
B			Passenger		..	..	..	10.10	..	..	Totnes	
K			Goods		..	..	..	10.20	..	..	Ashburton	
J	11/15	Banbury	Goods		10.22	11.0	11.50	..	..	..		
B			Passenger		..	10.10	10.50	..	..	..		
K			Goods		..	..	..	11.5	..	..	Stoneycombe	
A	5.30	Paddington	Passenger		10.37	10.47	11.19	11.28	12/25	12/36	Penzance	3/40
K			Goods		..	..	..	11.40	..	..	Ivybridge	
B			Passenger		..	11.30	12/12	12/20	..	..	Goodrington	12/46
B			Passenger		..	..	..	12/20	1/30	..		
E	5.30	Pontypool Rd.	Goods		12/0	12/35	1/20	..	..	..		
B			Passenger		..	12/0	..	..	..	..	Dawlish Warren	12/24
A	9.50	Bathampton	Passenger		12/25	12/30	1/7	1/12	2/5	..		
A	9.0	Paddington	Passenger		12/35	12/42	1/21	1/27	..	..	Kingswear	2/16
A	10.30	Paddington	Passenger		1/21	1/25	1/49		2/34	2/41	Penzance	4/58
B			Passenger		..	1/32	2/5	2/12	3/25	..		
B			Passenger		..	2/0	2/42	..	..	..		
A	11.10	Paddington	Passenger		2/6	2/12	2/38	2/42	3/38	3/44	Penzance	6/35
A	11.25	Cardiff	Passenger		2/16	2/21	2/58	3/3	..	..	Goodrington	3/30
A	12/0 nn	Paddington	Passenger		2/49	2/55	3/19		..	..	Kingswear	4/6
A	10.40	Wolverhampton	Passenger		3/18	3/25	3/56	4/5	4/52	5/0	Penzance	7/34
B	3/15	Kingswear	Passenger		..	..	3/56	4/20	5/30	..		
K			Goods		..	..	..	4/20	8/30	..		
B			Passenger		..	3/45	4/29	4/35	..	..	Kingswear	5/31
A	10.32	Crewe	Passenger		4/27	4/33	5/7	5/13	6/12	..		
A	1/30	Paddington	Passenger		4/58	5/6	5/42	5/49	6/36	6/45	Penzance	9/31
B			Passenger		..	5/16	5/58	6/3	7/11	..		
J			Goods		..	..	..	6/15	8/34	12.40	St. Blazey	
A	10.30	Bradford	Passenger		5/42	5/47	6/22	6/28	..	..	Kingswear	7/19
B			Passenger		..	6/10	6/53	..	..	..		
A	3/30	Paddington	Passenger		6/36	6/42	7/12	7/17	8/4	8/12	Truro	9/55
B			Passenger		..	6/50	7/34	7/40	..	..	Kingswear	8/26
B			Passenger		..	..	..	7/40	8/48	..		
J			Goods		..	..	..	8/45	11/0	11/33	Truro	
J	5.15	Rogerstone	Loco coal		3/45	7/15	8/5	9/25	11/55	..		
B	6/15	Taunton	Passenger		7/23	7/50	8/34	8/40	..	..	Kingswear	9/30
A	4/30	Paddington	Passenger		8/34	8/41	9/15	9/20	10/20	..		
J	3/10	Bristol	Goods		8/25	8/45	9/35	10/20	1.5	..		
B			Passenger		..	9/10	9/55	10/5	..	..	Paignton	10/27
B	8/20	Taunton	Passenger		9/29	10/0	10/44	..	..	..		
E	4/7	Swindon	Goods		10/15	11/20	12.5	1.35	3.15	..		
A	6/30	Paddington	Passenger		10/47	10/52	11/24	11/30	12.37	..		
C	9/55	Bristol			12.4		12.35	1.10	2.41		Penzance	7.20
H	5/5	Severn T. Jct.	Goods		12.18		1.15	..	..	..		
J	7/40	Bristol	Goods		12.28	12.40	1.30	..	..	..		

UP TRAINS

Class	Train	PLYMOUTH arr	PLYMOUTH dep	NEWTON ABBOT arr	NEWTON ABBOT dep	EXETER arr	EXETER dep	To
C	2/50 Penzance Goods	8/45	9/43	11/2	11/40	12.12		Paddington 5.55
J		..	2/55	5/30	10/50	11/40	12.15	Bordesley Jct
A	9/0 Penzance Passenger	12.2	12.20	1.8	1.18	1.44	1.55	Paddington 7.10
C	6/30 Drump Lane Goods	10/13	11/0	12.20	12.50	1.25	2.0	Bristol 4.7
J	Goods	..	8/10	11/45	12.15	2.0	2.32	Bristol 6.23
J	Goods	..	..	..	2.15	3.5	3.35	Bristol 7.35
H	Goods	..	11/55	2.28	3.0	3.50	4.10	Reading
H	Goods	..	1.15	3.48	4.10	5.0		Avonmouth
K	Goods	..	..	..	4.45	8.20	..	
J	11/40 Truro Goods	2.25	3.0	4.46	5.20	6.10	6.40	Banbury Jct.
H	Empties	..	3.30	5.18	5.45	6.33		Bristol 10.26
J	Goods	..	4.5	6.11	6.42	7.30	..	
B	6.37 Kingswear Passenger	..	..	7.19	7.24	8.8	8.15	Avonmouth
B	7.25 Totnes Auto	..	..	7.40	7.55	..	..	Moretonhampstead
A	7.5 Kingswear Passenger	..	..	7.44	8.4	8.47	8.55	Swansea (High St)
J	Goods	..	4.30	8.10	..	..	..	
B	Passenger	..	7.25	8.34	8.39	9.23	..	
B	8.15 Kingswear Passenger	..	..	9.0	9.5	9.42	..	
A	Passenger	..	8.35	9.27		9.52	10.0	Paddington 1/15
A	Passenger	..	8.45	9.40	9.46	10.22	10.27	Crewe 4/10
A	9.0 Kingswear Passenger	..	..	9.48	9.56	10.32	10.39	Bradford
H	Goods	..	5.50	7.35	8.50	10.32		Severn T. Jct.
B	Passenger	..	9.25	10.34	10.44	11.27	..	
B	10.50 Totnes Passenger	..	..	11.5		..	..	
A	7.45 Penzance Passenger	10.21	10.30	11.19	11.28	12/4	12/12	Crewe 6/6
B	Passenger	..	..	..	11.40	12/23	..	
A	8.15 Penzance Passenger	11.16	11.23	12/15	..	..	..	
A	11.25 Kingswear Passenger	..	..	12/11	12/20	12/46	12/50	Paddington 3/42
K	12/20 Stoneycombe Goods	..	..	12/33	..	..	..	
B	Passenger	..	11.0	12/15	12/25	1/8	..	
A	9.0 Penzance Passenger	11.42	11.50	12/44	12/52	1/19	1/30	Paddington 4/27
A	10.0 Penzance Passenger	12/23	12/30	1/15		1/39	1/46	Paddington 4/45
B	12/23 Kingswear Passenger	..	..	1/7	1/20	2/8	..	
B	Passenger	..	12/30	1/39	..	..	..	
A	Passenger	..	1/0	1/51	1/57	2/23	2/30	Crewe 8/3
B	Passenger	..	..	..	2/3	2/43	..	
A	10.45 Penzance Passenger	1/32	1/40	2/25		2/50	3/0	Wolverhampton 7/47
B	2/0 Goodrington Passenger	..	..	2/25	2/30	3/13	..	
A	11.10 Penzance Passenger	1/52	2/0	2/46	2/55	3/21	3/27	Paddington 6/50
B	3/20 Dawlish Warren Passenger	..	..	..	..	3/43	..	
J	Goods	..	..	..	12/25	1/15	2/0	Avonmouth
B	2/40 Paignton Passenger	..	..	3/1	3/5	3/49	..	
B	Passenger	..	2/15	3/27	4/5	4/52	..	
A	12/15 Penzance Passenger	3/37	3/55	4/41	4/49	5/15	5/26	Crewe 11/22
A	1/15 Penzance Passenger	4/1	4/10	4/56	5/5	5/31	5/40	Paddington 9/0
B	Passenger	..	..	..	5/15	5/58	..	
B	Passenger	..	4/25	5/39	5/45	6/33	6/51	Taunton 8/6
K	2/35 Ashburton Goods	..	..	6/20	..	..	..	
B	Passenger	..	5/15	6/23	..	..	..	
B	5/45 Kingswear Passenger	..	..	6/30	6/35	7/18	..	
B	2/5 Penzance Passenger	5/22	5/42	6/46	..	..	..	
A	Passenger	..	6/20	7/11	7/17	7/43	7/48	Paddington 2.40
E	Goods	..	..	..	5/25	6/23	7/30	Paddington 3.25
C	2/20 Penzance Perishables	6/14	6/40	7/35		8/3	8/23	Crewe 3.45
B	6/40 Kingswear Passenger	..	..	7/33	7/40	8/26	8/35	Taunton 9/42
B	Passenger	..	7/8	8/16	8/20	9/4	..	
C	4/25 Penzance Perishables	7/43	7/52	8/48		9/19		Paddington 1.50
A	5/5 Penzance Passenger	7/54	8/2	8/55	9/2	9/37	9/45	Crewe 4.0
B	8/50 Paignton Passenger	..	..	9/13	9/19	10/4	..	
K	5/20 Ivybridge Goods	..	..	9/23	..	..	..	
B	8/55 Kingswear Passenger	..	..	9/41	9/46	10/26	..	
A	6/48 Penzance Postal	9/5	9/16	10/4	10/10	10/36	10/45	Paddington 3.50
J	Goods	..	4/35	8/5	9/15	10/47		Bristol 2.8
B	Passenger	..	9/20	10/29	..	..	..	
B	9/46 Kingswear Passenger	..	..	10/32	10/40	11/20	..	

KINGSWEAR BRANCH

The Kingswear line was a branch in name only, being in all respects akin to a main route of the company, and having a comprehensive service of local passenger trains.

				Torquay arr.	Torquay dep.	Paignton arr.	Paignton dep.	Kingswear arr.	
K	3.25	Hackney	Goods	—	—	4.7	4.25	..	Brixham 5.32
B	4.0	Newton Abbot	Passenger	—	—	4.37	4.50	5.35	
K	4.15	Hackney	Goods	..	..	..	..	..	Torre 4.40
B	5.22	Newton Abbot	Passenger	5.44	5.46	5.51	5.59	6.23	
K	5.45	Hackney	Goods	6.21	6.23	6.30	6.43	8.54	
B	6.20	Newton Abbot	Passenger	6.42	6.44	6.49	6.56	7.26	
B	7.0	Newton Abbot	Passenger	7.20	7.21	7.26	7.28	7.49	
B	7.20	Newton Abbot	Passenger	7.39	7.40	7.45	..	..	
B	6.50	Exeter	Passenger	8.3	8.4	8.19	8.12	8.35	
B	8.15	Newton Abbot	Passenger	8.31	8.32	8.37	..	..	
B	8.40	Newton Abbot	Passenger	8.56	8.57	9.2	..	..	
B	8.7	Exeter	Passenger	9.11	9.12	9.17	..	..	
B	9.25	Newton Abbot	Passenger	9.43	9.45	9.50	9.52	10.14	
K	9.30	Hackney	Goods	10.42	10.44	—	—	12/55	
B	9.49	Newton Abbot	Auto	10.5	10.6	10.11	..	..	
B	9.20	Exeter	Passenger	10.23	10.24	10.29	10.30	10.52	
B	10.5	Moretonhampstead	Passenger	11.10	11.11	11.20	..	..	
B	11.15	Newton Abbot	Passenger	11.31	11.32	11.37	..	..	
B	11.31	Newton Abbot	Passenger	11.50	11.52	11.57	12/0	12/21	
B	11.30	Exeter	Passenger	12/36	12/37	12/42	12/44	..	Goodrington H. 12/46
B	12/40	Newton Abbot	Passenger	12/56	12/57	1/2	1/4	1/25	
B	1/13	Newton Abbot	Passenger	1/30	1/32	1/37	1/39	2/0	
A	9.0	Paddington	Passenger	1/44	1/47	1/52	1/55	2/16	
K	1/30	Hackney	Goods	2/58	3/0	—	—	..	Goodrington Yd 3/12
B	1/56	Newton Abbot	Passenger	2/12	2/13	2/18	2/20	..	Goodrington H. 2/22
B	2/12	Newton Abbot	Passenger	2/28	2/30	2/35	2/37	2/58	
A	11/25	Cardiff	Passenger	3/20	3/22	3/27	3/28		Goodrington H. 3/30
A	12/0 nn	Paddington	Passenger	3/30	3/35	3/40	3/44	4/6	
B	3/30	Newton Abbot	Passenger	3/47	3/49	3/54	3/56		Goodrington H. 3/58
B	4/5	Newton Abbot	Passenger	4/18	4/20	4/25	4/27	4/48	
G	4/10	Newton Abbot	Lt. Engine	—	—	—	—	..	Goodrington Yd 4/35
B	3/45	Exeter	Passenger	4/51	4/53	4/58	5/10	5/31	
B	4/15	Moretonhampstead	Auto	5/9	5/10	5/15	..	..	
B	5/15	Newton Abbot	Passenger	5/31	5/33	5/38	5/41	6/5	
B	5/49	Newton Abbot	Passenger	6/5	6/7	6/12	6/14	6/35	
A	10.30	Bradford	Passenger	6/44	6/46	6/51	6/57	7/19	
B	7/19	Newton Abbot	Passenger	7/33	7/35	7/40	7/42	8/3	
B	6/50	Exeter	Passenger	7/56	7/57	8/2	8/4	8/26	
B	6/15	Taunton	Passenger	8/56	8/58	9/3	9/6	9/30	
B	9/21	Newton Abbot	Passenger	9/36	9/38	9/43	9/45	10/6	
B	9/10	Exeter	Passenger	10/21	10/22	10/27	..	..	
B	10/50	Newton Abbot	Passenger	11/6	11/7	11/12	11/22	11/40	
B	11/32	Newton Abbot	Passenger	11/48	11/50	11/55	..	..	

				Kingswear dep.	Paignton arr.	Paignton dep.	Torquay arr.	Torquay dep.	
G			Lt. Engine	12.5	—	—	—	—	Newton Abbot 12.45
B			Passenger	..	..	12.35	12.40	12.42	Newton Abbot 12.57
K			Goods	12.30	—	—	—	—	Hackney 1.40
B			Passenger	6.37	6.55	6.57	7.2	7.3	Avonmouth 10.38
A			Passenger	7.5	7.22	7.23	7.28	7.29	Swansea (High St.) 2/55
B			Passenger	..	..	8.10	8.15	8.16	Moretonhampstead 9.37
B			Passenger	8.15	8.34	8.36	8.41	8.43	Exeter 9.42
B			Passenger	..	..	9.0	9.5	9.6	Plymouth 10.40
B			Passenger	..	..	9.15	9.20	9.23	Newton Abbot 9.37
B			Passenger	..	..	9.30	9.35	9.36	Newton Abbot 9.52
A			Passenger	9.0	9.19	9.22	9.27	9.32	Bradford 5/56
B			Passenger	9.36	9.55	9.56	10.1	10.2	Newton Abbot 10.18
B			Auto	..	..	10.16	10.21	10.22	Moretonhampstead 1.19
B			Passenger	10.30	10.51	10.33	10.58	11.1	Newton Abbot 11.17
K	11.15	Torre	Goods	..	..	..	..	..	Hackney 11.45
B			Passenger	..	..	11.35	11.40	11.41	Newton Abbot 11.57
A			Passenger	11.25	11.45	11.48	11.53	12/0	Paddington 3/42
B			Passenger	..	..	12/10	12/15	12/16	Newton Abbot 12/32
B			Passenger	12/23	12/42	12/45	12/50	12/51	Exeter 2/8
B			Passenger	1/5	1/23	1/25	1/30	1/32	Newton Abbot 1/48
B	2/0	Goodrington H.	Passenger	..	2/2	2/3	2/8	2/9	Exeter 3/13
B			Passenger	2/2	2/19	2/21	2/26	2/28	Newton Abbot 2/42
B			Passenger	..	..	2/40	2/45	2/46	Exeter 3/49
B			Passenger	2/36	2/56	2/58	3/3	3/4	Newton Abbot 3/20
B			Passenger	3/15	3/34	3/35	3/40	3/41	Plymouth 5/30
B			Passenger	3/45	4/6	4/10	4/15	4/19	Moretonhampstead 5/38
B			Passenger	..	..	4/30	4/35	4/38	Newton Abbot 4/52
B			Passenger	4/55	5/14	5/15	5/20	5/21	Newton Abbot 5/36
B			Auto	..	..	5/35	5/40	5/41	Moretonhampstead 6/45
B			Passenger	5/45	6/6	6/8	6/13	6/14	Exeter 7/18
K			Goods	3/30	—	—	5/5		Newton Abbot 6/50
B			Passenger	6/15	6/35	6/40	6/45	6/48	Newton Abbot 7/5
B			Passenger	6/40	7/1	7/6	7/11	7/14	Taunton 9/42
B			Passenger	7/26	7/45	7/48	7/53	7/55	Newton Abbot 8/11
K	6/48	Brixham	Goods	..		8/3	—	—	Hackney 8/28
B			Passenger	8/6	8/27	8/29	8/34	8/37	Newton Abbot 8/53
B			Passenger	..	..	8/50	8/55	8/57	Exeter 10/4
B			Passenger	8/55	9/13	9/15	9/20	9/25	Exeter 10/26
K			Goods	8/30	—	—	9/35	9/45	Hackney 10/5
B			Passenger	..	..	9/45	9/50	9/52	Exeter 11/1
B			Passenger	9/46	10/6	10/10	10/15	10/16	Exeter 11/20
K	6/20	Goodrington Yd	Goods	..	—	—	6/27		Hackney 10/47
B			Passenger	10/15	10/33	10/35	10/40	10/42	Newton Abbot 10/58
B			Passenger	..	..	10/50	10/55	10/56	Newton Abbot 11/11
G	10/35	Churston	Lt. Engine	—	—	—	—		Newton Abbot 11/5
B			Passenger	11/0	11/18	11/20	11/25	11/26	Newton Abbot 11/40

APPENDIX B.   ROUTE RESTRICTIONS (1947 Working Timetables)

MAIN LINE

Exeter to Keyham — all types authorised.
Keyham to Penzance — all types authorised except 60XX ('Kings') and 47XX.

BRANCH LINES

	Engines Authorised	*Prohibition*
WTT No. 5 Exeter Division		
City Basin (Exeter)	All uncoloured. Yellow and blue types.	
City Basin Junction–Heathfield	All uncoloured. Yellow types specially authorised. 2–6–2T, 0–6–0T, 2–4–0T.	
Newton Abbot–Heathfield and Chudleigh Knighton Siding	2–6–0s in blue group and 2–6–2T of 51XX type.	Not to exceed 20 mph and 5 mph in either direction between 0m 0ch and the ¼ MP.
Newton Abbot–Bovey	Blue types. All uncoloured and yellow types.	Blue 1 6 0 78XX restricted to 20 mph. Other blue types restricted to 25 mph.
Bovey–Moretonhampstead	All uncoloured types. Yellow types specially authorised: 2–6–2T 45XX and 55XX.	
Newton Abbot–Kingswear	All types.	Torre–Down Sidings. Only engines of the following types permitted to use siding next to loading bank: 0–6–0 tank and tender, 2–6–2T (yellow type), 2–4–0T, 0–4–2T. Kingswear. Red and blue engines prohibited over Mileage and Wharf lines.
Churston–Brixham	All uncoloured and yellow types except tenders. Blue engines specially authorised: 0–6–0T: 57XX–97XX.	Not to exceed speed of 20 mph.
WTT No. 6 Plymouth Division		
Totnes –Ashburton	0–6–0T uncoloured. 2–4–0T yellow. 0–4–2T 48XX, 58XX. 2–6–2T 44XX.	
Brent–Kingsbridge	Uncoloured. Yellows.	20XX–21XX.
Tavistock Jct–Yelverton, inclusive	All classes except 60XX and 47XX.	Marsh Mills–Clay Works Siding. No engine heavier than 45XX permitted.
Yelverton, exclusive, to Launceston	Uncoloured. Yellow 2–6–2T. 45XX specially authorised.	2251 Class.
Yelverton	Connection to Princetown Branch.	28XX, 30XX, 42XX, 52XX, 72XX
Yelverton, exclusive –Princetown	Uncoloured, not exceeding 12ft wheelbase. Yellow 2–6–2T. 19XX for emergency only. 45XX specially authorised.	
Mount Gould Jct–Yealmpton	Uncoloured. Yellow.	Blue engines not permitted: Billacombe – sidings leading to goods shed and loading bank. Steer Point – Junction to Brick Works Siding.
	Blue 4–4–0 'Bulldogs' 2–6–2T 41XX–61XX, 81XX for emergency only.	Yealmpton – 2–6–2T only. To goods yard and siding alongside cattle pens.
Friary Jct–Sutton Harbour	Uncoloured 0–6–0T 850–2021 Class. 'D' group 'red' engines except 'Castles' and 47XX specially authorised.	'Red' engines not permitted to pass Sutton Harbour Road Level Crossing gates, Northey Sidings and Gas Co.'s Siding.
North Quay Branch	Uncoloured 0–6–0T 850–2021 Class. 'Red' group except 'Castles' and 47XX specially authorised.	'Red' engines not permitted to pass points leading to Mileage Yard or siding to North Quay (SR).
Millbay Dock	For passenger and mail traffic: All classes except 60XX. Shunting – 0–6–0T 1361 class, 0–6–0T 1366 class, 0–6–0T* 19XX	Connection to back of Glasgow Wharf 4–6–0 and 2–6–2T (31XX) types. All sidings except Warehouse Line, 47XX
Keyham–Exchange Sidings, Dockyard	All classes except 47XX and 60XX.	
St. Budeaux East–Bull Point	33XX, 34XX, 45XX, 55XX 0–6–0T.	Outside siding beyond stop board.

* with front side rods disconnected.

APPENDIX C. MAIN LINE AND BRANCH LINE MAXIMUM LOADINGS (1947)
Passenger, Parcels, Milk, and Fish Trains

	'King'	'Castle' 'County'	'47XX' §	'Star' 'Hall' 'Grange'	Saint' '4300' 'Manor' Large 2—6—2T	'Bulldog' Small 2—6—2T '5700'
Exeter to Newton Abbot	500	455	440	420	420	
Newton Abbot to Rattery or Brent	360	315	300	288 'Hall' 275	252	200
Rattery or Brent to Plymouth	455	429	440	392	364	308
Plymouth to Hemerdon	360	315	300	288 'Hall' 275	252	200
Hemerdon to Totnes †	500	455	440	420	400	—
Hemerdon to Newton Abbot	385	350	340*	315 'Hall' 300	288	252

† Applicable to Perishable and Empty Passenger Stock Trains only.
* Totnes to Newton Abbot — 335 tons.
§ Only on local services, speed not to exceed 60 mph.

BRANCH LINES

	'King'	'Castle' 'County'		'Star' 'Hall' 'Grange'	Saint' '4300' 'Manor' Large 2—6—2T	'Bulldog' Small 2—6—2T '5700'
Newton Abbot to Paignton	485	450		420	394	320
Paignton to Kingswear	390	345		320	300	290
Kingswear to Paignton	410	365		340	320	300
Paignton to Torquay	460	420		392	364	308
Torquay to Newton Abbot (unassisted)	390	345		320	300	280
Torquay to Newton Abbot (assisted to Torre advance starting signal)	500	455		420	420	420
Plymouth to Yelverton	—	325		285	240	220
Yelverton to Plymouth	—	420		390	240	220

	'4300' '7800' Large 2—6—2Ts	'Bulldog' Small 2—6—2Ts '5700'	'2251' '3200'	'2301' Older 0—6—0Ts 54XX 64XX 74XX	'Metro' '4800'	'517'
Exeter to Heathfield	280 †	200	200 †	170	100	90
Heathfield to Exeter	300 †	220	220 †	200	110	110
Newton Abbot to Bovey	300 †	250	220 †	220	140	120
Bovey to Moreton		220		200	130	110
Moreton to Bovey		280		250	160	130
Bovey to Newton Abbot	280 †	280	200 †	250	150	126
Churston to Brixham		220		190	180	160
Brixham to Churston		196		168	144	120
Totnes to Buckfastleigh		240 §		200	140	120
Buckfastleigh to Ashburton		220 §		192	100	90
Ashburton to Totnes		280 §		240	160	140
Brent to Kingsbridge		200		144	120	
Kingsbridge to Brent		200		144	120	
Plymouth to Yelverton	240	220		190		
Yelverton to Launceston		240		190		
Launceston to Yelverton		220		170		
Yelverton to Plymouth	240	220		170		
Yelverton to Princetown		120				
Princetown to Yelverton		144				
Plymouth to Yealmpton	315*	252*		190		
Yealmpton to Plymouth	280*	220*		190		

† Specially agreed in connection with Diversion of Trains emergency working.
§ For '2021' class engines.
* Emergency working only — 'Bulldogs' and 41XX, 51XX, 61XX and 81XX only.

APPENDIX D
ENGINE ALLOCATIONS — SOUTH DEVON SHEDS

The following engine allocations are given for sheds in the South Devon area during five selected years between 1902 and 1946. The allocations are for 1st January each year, and include those engines undergoing repair at Swindon Factory (etc) at the time; in addition, locomotives at Swindon Factory which were earmarked for immediate transfer to South Devon sheds are also incorporated, although these are few in number.

The lists themselves also indicate the classes of engines that could most regularly be seen in the district, as sheds outside South Devon often used similar locomotives to work 'balancing' services into that area; thus, 'Kings' from Laira and Newton could be seen alongside sister engines from Old Oak Common, as in earlier years could 'Dukes' and 'Bulldogs' from Penzance and Truro be noted on shed at Plymouth and Newton.

1902 ALLOCATIONS
Of the original 88 indigenous SDR locomotives taken over by the Great Western in 1876, only 22 survived the gauge conversion of 1892. By 1902, twenty of these were still in service, twelve in the South Devon area. The bulk of the allocation, however, was made up of GWR standard classes such as 'Bulldog', 'Duke', 'Achilles', Dean Goods, and 'Buffalo' tanks, which had increasingly dominated the scene since the demise of the broad gauge.

EXETER

4—4—0

Atbara	3376 *Herschell*	3378 *Khartoum*
	3380 *Ladysmith*	3388 *Sir Redvers*
	3395 *Aden*	3403 *Hobart*
Badminton	3294 *Blenheim*	
Bulldog	3332 *Avalon*	3333 *Brasenose*
	3355 *Camelot*	3361 *Lyonesse*
	3364 *Pendragon*	
Duke	3268 *Tamar*	3283 *Mounts Bay*
	3285 *St. Erth*	3287 *St. Agnes*
	3312 *Bulldog*	

4—2—2

Achilles	3003 *Avalanche*	3007 *Dragon*
	3016 *Lightning*	3022 *Bessemer*
	3069 *Earl of Chester*	3079 *Thunderbolt*

0—6—0

| Dean Goods | 2301, 2377, 2447, 2476, 2488, 2523, 2542, 2544, 2553, 2574 |
| Std. Goods | 782, 784, 1101 |

0—6—0T

1854	1873, 1897
1076	1168, 1185 (Tiv. Jct.), 1269, 1569
850	1921
Mon. Rly.	1346
SDR	1325

2—4—0T

| SDR | 1298, 1300 (Hemyock) |
| Experimental | 1 |

0—4—2T

| 517 | 217, 524 (Tiv. Jct.), 533, 1476 |

NEWTON ABBOT

4—4—0

Bulldog	3347 *Tregothnan*	3354 *Bonaventura*
	3360 *Launceston*	3365 *Plymouth*
Duke	3252 *Duke of Cornwall*	3255 *Cornubia*
	3256 *Excalibur*	3264 *St. Anthony*
	3269 *Tintagel*	3278 *Eddystone*
	3290 *Torbay*	3321 *Mercury*
	3325 *St. Columb*	
3521	3553	

4—2—2

Achilles	3001 *Amazon*	3012 *Great Western*
	3025 *St. George*	3030 *Westward Ho*
	3033 *Albatross*	3047 *Lorna Doone*
	3049 *Nelson*	3063 *Duke of York*
	3064 *Duke of Edinburgh*	3065 *Duke of Connaught*
	3072 *North Star*	3078 *Shooting Star*

2—6—0

| 26XX | 2641 |

2—4—0

| Barnum | 3210 |
| Stella | 3508 |

0—6—0

| Dean Goods | 2305, 2483 |

0—6—0T

633	643
1854	905, 1713, 1736, 1751, 1756, 1767, 1895
1813	1831
1076	1138, 1148, 1171, 1181, 1235, 1252, 1265, 1286, 1562, 1564, 1578, 1646
1661	1689
1016	1070
850	1907, 1918, 1940
SDR	1317, 1323, 1326
Nth Pembroke	1380 *Ringing Rock*

2—4—0T

| Metro | 470, 1450 |

0—4—4T

| Experimental | 34 |

0—4—2T

| 517 | 540, 628 |

0—4—0T

| SDR | 1330, 1332 |

LAIRA

0—6—0

| Dean Goods | 2354, 2463, 2469, 2507 |

0—6—0T

1854	1752, 1865
2721	2748
1076	1239, 1271
850	1223, 1932
SDR	1320, 1321

2–4–0T			
Metro	1448, 1457		

0–4–0T			
SDR	1329		

PLYMOUTH

4–4–0

Bulldog	3348	*Titan*	3349	*The Wolf*
	3351	*Sedgemoor*	3353	*Blasius*
	3356	*Dartmouth*	3357	*Exeter*
	3362	*Newlyn*	3363	*One and All*
	3367	*St. Aubyn*	3371	*Tregeagle*
	3372	*Torquay*		
Duke	3261	*Mount Edgcumbe*	3271	*Tre Pol and Pen*
	3314	*Chepstow Castle*	3318	*Jupiter*
	3326	*St. Austell*	3328	*Severn*
	3329	*Thames*	3331	*Weymouth*
3521	3530, 3535, 3543, 3547, 3551, 3555, 3559			

2–4–0

Stella	3512

0–6–0

Dean Goods	2310, 2385, 2456, 2470, 2512, 2549, 2564
Std. Goods	1214
Sir Daniel	586

0–6–0T

1854	1738, 1764, 1768, 1800, 1883
1813	1815, 1817
1076	1174, 1268, 1605
1661	1679
1016	1051
850	992, 994, 1922, 1930, 1997

2–4–0T

Metro	1464

0–4–2T

517	218

0–4–0T		
SDR	1331, 1333	

ASHTON

0–4–2T

517	1468

MORETONHAMPSTEAD

0–6–0T

1076	731

KINGSWEAR

2–4–0T

Metro	3587

BRIXHAM

0–4–2T

517	1472

TOTNES

0–6–0T

SDR	1318
1661	1694

ASHBURTON

0–4–2T

517	1331

KINGSBRIDGE

0–4–2T

517	534

LAUNCESTON

4–4–0

3521	3528, 3554

PRINCETOWN

0–6–0T

850	2019

1914 ALLOCATIONS

By 1914, the 4–6–0s had arrived on the scene in some numbers, and members of the '40XX' and '29XX' classes were provided to work the best trains. The last of the 'Achilles' singles had left the area, and the 'Dukes' and 'Bulldogs' were now to be seen mostly on the Cornwall and secondary services. The first of the '43s' had arrived, and would gradually replace the 'Dean' and 'Standard' goods engines on the faster freights. The SDR was still represented in the district by the 1878 Ince Forge/Newton/Swindon 2–4–0Ts.

EXETER

4–6–0

40XX	4037	*Queen Philippa*		
29XX	2917	*Saint Bernard*	2925	*Saint Martin*
	2933	*Bibury Court*	2939	*Croome Court*
	2975	*Viscount Churchill*	2988	*Rob Roy*

4–4–0

38XX	3860	*County Kildare*	3827	*County of Gloucester*
City	3709	*Quebec*		
Atbara	4122	*Colonel Edgcumbe*		
Duke	3272	*Fowey*	3285	*Katerfelto*

2–6–0

26XX	2621
43XX	4336

0–6–0

Dean Goods	2305, 2445, 2456, 2544, 2560, 2563
Std. Goods	782, 1197

2–6–2T

31XX	3118, 3132

0–6–0T

1854	1751
1076	737, 1245, 1620, 1654
850	1932, 1956

2–4–0T

SDR	1298 (Hemyock), 1300

0–4–2T

517	559, 1158 (Tiv. Jct.), 1433, 1439, 1440, 1466

NEWTON ABBOT

4–6–0

29XX	2923 Saint George	2932 Ashton Court
	2934 Butleigh Court	2943 Hampton Court
	2984 Guy Mannering	

4–4–0

Bulldog	3300 Pendennis Castle	3301 Powderham
	3305 Tintagel	3316 St. Columb
	3348 Launceston	3350 Newlyn
	3353 Plymouth	3358 Tremayne
	3380 River Yealm	3398 Montreal
Duke	3273 Mounts Bay	3276 St. Agnes
	3277 Isle of Tresco	

2–6–0

| 26XX | 2650 |

0–6–0

| Dean Goods | 2371, 2483 |
| Std. Goods | 432, 1208 |

2–6–2T

| 44XX | 4405, 4407 |
| 45XX | 4508, 4512, 4514, 4529, 4531, 4537 |

0–6–0T

1854	1714
2721	2722, 2725, 2755
1813	1831
1076	1174, 1181, 1239, 1252, 1564, 1600
1016	1035, 1051, 1053
1361	1361
850	854, 863, 1985

2–4–0T

| Metro | 628, 1448 |

0–4–2T

| 517 | 217, 831, 832, 1431 |

| **Steam Railmotor** | 58, 61 |

LAIRA

4–6–0

40XX	4009 Shooting Star	4010 Western Star
	4011 Knight of the Garter	4016 Knight of the Golden Fleece
	4018 Knight of the Grand Cross	4020 Knight Commander
	4026 King Richard	4028 King John
	4029 King Stephen	4032 Queen Alexandra
	4038 Queen Berengaria	4041 Prince of Wales
	4042 Prince Albert	
29XX	2931 Arlington Court	2979 Quentin Durward

2–8–0

| 28XX | 2846 |

2–6–0

| 26XX | 2639, 2675 |
| 43XX | 4311, 4340 |

0–6–0

| Dean Goods | 2302, 2317, 2542 |
| Std. Goods | 597, 1188 |

2–6–2T

| 44XX | 4404, 4410 |
| 45XX | 4530 |

0–6–0T

2021	2074, 2118, 2120, 2125, 2126, 2132, 2140
1854	1755, 1800
1076	1168, 1244, 1284
1661	1662
850	1909, 1922, 1930

0–4–2T

| 517 | 530 |

PLYMOUTH

4–4–0

Bulldog	3308 Falmouth	3309 Maristow
	3312 Isle of Guernsey	3328 Marazion
	3335 Tregothnan	3347 Kingsbridge
	3351 One and All	3357 Trelawny
	3360 Torquay	3371 Sir Massey Lopes
	3376 River Plym	3377 Penzance
	3379 River Fal	3408 Bombay
	3417	3430
Duke	3252 Duke of Cornwall	3261 St. Germans
	3264 Trevithick	3265 Tre Pol and Pen
	3266 Amyas	3267 Cornishman
	3269 Dartmoor	3271 Eddystone
	3278 Trefusis	3279 Tor Bay
	3280 Tregenna	3282 Chepstow Castle
	3289 St. Austell	
3521	3536, 3551	

2–6–2T

| 3150 | 3180 |

0–6–0T

1076	1176, 1286, 1562, 1578, 1650
1361	1363, 1365
850	1925, 1973, 1992, 1997, 2020

MORETONHAMPSTEAD

2–6–2T

| 45XX | 4504 |

KINGSWEAR

2–6–2T

| 45XX | 4502, 4527 |

BRIXHAM

0–4–2T

| 517 | 845 |

ASHBURTON

0–4–2T

| 517 | 571 |

KINGSBRIDGE

2–6–2T

| 45XX | 4401, 4403 |

LAUNCESTON

4–4–0

| 3521 | 3556 |

2–6–2T

| 44XX | 4402 |

0–6–0T

| 1076 | 1139 |

PRINCETOWN

2–6–2T

| 44XX | 4408 |

1926 ALLOCATIONS

The '43XX' class engines had by now been supplied to South Devon sheds in significant numbers, replacing the 'Dukes', 'Bulldogs' and 'Dean Goods' on many of the passenger and goods turns. 'Castles' were now part of the scene, Laira housing five examples, whilst '45XX' class engines had taken over many of the local and branch services from the older types. There were, however, many of those ageing tank engines still resident in the area, working mainly on shunting, light freight and autotrain schedules.

EXETER

4—6—0
40XX	4001	Dog Star	4006	Red Star
	4008	Royal Star	4010	Western Star
	4011	Knight of the Garter	4012	Knight of the Thistle
	4012	Knight of the Thistle	4018	Knight of the Grand Cross
	4019	Knight Templar		

2—6—0
43XX   4304, 5346, 6303, 6340, 6363, 7312, 7316

0—6—0
Dean Goods   2483, 2522

2—6—2T
45XX   4512

0—6—0T
1854   1755, 1794, 1876
1076   737, 1148, 1564, 1654
850   854, 867

0—4—2T
517   205, 530 (Tiv. Jct.), 831, 845, 1165, 1431, 1487

Steam Railmotor   74, 82

NEWTON ABBOT

4—6—0
40XX	4025	King Charles	4039	Queen Matilda
	4044	Prince George	4048	Princess Victoria
	4053	Princess Alexandra	4054	Princess Charlotte
	4060	Princess Eugenie	4062	Malmesbury Abbey
	4066	Malvern Abbey	4068	Llanthony Abbey
	4070	Neath Abbey		

4—4—0
Bulldog   3357 Trelawny

2—8—0
28XX   2857

2—6—0
26XX   2674, 2675
43XX   4326, 4350, 4395, 5329, 5376, 6317, 6360, 7300

2—6—2T
31XX   3119, 3121, 3127, 3133, 3134, 3140
44XX   4402, 4403
45XX   4503, 4510, 4521, 4522, 4536, 4538, 4541, 4546, 4553, 4558, 4564, 4566, 4568

0—6—0T
2021   2125
1854   1728, 1729, 1895, 1899
2721   2725, 2785
1813   1815, 1831
1076   1176, 1286, 1562, 1650
1501   1557

2—4—0T
Metro   621

0—4—2T
517   571, 838, 1158, 1466

LAIRA

4—6—0
Castle	4084	Aberystwyth Castle	4085	Berkeley Castle
	4086	Builth Castle	4087	Cardigan Castle
	4088	Dartmouth Castle		
40XX	4014	Knight of the Bath	4020	Knight Commander
	4032	Queen Alexandra	4034	Queen Adelaide
	4036	Queen Elizabeth	4038	Queen Berengaria
	4046	Princess Mary	4052	Princess Beatrice
	4064	Reading Abbey	4069	Westminster Abbey
Rebuilt 29XX	2925	Saint Martin		

4—4—0
Bulldog   3416 John W. Wilson   3424
Duke   3253 Boscawen

2—8—0
28XX   2818, 2843, 2854
47XX   4707

2—6—0
26XX   2601, 2658
43XX   4352, 4354, 4380, 5307, 5323, 5345, 5356, 5377, 5396, 6313, 6319, 6331, 6343, 6349, 6350, 7310

2—6—2T
3150   3151, 3169
45XX   4514, 4523, 4551, 4557

0—6—0T
1854   1897, 1900
1076   738, 1168, 1235, 1252, 1265, 1284, 1600
1361   1363, 1365
850   863, 1905, 1922, 1930, 1932, 1997, 1999

PLYMOUTH

2—6—2T
45XX   4508, 4530, 4535, 4548
1076   1269, 1271
850   1909, 1927

MORETONHAMPSTEAD
2—6—2T
45XX   4565

BRIXHAM
0—6—0T
1076   1244

ASHBURTON
0—4—2T
517   1439

KINGSBRIDGE
2—6—2T
45XX   4525, 4542

LAUNCESTON
2—6—2T
45XX   4563

PRINCETOWN
2—6—2T
44XX   4405

1938 ALLOCATIONS

The late 'twenties and the 'thirties saw a major re-stocking of the GWR's engine stud, and this is reflected in the 1938 allocations. 'Kings' were now prevalent on the major London services, with increasing numbers of 'Castles' taking other important trains, having replaced the '40XX' ('Star') class on such duties. The ubiquitous '49s' had also arrived on the scene, as had the recently introduced '68XX' engines; these classes were used on main line fast, stopping, and fast goods services. The older '517' and '1076' auto-tanks had been replaced by the new '48XX' and '64XX' classes respectively, whilst '57XXs' were taking over light goods and shunting duties from the older 0–6–0Ts. Another class widespread throughout the Newton Division were the modified '43XX' class Moguls (with the heavy front end), which were re-numbered into the '83XX' series.

EXETER

4–6–0

Castle	4076 *Carmarthen Castle*	4098 *Kidwelly Castle*
	4099 *Kilgerran Castle*	5003 *Lulworth Castle*
	5026 *Criccieth Castle*	5059 *Earl St. Aldwyn*
	5065 *Newport Castle*	

| 68XX | 6813 *Eastbury Grange* | 6814 *Enborne Grange* |
| | 6822 *Manton Grange* | 6825 *Llanvair Grange* |

4–4–0

| Bulldog | 3395 *Tasmania* | 3451 *Pelican* |

2–8–0

| 47XX | 4707 |

2–6–0

| 43XX | 8338, 8361, 8363, 8391 |

2–6–2T

| 44XX | 4405 |
| 45XX | 4530, 5543, 5551 |

0–6–0T

57XX	5760, 7716, 7761, 9718
2021	2050, 2148
1854	1897
850	1930, 1956

0–4–2T

| 48XX | 4805, 4819, 4827, 4835, 4840 (Tiv. Jct.) |
| | 4849 (Tiv. Jct.), 4851, 4868, 4869 |

NEWTON ABBOT

4–6–0

| King | 6002 *King William IV* | 6018 *King Henry VI* |
| | 6023 *King Edward II* | 6024 *King Edward I* |

Castle	4077 *Chepstow Castle*	5009 *Shrewsbury Castle*
	5011 *Tintagel Castle*	5017 *St. Donats Castle*
	5028 *Llantilio Castle*	5034 *Corfe Castle*
	5057 *Earl Waldegrave*	5058 *Earl of Clancarty*
	5062 *Earl of Shaftesbury*	

| 49XX | 4901 *Adderley Hall* | 4908 *Broome Hall* |
| | 5975 *Winslow Hall* | |

4–4–0

| Bulldog | 3375 *Sir Watkin Wynn* | 3383 *Winnipeg* |

2–8–0

| 28XX | 2846 |

2–6–0

| 43XX | 6305, 8318, 8325, 8340, 8353, 8364, 8366, 8372, |
| | 8374, 8383 |

2–6–2T

51XX	4109, 4117
3150	3151, 3166, 3181, 3185
45XX	4528, 4547, 4550, 4574, 4587, 5500, 5505, 5516,
	5552, 5567

0–6–0T

57XX	3705, 5798, 8709, 9717
1854	1736, 1797, 1895
74XX	7427
2721	2737
655	1782
1361	1365

2–4–0T

| Metro | 3590 |

0–4–2T

| 48XX | 4829, 4865, 4870 |

LAIRA

4–6–0

King	6004 *King George III*	6010 *King Charles I*
	6012 *King Edward VI*	6016 *King Edward V*
	6019 *King Henry V*	6020 *King Henry IV*
	6022 *King Edward III*	

Castle	4032 *Queen Alexandra*	4090 *Dorchester Castle*
	4092 *Dunraven Castle*	4093 *Dunster Castle*
	4097 *Kenilworth Castle*	5013 *Abergavenny Castle*
	5015 *Kingswear Castle*	5019 *Treago Castle*
	5021 *Whittington Castle*	5024 *Carew Castle*
	5041 *Tiverton Castle*	

49XX	4910 *Blaisdon Hall*	4932 *Hatherton Hall*
	4951 *Pendeford Hall*	4966 *Shakenhurst Hall*
	4982 *Acton Hall*	4991 *Cobham Hall*
	4999 *Gopsal Hall*	5902 *Howick Hall*
	5926 *Grotrian Hall*	

| 68XX | 6801 *Aylburton Grange* | |

4–4–0

Bulldog	3313 *Jupiter*	3393 *Australia*
	3427	3431
	3441 *Blackbird*	3449 *Nightingale*
	3453 *Seagull*	

2–8–0

| 28XX | 2818, 2819, 2839 |
| 47XX | 4703 |

2–6–0

| 43XX | 8337, 8341, 8357, 8376, 8381, 8388 |

2–6–2T

3150	3180, 3186
44XX	4410
45XX	4531, 4534, 4545, 4582, 5519, 5531, 5573

0–6–0T

57XX	7760, 8719, 9711, 9770
2021	2097, 2103, 2116
64XX	6406, 6407, 6414, 6417, 6419, 6420, 6421
74XX	7422
2721	2725, 2755, 2780
1361	1361
850	1909, 1993

PLYMOUTH

0—6—0T
1361   1362, 1363, 1364

MORETONHAMPSTEAD

2—6—2T
45XX   5557

ASHBURTON

0—4—2T
48XX   4866

KINGSBRIDGE

2—6—2T
45XX   4542

LAUNCESTON

2—6—2T
45XX   4598

PRINCETOWN

2—6—2T
44XX   4402

1946 ALLOCATIONS

An era of consolidation, extending the numbers of proven designs to fulfil the needs of traffic. Curiously, the 'Bulldogs' made a comeback, mainly on pilot and banking duties. In fact, the only new class to appear at this time was the '10XX' ('County'), which eventually became so familiar a part of the West Country locomotive scene. It is perhaps fitting that members of the '850' and '1854' classes were still on hand in the area to see the end of the old company, having served on the ex-SDR line since the gauge conversion.

EXETER

4—6—0

| Castle | 5012 | *Berry Pomeroy Castle* | | |
| | 5026 | *Criccieth Castle* | 5059 | *Earl St. Aldwyn* |

| 40XX | 4054 | *Princess Charlotte* |
| 49XX | 6957 | *Norcliffe Hall* |

4—4—0

| Bulldog | 3335 | | 3395 | *Tasmania* |
| | 3451 | *Pelican* | | |

2—8—0

| 47XX | 4706 |
| LMS 8F | 8420, 8432 (on loan) |

2—6—0

| 43XX | 5321, 6301, 6323, 6385, 6397 |

0—6—0

| 2251 | 2230 |

2—6—2T

| 44XX | 4405 |
| 45XX | 4530, 5502, 5525 |

0—6—0T

57XX	3603, 3606, 3794, 5760, 7716, 7761
2021	2088
2721	2785
850	1909, 1999

0—4—2T

| 48XX | 4805 (Tiv. Jct), 4829, 4835 (Tiv. Jct.), 4840, 4849, 4851, 4868, 4869 |

NEWTON ABBOT

4—6—0

King	6018	*King Henry VI*	6023	*King Edward II*
	6024	*King Edward I*	6027	*King Richard I*
	6028	*King George VI*		

Castle	4016	*The Somerset Light Infantry (Prince Albert's)*		
	4077	*Chepstow Castle*	4099	*Kilgerran Castle*
	5011	*Tintagel Castle*	5028	*Llantilio Castle*
	5034	*Corfe Castle*	5047	*Earl of Dartmouth*
	5058	*Earl of Clancarty*	5062	*Earl of Shaftesbury*
	5071	*Spitfire*	5072	*Hurricane*
	5078	*Beaufort*	5094	*Tretower Castle*

40XX	4012	*Knight of the Thistle*		
10XX	1001			
49XX	4983	*Albert Hall*	4992	*Crosby Hall*
	6934	*Beachamwell Hall*		
68XX	6813	*Eastbury Grange*	6814	*Enborne Grange*
	6822	*Manton Grange*		

4—4—0

Bulldog	3313	*Jupiter*	3341	*Blasius*
	3375	*Sir Watkin Wynn*	3383	
	3400	*Winnipeg*	3430	*Inchcape*

2—8—0

| LMS 8F | 8407, 8408, 8409, 8425 (on loan) |

2—6—0

| 43XX | 6345 |

2—6—2T

| 51XX | 4109, 4133, 5108, 5113, 5132, 5142, 5150, 5153, 5157 |
| 45XX | 4516, 4526, 4547, 4587, 5505, 5530, 5551, 5552, 5557 |

0—6—0T

57XX	5798, 9717
1854	1761, 1795
74XX	7422, 7427
1361	1362

0—4—2T

| 48XX | 4839, 4866 |

LAIRA

4—6—0

King	6000	*King George V*	6002	*King William IV*
	6004	*King George III*	6010	*King Charles I*
	6012	*King Edward VI*	6016	*King Edward V*
	6017	*King Edward IV*	6019	*King Henry V*
	6020	*King Henry IV*	6022	*King Edward III*
	6026	*King John*	6029	*King Edward VIII*

Castle	4032	*Queen Alexandra*	4087	*Cardigan Castle*
	4088	*Dartmouth Castle*	4090	*Dorchester Castle*
	4097	*Kenilworth Castle*	4098	*Kidwelly Castle*
	5009	*Shrewsbury Castle*	5041	*Tiverton Castle*
	5050	*Earl of St. Germans*	5057	*Earl Waldegrave*
	5060	*Earl of Berkeley*	5090	*Neath Abbey*
	5095	*Barbury Castle*		

10XX	1004, 1006, 1009

49XX	4908	*Broome Hall*	4937	*Lanelay Hall*
	4951	*Pendeford Hall*	4958	*Priory Hall*
	4961	*Pyrland Hall*	4962	*Ragley Hall*
	4966	*Shakenhurst Hall*	4991	*Cobham Hall*
	6907	*Davenham Hall*	6911	*Holker Hall*
	6913	*Levens Hall*		

68XX	6800	*Arlington Grange*	6872	*Crawley Grange*

4—4—0

Bulldog	3391	*Dominion of Canada*	
	3401	*Vancouver*	3431
	3441	*Blackbird*	3445	*Flamingo*
	3446	*Goldfinch*	

2—8—0

28XX	2835, 3811
47XX	4703
LMS 8F	8414, 8427, 8434, 8435 (on loan)

2—6—0

43XX	5318, 5350, 5361, 5376, 5391, 6319, 7312, 7321

2—6—2T

51XX	5172
3150	3186, 3187
44XX	4410
45XX	4517, 4531, 4542, 4583, 4591, 5519, 5540, 5567, 5569

0—6—0T

57XX	3629, 3639, 3675, 3686, 3705, 3787, 3790, 4653, 4656, 5658, 5679, 5693, 7762, 8709, 8719, 9711, 9716, 9765, 9770
2021	2103
1854	1799
64XX	6406, 6407, 6414, 6417, 6419, 6421
2721	2752, 2776
54XX	5412
1361	1361, 1364, 1365
850	1973

4658, 4679, 4693

PLYMOUTH

0—6—0T

1361	1363

MORETONHAMPSTEAD

0—4—2T

48XX	4827

ASHBURTON

0—4—2T

48XX	4870

KINGSBRIDGE

2—6—2T

45XX	4582

LAUNCESTON

2—6—2T

45XX	4528

PRINCETOWN

2—6—2T

44XX	4402

ACKNOWLEDGEMENTS

The authors and publishers would like to thank Michael Wyatt for the loan of his original GWR publicity material which has so much enhanced this volume. We should also like to thank Dick Riley, Roger Carpenter and Pat Garland for so generously putting their collections at our disposal, and Gerry Beale who played such a large part in the selection and assembly of material.

GREAT WESTERN RAILWAY.

Special Easter Announcement

THE

"TORQUAY PULLMAN LIMITED"

(FIRST AND THIRD CLASS)

BETWEEN

LONDON (Paddington)

AND

TORQUAY and

PAIGNTON

WILL RUN ADDITIONALLY ON

Thursday, April 17th & Tuesday, April 22nd

at the undermentioned times :—

			a.m.				p.m.
LONDON (Paddington)	dep.	11 0		PAIGNTON	...	dep.	4 30
Newton Abbot	...	arr.	p.m. 2 25	TORQUAY	...	„	4 38
TORQUAY	...	„	2 40	Newton Abbot	...	„	4 58
PAIGNTON	...	„	2 50	LONDON (Paddington)	arr.	8 30

A supplementary charge of **7/6** 1st Class and **5/-** 3rd Class will be made
for accommodation in these trains, in addition to the Ordinary Fares.

Applications for seats should be made to the Reserved Seats Office, Paddington Station, the Company's
Offices and certain Agencies in London, or the Station Master's Offices at Torquay or Paignton.

LUNCHEON, DINNER AND OTHER REFRESHMENTS CAN BE OBTAINED ON THE CARS.

THE TRAINS WILL NOT RUN ON

FRIDAY, SATURDAY & MONDAY, APRIL 18th, 19th & 21st.

Paddington Station,
March, 1930.

JAMES MILNE,
General Manager.

B. 268641

Great Western Railway

YEALMPTON BRANCH.

The Great Western Company give notice that on and from July 7th, 1930, the passenger train service on this Branch will be entirely withdrawn and the following stations closed for passenger traffic :—

Billacombe,
Elburton Cross,
Brixton Road,
Steer Point,
Yealmpton.

Arrangements have been made with the Western National Omnibus Company for their omnibus services between Plymouth and the above mentioned points to be augmented as occasion demands.

The existing Merchandise and Mineral train service will continue to operate over the Branch and will not be affected by the withdrawal of the passenger train service.

JAMES MILNE,
General Manager.

Paddington Station,
London, W. 2.
June, 1930.

B. 268836.